The Universal Social Safety-Net and the Attack on World Poverty

World poverty is a many-headed hydra. Eliminating its most extreme manifestations demands a variety of weapons. This book concerns one central element in extreme poverty: the inadequacy of many people's capacity for obtaining food (together with some other basic necessities) – because they cannot either produce enough themselves or earn the cash that they would need to buy it. To put it another way: they don't have enough 'disposable income' – not enough of cash and their own production combined – to meet some basic minimum for survival with dignity. How can that crucial element of extreme poverty be eliminated?

Simply increasing the output of food may help but provides no solution. People need not only to have enough food produced or imported where they live. They must also have adequate 'entitlements': claims (in cash or otherwise) to their individual shares in the food supply. How far in total those entitlements fall below the internationally accepted extreme-poverty line is the meaning of the (extreme) total poverty gap (TPG). The size of the extreme TPG is estimated from official figures, country by country and as a world total, and the authors consider how that gap might be filled.

A tantalizing finding is that the size of that gap is surprisingly low: for the low-income and low-middle-income countries combined, only about 0.2 per cent of world output. The book is concerned with strategy and tactics for directing that small slice of world income into filling the gap. This must be done country by country, on the initiative of each country's government: with the maximum involvement of its own civil society, and with the rich world also making a contribution. To add momentum, the international community needs to adopt targets far more specific than the 50 per cent extreme 'poverty reduction' of the first Millennium Development Goal.

Anthony Clunies-Ross is Emeritus Professor at the University of Strathclyde in Glasgow. His publications include *Taxation of Mineral Rents* (jointly wth Ross Garnaut, Clarendon Press, 1983), and he is co-author (with David Forsyth and Mozammel Huq) of *Development Economics* (McGraw-Hill, 2009).

Mozammel Huq teaches at the University of Strathclyde in Glasgow and is also Visiting Professor of Economics at Uttar Bangla College (National University, Bangladesh). He is the author of a number of books including *The Economy of Ghana: The First 25 Years since Independence* (Macmillan, 1989), and is co-author (with David Forsyth and Anthony Clunies-Ross) of *Development Economics* (McGraw-Hill, 2009).

Routledge studies in development economics

1 **Economic Development in the Middle East**
Rodney Wilson

2 **Monetary and Financial Policies in Developing Countries**
Growth and stabilization
Akhtar Hossain and Anis Chowdhury

3 **New Directions in Development Economics**
Growth, environmental concerns and government in the 1990s
Edited by Mats Lundahl and Benno J. Ndulu

4 **Financial Liberalization and Investment**
Kanhaya L. Gupta and Robert Lensink

5 **Liberalization in the Developing World**
Institutional and economic changes in Latin America, Africa and Asia
Edited by Alex E. Fernández Jilberto and André Mommen

6 **Financial Development and Economic Growth**
Theory and experiences from developing countries
Edited by Niels Hermes and Robert Lensink

7 **The South African Economy**
Macroeconomic prospects for the medium term
Finn Tarp and Peter Brixen

8 **Public Sector Pay and Adjustment**
Lessons from five countries
Edited by Christopher Colclough

9 **Europe and Economic Reform in Africa**
Structural adjustment and economic diplomacy
Obed O. Mailafia

10 **Post-apartheid Southern Africa**
Economic challenges and policies for the future
Edited by Lennart Petersson

11 **Financial Integration and Development**
Liberalization and reform in sub-Saharan Africa
Ernest Aryeetey and Machiko Nissanke

12 **Regionalization and Globalization in the Modern World Economy**
Perspectives on the Third World and transitional economies
Edited by Alex E. Fernández Jilberto and André Mommen

13 **The African Economy**
Policy, institutions and the future
Steve Kayizzi-Mugerwa

14 **Recovery from Armed Conflict in Developing Countries**
Edited by Geoff Harris

15 **Small Enterprises and Economic Development**
The dynamics of micro and small enterprises
Carl Liedholm and Donald C. Mead

16 **The World Bank**
New agendas in a changing world
Michelle Miller-Adams

17 **Development Policy in the Twenty-First Century**
Beyond the post-Washington consensus
Edited by Ben Fine, Costas Lapavitsas and Jonathan Pincus

18 **State-Owned Enterprises in the Middle East and North Africa**
Privatization, performance and reform
Edited by Merih Celasun

19 **Finance and Competitiveness in Developing Countries**
Edited by José María Fanelli and Rohinton Medhora

20 **Contemporary Issues in Development Economics**
Edited by B.N. Ghosh

21 **Mexico Beyond NAFTA**
Edited by Martín Puchet Anyul and Lionello F. Punzo

22 **Economies in Transition**
A guide to China, Cuba, Mongolia, North Korea and Vietnam at the turn of the twenty-first century
Ian Jeffries

23 **Population, Economic Growth and Agriculture in Less Developed Countries**
Nadia Cuffaro

24 **From Crisis to Growth in Africa?**
Edited by Mats Lundal

25 **The Macroeconomics of Monetary Union**
An analysis of the CFA franc zone
David Fielding

26 **Endogenous Development**
Networking, innovation, institutions and cities
Antonio Vasquez-Barquero

27 **Labour Relations in Development**
Edited by Alex E. Fernández Jilberto and Marieke Riethof

28 **Globalization, Marginalization and Development**
Edited by S. Mansoob Murshed

29 **Programme Aid and Development**
Beyond conditionality
Howard White and Geske Dijkstra

30 **Competitiveness Strategy in Developing Countries**
A manual for policy analysis
Edited by Ganeshan Wignaraja

31 **The African Manufacturing Firm**
An analysis based on firm surveys in sub-Saharan Africa
Dipak Mazumdar and Ata Mazaheri

32 **Trade Policy, Growth and Poverty in Asian Developing Countries**
Edited by Kishor Sharma

33 **International Competitiveness, Investment and Finance**
A case study of India
Edited by A. Ganesh Kumar, Kunal Sen and Rajendra R. Vaidya

34 **The Pattern of Aid Giving**
The impact of good governance on development assistance
Eric Neumayer

35 **New International Poverty Reduction Strategies**
Edited by Jean-Pierre Cling, Mireille Razafindrakoto and François Roubaud

36 **Targeting Development**
Critical perspectives on the millennium development goals
Edited by Richard Black and Howard White

37 **Essays on Balance of Payments Constrained Growth**
Theory and evidence
Edited by J.S.L. McCombie and A.P. Thirlwall

38 **The Private Sector After Communism**
New entrepreneurial firms in transition economies
Jan Winiecki, Vladimir Benacek and Mihaly Laki

39 **Information Technology and Development**
A new paradigm for delivering the internet to rural areas in developing countries
Jeffrey James

40 **The Economics of Palestine**
Economic policy and institutional reform for a viable Palestine state
Edited by David Cobham and Nu'man Kanafani

41 **Development Dilemmas**
The methods and political ethics of growth policy
Melvin Ayogu and Don Ross

42 **Rural Livelihoods and Poverty Reduction Policies**
Edited by Frank Ellis and H. Ade Freeman

43 Beyond Market-Driven Development
Drawing on the experience of Asia and Latin America
Edited by Makoto Noguchi and Costas Lapavitsas

44 The Political Economy of Reform Failure
Edited by Mats Lundahl and Michael L. Wyzan

45 Overcoming Inequality in Latin America
Issues and challenges for the twenty-first century
Edited by Ricardo Gottschalk and Patricia Justino

46 Trade, Growth and Inequality in the Era of Globalization
Edited by Kishor Sharma and Oliver Morrissey

47 Microfinance
Perils and prospects
Edited by Jude L. Fernando

48 The IMF, World Bank and Policy Reform
Edited by Alberto Paloni and Maurizio Zanardi

49 Managing Development
Globalization, economic restructuring and social policy
Edited by Junji Nakagawa

50 Who Gains from Free Trade?
Export-led growth, inequality and poverty in Latin America
Edited by Rob Vos, Enrique Ganuza, Samuel Morley, and Sherman Robinson

51 Evolution of Markets and Institutions
A study of an emerging economy
Murali Patibandla

52 The New Famines
Why famines exist in an era of globalization
Edited by Stephen Devereux

53 Development Ethics at work
Explorations – 1960–2002
Denis Goulet

54 Law Reform in Developing and Transitional States
Edited by Tim Lindsey

55 The Assymetries of Globalization
Edited by Pan A. Yotopoulos and Donato Romano

56 Ideas, Policies and Economic Development in the Americas
Edited by Esteban Pérez-Caldentey and Matias Vernengo

57 European Union Trade Politics and Development
Everything but arms unravelled
Edited by Gerrit Faber and Jan Orbie

58 Membership Based Organizations of the Poor
Edited by Martha Chen, Renana Jhabvala, Ravi Kanbur and Carol Richards

59 The Politics of Aid Selectivity
Good governance criteria in World Bank, U.S. and Dutch development assistance
Wil Hout

60 **Economic Development, Education and Transnational Corporations**
Mark Hanson

61 **Achieving Economic Development in the Era of Globalization**
Shalendra Sharma

62 **Sustainable Development and Free Trade**
Shawkat Alam

63 **The Impact of International Debt Relief**
Geske Dijkstra

64 **Europe's Troubled Region**
Economic development, institutional reform and social welfare in the Western Balkans
William Bartlett

65 **Work, Female Empowerment and Economic Development**
Sara Horrell, Hazel Johnson and Paul Mosley

66 **The Chronically Poor in Rural Bangladesh**
Livelihood constraints and capabilities
Pk. Md. Motiur Rahman, Noriatsu Matsui and Yukio Ikemoto

67 **Public–Private Partnerships in Health Care in India**
Lessons for developing countries
A. Venkat Raman and James Warner Björkman

68 **Rural Poverty and Income Dynamics in Asia and Africa**
Edited by Keijiro Otsuka, Jonna P. Estudillo and Yasuyuki Sawada

69 **Microfinance**
A reader
David Hulme and Thankom Arun

70 **Aid and International NGOs**
Dirk-Jan Koch

71 **Development Macroeconomics**
Essays in memory of Anita Ghatak
Edited by Subrata Ghatak and Paul Levine

72 **Taxation in a Low Income Economy**
The case of Mozambique
Channing Arndt and Finn Tarp

73 **Labour Markets and Economic Development**
Edited by Ravi Kanbur and Jan Svejnar

74 **Economic Transitions to Neoliberalism in Middle-Income Countries**
Policy dilemmas, crises, mass resistance
Edited by Alfedo Saad-Filho and Galip L. Yalman

75 **Latecomer Development**
Innovation and knowledge for economic growth
Banji Oyelaran-Oyeyinka and Padmashree Gehl Sampath

76 **Trade Relations between the EU and Africa**
Development, challenges and options beyond the Cotonou Agreement
Edited by Yenkong Ngangjoh-Hodu and Francis A. S. T Matambalya

77 **The Comparative Political Economy of Development**
Africa and South Asia
Edited by Barbara Harriss-White and Judith Heyer

78 **Credit Cooperatives in India**
Past, present and future
Biswa Swarup Misra

79 **Development Economics in Action (2nd edition)**
A study of economic policies in Ghana
Tony Killick

80 **The Multinational Enterprise in Developing Countries**
Local versus global logic
Edited by Rick Molz, Cătălin Ratiu and Ali Taleb

81 **Monetary and Financial Integration in West Africa**
Temitope W. Oshikoya

82 **Reform and Development in China**
What can China offer the developing world
Edited by Ho-Mou Wu and Yang L. Yao

83 **Towards New Developmentalism**
Market as means rather than master
Edited by Shahrukh Rafi Khan and Jens Christiansen

84 **Culture, Institutions, and Development**
New insights into an old debate
Edited by Jean-Philippe Platteau and Robert Peccoud

85 **Assessing Prospective Trade Policy**
Methods applied to EU–ACP economic partnership agreements
Edited by Oliver Morrissey

86 **Social Protection for Africa's Children**
Edited by Sudhanshu Handa, Stephen Devereux and Douglas Webb

87 **Energy, Bio Fuels and Development**
Comparing Brazil and the United States
Edited by Edmund Amann, Werner Baer and Don Coes

88 **Value Chains, Social Inclusion and Economic Development**
Contrasting theories and realities
Edited by A.H.J. (Bert) Helmsing and Sietze Vellema

89 **Market Liberalism, Growth, and Economic Development in Latin America**
Edited by Gerardo Angeles Castro, Ignacio Perrotini-Hernández and Humberto Ríos-Bolivar

90 **South–South Globalization**
Challenges and opportunities for development
Edited by S. Mansoob Murshed, Pedro Goulart and Leandro A. Serino

91 **Trade Infrastructure and Economic Development**
Edited by Olu Ajakaiye and T. Ademola Oyejide

92 **Microcredit and International Development**
Contexts, achievements and challenges
Edited by Farhad Hossain, Christopher Rees and Tonya Knight-Millar

93 **Business Regulation and Non-State Actors**
Whose standards? Whose development?
Edited by Darryl Reed and Peter Utting and Ananya Mukherjee Reed

94 **Public Expenditures for Agricultural and Rural Development in Africa**
Edited by Tewodaj Mogues and Samuel Benin

95 **The Global Economic Crisis and the Developing World**
Implications and prospects for recovery and growth
Edited by Ashwini Deshpande and Keith Nurse

96 **The Microfinance Impact**
Ranjula Bali Swain

97 **Gendered Insecurities, Health and Development in Africa**
Edited by Howard Stein and Amal Hassan Fadlalla

98 **Financial Cooperatives and Local Development**
Edited by Silvio Goglio and Yiorgos Alexopoulos

99 **Digital Interactions in Developing Countries**
An economic perspective
Jeffrey James

100 **Migration and Inequality**
Edited by Tanja Bastia

101 **Financing Regional Growth and the Inter-American Development Bank**
The case of Argentina
Ernesto Vivares

102 **Globalization and Development**
Rethinking interventions and governance
Edited by Arne Bigsten

103 **Disasters and the Networked Economy**
J.M. Albala-Bertrand

104 **Microfinance, Debt and Over-Indebtedness**
Juggling with money
Edited by Isabelle Guérin, Solène Morvant-Roux and Magdalena Villarreal

105 **The Universal Social Safety-Net and the Attack on World Poverty**
Pressing need, manageable cost, practical possibilities, favourable spillovers
Anthony Clunies-Ross and Mozammel Huq

The Universal Social Safety-Net and the Attack on World Poverty

Pressing need, manageable cost, practical possibilities, favourable spillovers

Anthony Clunies-Ross and Mozammel Huq

Routledge
Taylor & Francis Group
LONDON AND NEW YORK

First published 2014
by Routledge
2 Park Square, Milton Park, Abingdon, Oxfordshire OX14 4RN

and by Routledge
711 Third Avenue, New York, NY 10017

First issued in paperback 2016

Routledge is an imprint of the Taylor & Francis Group, an informa business

British Library Cataloguing in Publication Data
A catalogue record for this book is available from the British Library

Library of Congress Cataloging in Publication Data
Clunies Ross, Anthony
The universal social safety-net and the attack on world poverty: pressing need, manageable cost, practical possibilities, favourable spillovers / Anthony Clunies-Ross and Mozammel Huq.
1. Poverty. 2. Income. 3. Economic security. 4. Public welfare. 5. Welfare economics. I. Huq, M. M. II. Title.
HC79.P6C58 2013
362.5'52–dc23 2013015361

ISBN 13: 978-1-138-24399-6 (pbk)
ISBN 13: 978-0-415-52766-8 (hbk)

Typeset in Times New Roman
by Wearset Ltd, Boldon, Tyne and Wear

Contents

Figures

Tables

Preface

Both authors of this book have spent most of their lives believing in 'the welfare state'. We have taken this to mean a society in which everyone can obtain at least a basic minimum of essentials, and we had hoped that societies like that might be established everywhere: not only in high-income countries but also in those of middle income and even low income. But we had little idea of how that ideal could be realized. Insofar as we tried to think of solutions to the problem of providing something better than a starvation diet, year in and year out, for hundreds of millions of people who would otherwise live in extreme poverty or destitution, we probably assumed implicitly that filling the gap – meeting the most glaring deficiencies – would be both far too expensive and far too complicated to administer.

Mozammel Huq was born and brought up in Bangladesh which at the time of its independence in 1971 was regarded as hopelessly poor. He came from an especially impoverished northern region, Greater Rangpur, subject even in normal times to a type of seasonal two-month famine, the *monga*, during which many people had to experience serious starvation, often living on a highly inadequate food supply for days. Real hunger was, and had been before the last decade or so, a regular part of most people's lives. And across the whole country, until now or very recently, a large proportion of children have shown clinical signs of undernourishment.

Fully aware as we are of the weaknesses of governments, we yet believe that our intuitions are right when they tell us that situations of such impoverishment, affecting either the many or the few, and by no means confined to very poor countries, call for some imposed redistribution of income that only governments can consistently provide. But conventional wisdom seemed to be telling us that, for the low-income and lower-middle-income countries at least, bringing everyone up to even the most meagre view of a basic-needs level of cash income or equivalent would be simply impossible.

When, with a third colleague, David Forsyth, over 2006 to 2008 we had the temerity to prepare a textbook on development economics,[1] we were of course aware that overcoming extreme poverty required more than ensuring that every family had enough cash or equivalent to obtain food and the other essentials that can be bought in the market or home-grown. There is also much that can and must be done across the world to provide clean and accessible water and schooling and sanitation and clinical services and control of infectious diseases and much else that economists would call public goods or merit goods. We did also believe that economic growth, as and when it occurred, could *eventually* be expected to raise living standards *on average*, and that small enclaves subject to special attention and with a certain amount of internal redistribution might be able to set a floor to income among their own members. But we had no clear idea of what could and should be done *now*, across national populations, *not to raise the average* – that could only be done, or happen, gradually, and even if it did would not in itself eradicate severe poverty in cash income at the bottom levels of societies – but to ensure as nearly as possible that the huge cohort of human beings who would otherwise fall below the most miserable standard of basic needs might be given the means of living a materially tolerable life, and of doing so without running the risk of burdensome debt or labour-servitude.

From an issue of the *Human Development Report*, we got the idea of calculating the total poverty gaps of various developing countries: namely the amounts that it would take, in 'international' (PPP) dollars, to bring everyone up to the 'extreme-poverty' borderline as that line had been set after the big revision of World Bank real-income figures made in 2005. But to get an idea of the cost in actual convertible currency of 'filling the extreme-poverty gap' we had to take account of the fact that each US dollar would exchange for several (usually 2–4) 'international dollars'. World Bank figures existed which allowed these calculations of the numbers of actual US dollars needed to fill the extreme-poverty gap to be made for almost all of the low-income and lower-middle-income countries. And the total gap turned out to be surprisingly low: well below, for example, the total foreign aid from the rich OECD countries for the year concerned. It seemed that finding the sheer amount of cash transfers needed – for bringing above the extreme-poverty line all those whose 'disposable' income would otherwise be below it – would not be so much of a difficulty after all.

To provide further encouragement, in 2008 the International Labour Organization (ILO) brought forward a proposal designed for low-income countries. This would include (virtually) universal cash stipends for children and old and handicapped people; guaranteed employment up to a certain number of days a year for the able-bodied who were willing to undertake it; and a health service financially accessible to the poor and based on models actually in being. This was roughly costed for the next several decades and judged affordable even without external help for several of the countries in the sample. The ILO has now moved well beyond this outline, but the fact that the costs it projected were *of the same order* as those we derived, by simple calculation from World Bank data, of the extreme-poverty gap in disposable income for the same countries taken together was certainly encouraging. It suggested that the costs estimated would be at least of the right general order.

But what about the administrative challenge? When we looked about us in the years 2010–12 we realized that a wealth of study and experience was building up. The big resource-book *For Protection and Promotion: the design and implementation of effective safety nets*, by Margaret Grosh, Carlo del Ninno, Emil Tesliuc and Azedine Ouerghi, published by the World Bank in 2008, provides a wealth of analysis and factual evidence, and a huge assortment of 'boxes' purveying items of practical experience. Also, refreshingly original and reading like a novel though at the same time building its story rigorously on empirical results, is *Poor Economics*, by Abhijit Banerjee and Esther Duflo, published in 2011.

But at the same time, since just before the turn of the century, large events have been happening in big countries – India, China, Mexico, Brazil, Thailand, Indonesia – with some most ambitious endeavours that can be seen as directed toward providing genuine safety-nets of disposable income for the extremely poor. At the same time the ILO and other multilaterals, under UN auspices, have been working away over the last couple of years with the governments of generally smaller and less spectacular countries that have expressed serious commitments to the goal of an income floor. It also seemed impossible to avoid considering the extraordinary phenomenon of microcredit in Bangladesh – which is now largely financed, and also almost entirely operated, by non-government sources – serving some 30 million borrowers, many of whom show their satisfaction by coming back for more. How does Bangladesh microcredit fit into the safety-net scene?

In this short book, we seek to put the case for safety-nets, floors to disposable-income: in effect for extending the welfare state beyond its heartlands. We aim to explain how that can happen and is indeed already happening.

But we are only too well aware how dependent we have been on other writers, especially those we mention in our Acknowledgements below, and on a number of other individual friends, colleagues and associates.

With 2015 approaching, and so the time set for the achievement of the Millennium Development Goals coming to an end in a couple of years, the UN and its sister organizations will no doubt continue to analyse the world's achievements in these matters of basic welfare. One thing will very probably remain true for the time being: we shall still be left after 2015 with over one billion people in the world living in extreme (disposable-income) poverty. But there is a variety of evidence suggesting, though still without any certainty, that not only the proportions but also the numbers of the extremely poor have been most recently on a falling trend. This book, which we aim to be accessible enough to the general reader, attempts to present the case and to show grounds for hope that it will prevail.

We would, indeed, feel delighted if our modest attempt provides an additional stimulus for governments, rich and poor, and the international organizations to take ever more seriously the commitments that have been made in their names to prevent *any person's* disposable income from falling below a critical level.

14 April, 2013
A.C.-R. and M.H.

Note

1 Clunies-Ross, A.I., Forsyth, D.J.C. and Huq, M.M. (2009) *Development Economics*, London: McGraw-Hill.

Acknowledgements

In the course of writing the book, beside various discussions that we have had with colleagues and friends, we have also naturally depended heavily on both secondary and primary sources, and in the process have accumulated a heavy debt to a large number of people. While acknowledging our gratitude to all of them, we should like to mention at least some of them by name.

Krzysztof Hagemejer of the ILO has been extremely obliging in answering questions and in sending filenames and addresses of ILO publications, some of which have been quite exceptionally valuable for our purposes. One or other of us has also greatly benefited from useful discussions with Mohammad Yunus of Grameen Bank; Shafiq Chowdhury of ASA; Rehman Sobhan and Debapriya Bhattacharya of Centre for Policy Dialogue (Dhaka); Siddiq Osmani of the University of Ulster; Sharifa Begum, Abdul Mannan, Mustafa Mujeri, Binayek Sen and Quazi Shahabuddin of Bangladesh Institute of Development Studies; and Baqui Khalili and Abdul Latif of the Institute of Microfinance. Our colleagues, in particular, Roy Grieve, H.P. Kushari, Eric Rahim, Roger Sandilands and Mike Tribe of the University of Strathclyde; and John Struthers of the University of the West of Scotland, often provided vital inspiration as and when it was needed. We are also grateful for help and advice, as ever, from John Langmore of the University of Melbourne and Geoff Harris of the Durban University of Technology.

A huge amount of primary data was collected in Bangladesh concerning the contributions to safety-nets made by state transfers, and also on microcredit programmes in both rural and urban areas. These information-collecting activities received generous funding from the Carnegie Trust for the Universities of Scotland. Although we have used mainly the extensive data that we collected with fellow-workers on microcredit, the other information collected has also been helpful. We are very grateful to Mohammed Salimullah who, besides remaining a key collaborator in our Bangladesh investigations, helped enormously at various stages of the work and, along with Ayub Ali Khan of BIDS, was particularly instrumental in guiding the data-collection process, as well as carefully checking the questionnaires and advising on the selection of the samples. Majedul Islam remained the key figure in the actual data-collection drive which he successfully carried out with active help from a number of research assistants including Nuruzzaman Ahmed, Piari Banu, Bilkis Begum, Ashadul Huq, Mahmud Khan, Robiul Alam Khan, Babul Mia, Abdur Rahim and Daudur Rahman.

A number of authors (including Quazi Khaliquzzaman Ahmad, Salehuddin Ahmed, Shahid Khandker, Rubana Mahjabeen, Hassan Zaman and Sajjad Zohir) kindly responded immediately allowing us to quote from their published works. We are also grateful to the World Bank and the Microcredit Regulatory Authority of Bangladesh for their immediate responses, which kindly allowed us to reproduce some of their sources.

At various stages of the work, we also received strong support from a number of individuals including Molly Huq, Fiona McIntosh, Kirsty Fontanella, Chuma Ozougwu and Twyeafur Rahman in Glasgow; and Montosh Roy, Ibrahim Khalil, ASM Tariq, Zulfikar Ali Khan and Rafiqul Islam Rupchad in Bangladesh. Support and help received from several microcredit providers in Bangladesh including ASA, Grameen Bank, BRAC, POPI and TMSS are gratefully acknowledged. Thanks are also due to Uttar Bangla University College (at Kakina, Lalmonirhat, Bangladesh) where one of us was based for several periods during part of the time of the data collection in Bangladesh.

Abbreviations

ADB	Asian Development Bank
ASA	Association for Social Advancement
BAA	Birth-attended access
BBS	Bangladesh Bureau of Statistics
BHB	Bangladesh Handloom Board
BIDS	Bangladesh Institute of Development Studies
BRAC	Bangladesh Rural Advancement Committee
CCT	Conditional Cash Transfer
CLP	Chars Livelihood Programme
CSMBS	Civil Servant Medical Benefit Scheme
GDP	Gross Domestic Product
GNI	Gross National Income
GOB	Government of Bangladesh
IAS	Impact Assessment Study
ILO	International Labour Office
IMF	International Monetary Fund
MDGs	Millennium Development Goals
MFI	Micro-finance Institution
MRA	Microcredit Regulatory Authority
NAB	NGO Affairs Bureau
n.d.	non-dated
NGO	Non-government Organization
NOAB	Newspaper Owners' Association of Bangladesh
NPG	Normalized Poverty Gap
ODA	Overseas Development Assistance
OECD	Organisation for Economic Co-operation and Development
OOP	Out-of-pocket
PKSF	Palli Karma Sahayak Foundation
POs	Partners Organizations
POPI	People Oriented Program Implementation
PPP	Purchasing Power Parity
PROGRESA	Programa de Educación, Salud, y Alimenación
RAP	Rapid Assessment Protocol

RSBY	Rastrya Swasthya Bima Yojana (National Health Insurance Scheme)
RWDP	Rural Women's Development Project
SEMBS	State Enterprise Medical Benefit Scheme
SPF	Social Protection Floor
SRA	Staff-related access
SSN	Social Safety-net
Tk.	Taka
TMSS	Thengamara Mohila Sabuj Sangha
TPG	Total Poverty Gap
UC	Universal Cover
UHC	Universal Health Coverage
UID	Unique Identifications
UNICEF	United Nations Children's Emergency Fund
WDI	*World Development Indicators*
WDR	*World Development Report*
WHO	World Health Organization

Part I

Case for a safety-net

1 Paradox

Need and opportunity

1.1 Quest for a disposable-income floor...

This book is about the quest, the demand, the urgent need, that every household and every solitary individual should have *at least* a certain basic minimum of *disposable income* – spending-power in cash or in kind – to provide the essentials: food and whatever other material goods – of those that can be bought for cash or home-produced – are needed to sustain life and make it tolerable. That is what is meant here by a *safety-net:* in other words a *floor* to everyone's income below which it will not be allowed to fall.

That net, that floor, will have to be set and maintained for the people of each country *primarily* by its *government*, though other people and institutions – its own 'civil society', foreign governments, foreign organizations and benefactors, international institutions – may also have important parts to play. The level of the floor will thus almost inevitably vary from one country to another.

1.2 ...and for a floor of floors

What we mean in our title by calling for a *universal* social safety-net is that each of the national safety-nets should be no lower than a certain agreed minimum, a floor of floors.

We are taking it that, for a start and in default of something better, that floor of floors should be set at the level that the international community has effectively agreed to regard as the limit of *extreme poverty.* That level was originally expressed as a dollar per person per day. It has had to be more precisely defined and redefined to make it independent of exchange-rates and the purchasing-power of currencies. More of that below.

From an ideal standpoint, that standard is far too low. But quite a large proportion of the world's people – recently it appeared to be about a fifth – do actually have incomes below that ludicrously low level. Raising most of them, and seriously aiming to raise them all, above that extreme-poverty limit, would represent an immense step forward. Yet, as we shall argue, it is not nearly as difficult a step as those numbers suggest.

Moreover, movement toward providing a basic minimum of purchasable goods *for every household or individual* – not for nations but for *people* – has begun to happen over the past 10–15 years, without fanfare or sometimes even very explicit policy, and most strikingly in some of the huge developing countries that account for such a large proportion of the world's population.

1.3 Shift of concern from national incomes to individual poverty

Over the first quarter-century of 'development economics', roughly the 25 years after 1945, the poverty of much of the world – in relation to the living standards of Western Europe and North America – was widely recognized and deplored. Yet the usual assumption was that the misery that much of this poverty entailed was unlikely to be fixed *except by economic growth* in the countries affected. Attempts were made to *understand* the wide inequalities of income per head between the 'developed' and the 'underdeveloped' or 'less developed' countries, but, to remedy poverty, economic growth was taken to be the thing. And, especially among the newly independent countries, there was plenty of optimism over how *economic growth* might be accelerated by government policy. Little attention was paid to the possibilities of *imposed redistribution* of income and wealth in favour of the poorer or poorest, redistribution of the kind that paradoxically was at the same time having its heyday *within* the countries of the affluent fifth or so of the world.

By the 1970s interest had extended from how the *distribution* of income in the lower-income countries was determined, and how it might be changing, to how the change might be deliberately brought about. Distribution objectives came to be written in to methods of cost-benefit analysis. Non-government organizations (NGOs) ministered, as they had in the past, to particular disadvantaged individuals and communities, but *governments* of the poorer countries, however humane and concerned, generally had a broad-brush approach, not concerning themselves, as the affluent 'welfare-states' had begun to do, with providing a safety-net that would serve as a last-resort protection for each and every individual.

New ground was broken from 1981 by Amartya Sen and those who worked with and followed him in the study of famines and chronic under-nutrition, especially bringing to light the strongly political elements in the causation of famines, how democracy and freedom of expression can normally preclude their occurrence, how policy mistakes backed by coercive power can be disastrous, and on the other hand how enlightened policy responses in some states can actually lead to improved nutrition even in the face of interruptions to normal food-supply of magnitudes that elsewhere have left many dead.

1.4 Everyone's extreme poverty matters

All this has led to doubts over the easy acceptance of extreme poverty – *anyone's* extreme poverty – in disposable income. So long as there was a possibility of doing something to remedy it, there was a point in recognizing that *everyone*'s extreme poverty mattered.

In the senses that are important, it is *people* – individuals and households – that are poor, not nations, not localities. And of course poverty comes in vastly varying degrees and multiple forms and aspects. We talk of poor countries to mean those of low average incomes by the standards of the rest of the world. But this risks being misleading: of giving a sense of satisfaction where *average* incomes are reasonably high even though there may still be plenty of extremely poor people: people who are not only poor by local standards, *relatively* poor, but also poor by anyone's standards, *absolutely* poor. Though *relative* poverty matters in itself to many of those who suffer from it, we are concerned in this book only with *absolute* poverty.

World poverty – in the absolute sense – is a huge and amorphous concept, with no recognized or recognizable boundaries: essentially a low level of the ingredients of material well-being for a substantial part of the human family. On any understanding it has numerous strands: water poverty; nutritional poverty; poverty in susceptibility to infectious diseases; poverty in medical services; educational poverty. Any and all of these, insofar as they are technically remediable, may be serious enough to matter and to matter urgently. And frequently many or all the strands appear together.

1.5 Poverty in disposable income one key strand ... its limitation our agenda

This book, as implied above, is designed to pursue with a sense of pressing need *a particular path* to *reducing* absolute poverty, *limiting* it both qualitatively and quantitatively: *qualitatively* in the sense of ameliorating a particular fundamental and vital strand or aspect of poverty; *quantitatively* in setting an upper limit to that strand.

That strand is *poverty in disposable income*, and the path is the setting of a *social safety-net*, as we have described. This means, as we have said, setting *a lower limit, a floor*, to any household's *disposable income* per person. The *disposable income* of a household is a measure of its capacity for obtaining goods that are of a purchasable nature.[1] We interpret this as its cash income together with the value of the purchasable goods that it produces for its members' own use. That appears to correspond to the understanding of household income used by the multilateral organizations such as the World Bank and intended to be applied in national household-income surveys. The World Bank uses two cut-off levels of household income per person per day to define, for purposes of international comparison, the limits of what we are calling – following most current practice – 'poverty' and 'extreme poverty' respectively. These are the so-called 'two-dollar-a-day' and 'one-dollar-a-day' standards, which of course have to be more precisely specified than in these expressions. The first of the Millennium Development Goals requires that 'poverty' be reduced by half across the world between 1990 and 2015. 'Poverty' in the sense intended is taken to be '*extreme* poverty' *in disposable income*: household incomes in cash or in kind below the level of a (conventionally interpreted) 'one dollar a day' per person. It is what we are calling '*extreme disposable-income poverty*'.

1.6 Filling the gap: the benign (500 to 1) paradox

To eliminate extreme disposable-income poverty, there is a *gap* to be filled: a gap that could in principle be eliminated by handing over in each period the necessary amount of cash (expressed for example in US dollars) into the hands of each of the extremely poor 'as each has need'. That is the idea, potentially the ideal. It seems understandably to constitute an immense mountain for the rest of the world to climb. Maybe it is. But the difficulty is not so much in the amount of income that would need to be transferred as in how to do it – by what administrative means.

It is of course important to be aware that a household's level of material well-being depends on much more than its disposable income. This is part at least of what is meant by treating a social safety-net as a part, a subset, of what is meant by *social security* or *social protection* (Barrientos and Hulme 2008, *passim*). Two households with the same level of disposable income per head may differ greatly in material well-being. One may have a permanent source of clean water readily accessible and close at hand, while the other has to rely on water that may well be polluted and can only be obtained by long and arduous daily journeys. One may live where malaria is endemic and the other where it is not. One may have free schooling near home, with regular and conscientious teachers, while the other falls down on both scores. In brief, the two households may differ with respect to the natural endowments of the places where they live, and to the socially provided amenities that they enjoy.

So, if we were considering the whole potential gamut of the attack on extreme poverty, we should need to be concerned with far more than setting a lower limit to people's *disposable incomes*. These other requirements include so-called *public goods* and *merit goods* that can only be provided, or are most likely to be provided, or are best provided, by social action: that is, by the state or by society. With the exception of one particular merit good[2] (financial access to health services) that has been added to the safety-net agenda for reasons explained below in Chapter 10, we shall not *here* be concerned explicitly with these public goods and merit goods, extremely important as they are.

So setting a floor to disposable income can be regarded as *a necessary condition*, though far from being in itself *a sufficient condition*, for eliminating extreme poverty.

Yet setting a floor to disposable income – the objective presented in this book – even if that floor is set right down at the extreme-poverty margin, must be of immense importance to people *who otherwise are, or risk being, below that margin*. Those who *actually were below* that margin around the year 2005, appear to have numbered about 1.3–1.4 billion, around one-fifth of the world's people (and not many fewer in absolute numbers three years later in spite of some promising developments in the interim). But not only that: also many tens of millions of others who *happened to be above the margin at that time* must have *lived with the threat of extreme destitution* – through crop failure, loss of employment, or one of a number of other personal or communal disasters – a threat that would surely be ever-present to those already close to the margin.

If the safety-net, the floor to disposable income, could credibly *eliminate that threat* for those currently above, but close to, the margin, as well as *correcting the reality* for those below it, this would necessarily be a huge additional bonus. Moreover, the *possibilities entailed* by the extra disposable household income – of enhanced health, nutrition, education and risk-reduction – could, as we shall argue, be highly fruitful in other benefits: for today's children, their families and their communities and nations.

And, if we believe that our common status as human persons implies an acceptance of responsibility for each other's material welfare – and that this demands *at least* some minimum provision *for everyone* of access to food and a few comparable necessities – then our responsibility, insofar as it may be capable of fulfilment, extends to providing, country by country but universally, a social safety-net. Right now too, it seems, various strands of thought and practice have been coming together to make that outcome seem no longer unthinkable but on the contrary necessary and possible.[3]

Moreover, if we set our aims so that the safety-net is to be at the 'one-dollar-a-day' standard,[4] an encouraging message of this book is that the cash cost of providing it is, in highly relevant senses, 'affordable'. *In particular societies*, no doubt, the effective administration may be too difficult: 'governability' may be inadequate; 'civil society' may be too feeble. *In particular states* and *across the rich world* the will among those sufficiently influential to take the necessary action may be lacking.

But the outlook on these points is far from entirely gloomy. In the few years since the start of the century several of the giants of the developing world, as we have hinted above, have been making ambitious moves toward providing safety-nets for their own people. And the sheer cash amount of the purchasing power that would need to be put into the hands of very poor people in order to fill the gap is by world standards utterly trivial. The rest of the world – the richer four-fifths of *people* – would appear to have the income flows that could fill that gap for those poorest 1.3 billion people *about 500 times over*: the ratio between US$40 trillion[5] and US$80 billion a year.

Conclusion

We are faced with an amazing, but surely also encouraging, paradox: the number of people living in households below the extreme-poverty margin is immense; but the total amount of annual income needed to bring them up to that margin – to fill the extreme-poverty gap – is a tiny fraction of the world's income.

The resources are there to fill the gap. The sacrifices required, properly apportioned, need hardly be noticeable on the part of those that would have to make them. Also, as we aim to show, there are plenty of ideas around, some already well tested, on how to do it. What is required is the administrative capacity, the ingenuity and the combination of hope, responsibility and determination that we call the will, for meeting the challenge.

Notes

1 The term 'disposable income' is commonly used to emphasize that it is income after taxes have been deducted and any positive state transfers have been added. But the broader (but not inconsistent use we are making of it here – to mean that it is income *over which the recipient can determine the disposition* – seems to accord with the plain sense of the words and to make a useful distinction.
2 This refers to essential financial cover for clinical health services so that no household's out-of-pocket costs in paying for them should risk its 'impoverishment'.
3 See for example *The Economist* (2012a).
4 Now in fact the purchasing-power equivalent of US$1.25 a day in 2005 (US) prices.
5 The size of 2005 world income in US dollars translated at current exchange-rates in the numerator, with a reduction of 11 per cent (excessively generous for the sake of convenience) to remove the income of the poorest fifth themselves from the total.

2 Three sages and two new messages

2.1 Three economists on growth and current improvement

There are in fact four books considered here. They are: William Easterly, *The White Man's Burden: why the West's efforts to aid the rest have done so much harm and so little good*, New York: Penguin Press, 2006; Paul Collier, *The Bottom Billion: why the poorest countries are failing and what can be done about it*, Oxford: Oxford University Press, 2007; Jeffrey Sachs, *The End of Poverty: how we can make it happen in our lifetime*, London: Penguin Books, 2005; and Abhijit V. Banerjee and Esther Duflo, *Poor Economics: a radical rethinking of the way to fight global poverty*, New York: Public Affairs, 2011. The issue on which we represent the views, initially of the first three authors, is the priority to be given to growth-promoting policies as against those of immediate material betterment for the poor.

All four deal, either more or less directly, with the form, that *intervention* on the part of the national or international public sector or the institutions of civil society should take. They are concerned, directly or by implication, with the question whether motivation of the intervention should be primarily or exclusively ameliorative, concerned with immediate improvement in standards of life, especially for the poorest, or whether it should be primarily growth-directed; and whether apparent conflict between those options can be mitigated or avoided.

Easterly argues in effect for aid that is exclusively humanitarian in its immediate purpose. He bases this in part on the view that 'we' – governments native or foreign – do not know how to promote economic growth and might as well use aid resources on interventions that are asked-for by members of the communities that they are intended to benefit or that make a manifest direct contribution to the welfare of the poor, such as rehydration therapy or cash transfers to households on condition they have certain vaccinations. Economic growth comes about through the coincidence of numerous private decisions. If it occurs, that will of course be good, but we should not pretend that we know the secret for bringing it about. Attempts to generate it by international aid, financial or otherwise, have been demonstrably futile.

Collier, toward the other extreme, in the sense of seeing growth as something to be analysed with a view to influencing it, treats the role of intervention in promoting economic growth as that of removing 'traps' that have prevented much of Sub-Saharan Africa, together with Central Asia and a few states elsewhere, from getting on to a continuous growth path. The traps may generate vicious circles in which poverty and stagnation lead to coups and armed conflict, which aggravate bad governance, and hence perpetuate poverty and stagnation. Though a mineral bonanza in a country will increase the country's income while it lasts, it will often increase the temptations and the grievances that beget coups and civil wars. Aid may be useful but only provided that it can be used in such a way as to help break the traps rather than multiplying them. One of the traps most difficult to break where it occurs is geographical isolation from world markets, as in landlocked states. Otherwise, it would seem, the traps most worthy of attention are those of bad governance and armed conflict. It is taken for granted that, if a country has the potential for entering upon a continuous growth path, policies for putting it on such a path must have priority. Welfare gains from continuing and sustainable income growth are likely to spread to most sections of society. But, if there are countries that have no foreseeable prospect of continuing and sustainable growth – because they are landlocked or otherwise largely cut off from profitable international trade other than in raw materials (*and* have little raw-material potential), or have irretrievably poor governance, or are chronically engaged in fighting – the best the outside world can do to help in these cases may take the form of short-term expedients to make life more tolerable unless and until these limiting conditions change. UN-type peacekeeping is one such possible expedient for amelioration, though it may also play a critical part in breaking one of the crucial traps.

Sachs works on the more consistently hopeful view that there will often, even in the short term, be synergies to be found, rather than competition, between growth promotion and measures of immediate direct benefit even to the poorest. Apart from the ten major programmes, mostly concerning disease-prevention or agricultural improvement, that he cites as examples of the manifest benefits resulting from 'aid' of public or private provenance, he mentions the venture he has recently promoted in the Sauri villages of western Kenya: what was in 2005 'a miserably and increasingly poor rural community of 5000 people', two-thirds of them below the extreme-poverty margin. This appeared to provide a striking example of how vicious circles could be turned, by appropriate, fairly modest, inputs, into virtuous ones.

> These inputs – to be funded initially through outside finance at a cost roughly estimated in 2005 at $70 per person per year for about five years – would, it was hoped, reduce malaria transmission by about 90 per cent, cut mass deaths from AIDS, double or triple food yields per hectare, improve school attendance, reduce water-borne disease, and raise cash incomes … in consequence drastically reducing chronic hunger and malnutrition
>
> (Clunies-Ross *et al.* 2009, p. 603; citing Sachs 2005, pp. 234–5)

A report after two years suggested that much of the aspiration was on course toward fulfilment.

Could the success simply be extended by providing more of the same? Merely multiplying the overt cost of the Sauri venture in proportion to the numbers of people covered would suggest that extending the process across rural Kenya, or even across the whole of rural Sub-Saharan Africa, need not be completely out of the question on purely financial grounds, at least if undertaken in phases. But, even if finance on the necessary scale were available, there are probably compelling reasons why the inputs of the Sauri project cannot simply be multiplied up proportionately. The plan on which it had been based depended on a single many-sided *ad-hoc* prescription tailored to the actual conditions in the area, and for this purpose drawing on the considerable intellectual resources of the Earth Institute at Columbia University. And it would seem that not only drawing up the plan but also translating the ideas and the finance into their implementation on the ground in any locality would necessarily be a delicate management task, requiring a variety of skills – in instruction, persuasion, mobilization, bookkeeping, agronomy, health education – all ready to be enlisted to meeting the expectations and desires of the people of the area, plus an administrative structure to ensure that what was projected actually happened. Introducing such a set of projects, however gradually, right across the rural areas of an African country would require not only the many *ad-hoc* plans and the finance but also in effect a new civil service free of the vices and inadequacies of the old one. It would demand the manifold multiplication of that very administrative *capacity* that appears actually to be in such short supply. Sachs's solutions, in other words, seem highly intensive in intellectual skills and competent administration.

Unlike Easterly but to a point like Collier, Sachs seems to regard significant economic growth as a normal state or process, so that, if it is not happening, he asks for *diagnoses* that might point to the possibilities of complex *therapy* that is welfare-enhancing in both the short run and the long run – just as Collier looks for *traps* that may need to be removed.

Sachs can claim to have some ground for hope that vicious circles can be converted, as in Sauri, into virtuous ones. Beside the Sauris, further big transformational projects analogous to the Green Revolution of the 1970s and the mass disease-eradication campaigns (smallpox, polio, river-blindness) are still to be mounted or carried through.

But, without necessarily rejecting Easterly's debunking of all but the most directly and unambiguously welfare-enhancing (or locally popular) works of mercy emerging from the rich world; without rejecting Collier's hard-headed politico-economic modelling of the often wasteful and malign nexuses in which the states representing many of the poorest of the earth's peoples are entangled; certainly without rejecting the hopes placed by Sachs in vast cooperative projects under UN or other leadership, making ever fuller use of the human family's treasury of technical knowledge, ideas and experience – without rejecting any of this, we may find scope for considering more fully how the creative powers of the very poor may be released and how in the interim they may be sheltered from the worst disasters.

2.2 Two lessons from Banerjee and Duflo

This brings us to the fourth recently foreshadowed approach to dealing with extreme poverty: that of *Banerjee and Duflo*, which seems at least to provide additional insights. Their book, *Poor Economics*, views the position of the poor at the ground level, calling on a mass of recent research to illuminate the positions in which the very poor are likely to find themselves and how they react and why. The two authors put the ameliorative versus growth-promoting dilemma in a somewhat different light, suggesting how 'insuring' against the many hazards and grounds of anxiety faced by the poorest may itself have growth potential.

The enduring impressions from their book comprise *first* an awareness of the difficulties faced by very poor people: difficulties that go beyond the sheer consumer-deprivations springing from their poverty, to include also (a) the anxiety entailed by the multiple uncertainties and precariousness of their position, often in highly changeable informal labour markets; (b) in consequence, their need to minimize risk even at the cost of missed opportunities; and (c) the obstacles they face to achieving material improvement for themselves or their children (through more adequate nutrition, through education, through access at need and at manageable cost to medical and surgical treatment, through saving, through borrowing for investment, or through insured risk-taking).

Though these authors are cautious and selective about diagnosing vicious – and potentially virtuous – circles faced in the course of individual and social attempts at cultivating economic growth, they recognize a number of factors that help to explain why extreme poverty persists. It is not because very poor people are generally stupid, or ignorant (though many do lack elements of highly relevant information), or lazy, or unenterprising, or lacking in ingenuity. It is rather that a number of the financial devices and material inputs readily available to more affluent households or in more affluent societies for removing the obstacles and mitigating the handicaps to improvement are simply not available to the very poor except at costs or risks that are too high, or for prospective rewards that are too low, to be attractive. Highly exceptional individuals may overcome the barriers to securely remunerative activity, but many who are reasonably hardworking, intelligent, patient, self-disciplined and ingenious are not able to do so.

What we read from this, and what the authors themselves seem to be saying or implying, if we may draw the necessary inferences, is that either government or civil society (which might include for this purpose, we suppose, socially motivated business and informal combinations of people at any level of the hierarchy of influence and privilege) will need to take action for introducing the missing financial devices and supplying the material inputs needed for backing them. There are investments in finance and in time and attention to be made by 'society'. 'Insurance' in the broadest sense will be needed to provide a floor to disposable income; instruments to facilitate saving, low-cost borrowing, hedged risk-taking and investment; a critical modicum accessible to all of schooling, nutrition and prophylaxis against disease; and affordable clinical health services.

Very poor people are often stuck in miserable equilibria, inescapable traps, because the ostensible ways out are largely closed to them.

The *second* message is one of cautious and qualified optimism: optimism over small things but small things that may have the potential to add up, if they are numerous enough, to real improvements in the conditions of life that the poor typically experience. The authors, it seems, are not looking for social revolution from below or for enlightened despotism from above or for a cohort of technical devices tailor-made for each of the great variety of situations in which very poor people may find themselves, but rather – from all those with authority or influence – for a bit more integrity, a bit more courage, a bit more imagination, a bit more exercise of ingenuity, a bit less inertia, in the design and day-to-day administration of the existing public services, and in the creation of financial institutions (from which variants of microcredit are certainly not excluded) framed to meet the needs of people who depend on the meagre and volatile sources of income in the 'informal sector'.

In all this, setting a credible floor to disposable income, especially if it can be combined with insurance (contributory or not) against catastrophic household health expenses, will do more than just relieve current need. It will provide a shelter for risk-taking. If a household can be reasonably confident that a novel venture will not be allowed to plunge it into complete destitution, it may risk investments in new activities or new ways of doing things that otherwise it might feel obliged to avoid. There is good reason to believe that this is more likely to release enterprise than to discourage it.

Conclusion

After 70 years or so of thought and debate on 'development economics' and where it should be driving us there are fundamental differences of outlook among some of the leading recent thinkers in the field. The differences become striking over the relative priorities that should be given in national and international intervention to current welfare and economic growth.

Easterly's view at its simplest is that, as we don't know how to promote economic growth., it would be better for governments and societies that seek to relieve poverty to confine their benevolence to acts directed at what is of manifest immediate value to poor people or responds directly to the requests of their representatives.

Collier, believing that judgements can be made through politico-economic analysis backed by empirical research on how to promote or release economic growth, and that only through its release can the very poor look for consistent improvement in their living standards, would concentrate any help from the rich world on pulling whatever levers seem likely to be most effective for that purpose.

Sachs works on the assumption that no such choice between growth and current welfare needs to be made: that suitable state and social-sector interventions need only to be framed out of the vast choice of techniques that allow both ends to be served simultaneously.

Banerjee and Duflo introduce a new perspective, though one not necessarily inconsistent with any of the other three, in looking at choices and opportunities from the viewpoint of the very poor, with the informal household enterprises on which so many of them depend for a livelihood. In so doing they reveal further prospects of avoiding the need to choose between what is directly welfare-enhancing and what is growth-promoting. The very poor are hobbled by downside risks against which they typically lack serviceable means of protection. A credible determination on the part of the wider society to shield poor families from the fear of complete destitution encourages the taking of a step forward through the assurance that it will not lead to two steps back. Those who feel themselves more secure are the ones that can afford to be more enterprising, more 'progressive' over education and health and productivity: to be more concerned for building their material and human capital.

Though the Banerjee and Duflo book is not framed as an argument for a disposable-income safety-net, and conveys an abundance of insights not directly connected with that case, including a sympathetic but qualified appraisal of the possibilities of microcredit in its standard form, their close examination of the economics of the very poor seems to lead fairly clearly in that direction.

3 The basic case

3.1 Case for a disposable-income safety-net

The simple, basic and obvious case for a 'safety-net' that sets a lower limit to everyone's disposable income is that it would stop people from suffering extremes of hunger and undernourishment and of other forms of deprivation rated as comparably serious for those who have to experience them. It would also reduce, though it would not eliminate, except for those who were already very poor, those *falls* in income below accustomed levels that typically cause such grief.

Banerjee and Duflo (2011, ch. 1) warn against seeing deprivation exclusively as a matter of lack of food. They mention (ibid., p. 22) that in an 18-country study food represented only 'from 36 to 79 per cent of consumption among the rural extremely poor, and 53 to 74 per cent among their urban counterparts', and they offer evidence that extra income, even among the very poor, need not generate extra spending on food, let alone consumption of a greater quantity of food or more calories. They accept the possibility of a food-poverty trap, a vicious circle in which lack of access to food reduces people's productivity and hence their income, but do not consider this a clearly prevalent reality among working-age adults. Critical undernourishment seems to arise largely in childhood or even in the womb, with deficiencies of micronutrients or effects of certain infestations or both. Some of the damage done may not appear until even two generations later, and for this reason the special nutritional needs of children and pregnant and nursing mothers must be met as a matter of particular priority. Famines do of course occur, when lack of access to food may dominate over other deprivations for people of all ages. But the varied patterns of spending, even in normal times, among the extremely poor suggest that we should not necessarily give privileged consideration to particular forms of consumption but focus concern on overall lack of disposable income. However, in this book we shall continue to speak of lack of food as the representative deprivation and suppose that those who lack what they themselves would see as a minimally acceptable diet will lack other goods that they also value highly.

Ensuring that everyone in a country can be fed, even at a very meagre level, will not necessarily be achieved by simply maintaining the sum of the country's food production and its net food imports together at some target level. It also requires that every household should receive *entitlements* to food (and to other marketable essentials ranked as comparably important) in cash or in kind. These need to be provided, if necessary as 'transfers' (free grants), insofar as any household's other sources of income would otherwise fall below whatever lower limit is targeted. The objective of a safety-net, in the sense considered here, is to ensure that, as far as possible, no one – no household given its size – should see its disposable income fall below the extreme-poverty borderline. Given a roughly fair distribution *within* each household and *no extraordinary expenditure requirements* such as catastrophic medical outlays, this would *protect all from suffering the extremes of destitution*.

But these *immediate consumer benefits* are only the beginning. As we have mentioned in Chapter 1, *if continuance of the safety-net can be credibly guaranteed*, this also removes or *relieves a major source of anxiety about the future* for anyone who is above but close to the level of the guarantee or who on other grounds may fear falling below it. Reduction of such anxiety is another highly important consumer benefit. If, as the 2005 figures suggest, the number of people in the world below the extreme-poverty threshold at that time was of the order of 1.3–1.4 billion, we can be sure that there must have been many more millions who, though not currently in that extreme-poverty category, could easily, through any number of possible kinds of accidents, find their own households more or less destitute. The high rate of suicides of able-bodied farmers in certain countries such as India at times of serious crop failure is a reminder of the abyss yawning at the feet of many of those who normally just manage to make do.

A third strand of potential benefits results from that very reduction in risks that a fully credible safety-net provides. If the household contemplates an investment of any sort – or a change in its accustomed mode of production – one that offers a plausible (but uncertain) expectation of being profitable – the safety-net *may make the risk worth taking*. Any new outlay or any change from the familiar way of doing things involves risk. When the cost of failure is high, caution may seem to be the best policy. Avoiding risk, even at the probable cost of missed opportunities, may be perfectly rational. One way of reducing the risk is reducing the cost of failure. Two courses of action may face a decision-maker: one course with lower 'expected' returns but low perceived probability of failure, the other with higher expected returns but also higher probability of failure. Reducing the severity of failure if it should occur, which is what a credible safety-net would do, could easily alter the balance of advantage for the decision-maker in favour of the one with higher expected returns, and the repetition of similar reductions in the cost of failure across the country could increase the rate of growth in the economy at large.

Investment in education is one case of household investment from which parents commonly hope for an eventual increase in family income. Banerjee and Duflo (2011, pp. 86–9) incidentally cite evidence *against* the view that what is spent on educational investment generally brings higher returns if it is concentrated on what are thought to be the most gifted members of the family. Rather, it would appear, the relationship between educational investment and absolute return may well be approximately linear. But there *is* a reasonable expectation of return; and again reducing, by the presence of a safety-net, what the net cost of the investment will be in case the hoped-for return fails to eventuate shifts the balance in favour of the investment. The same goes for *other investments in human resources* such as the use of nutritional supplements, water-chlorination and de-worming[1] treatment, even if they involve out-of-pocket costs for the households. And these investments – in capacities such as literacy and in children's health – do of course also bring significant consumer-benefits, some immediate and obvious, some concealed or realized only over time.

Insofar as a healthier and better intellectually equipped community is recognized as a common interest, so that the standards of education and health of the population can be regarded as 'public goods', the safety-net, because it could be expected to *reduce any tendencies on the part of households to underinvestment in education and health, would enhance the community's investment in human capital.*

A related and very important use of a safety-net is in *avoiding indebtedness.* Borrowing – often at high interest rates that will make servicing the debt an increasing burden and ultimate repayment a receding possibility – may seem an unavoidable response when crops have failed or other disasters have occurred. It is one way in which young children may be drawn into the horrors of debt-slavery.

More generally, a safety-net may be an effective way of *avoiding the need for putting young children to work.* (Some evidence relevant to this assertion is cited in Chapter 8 below on conditional cash transfers.) Where the disaster is a crop failure, for example, we might hope that a safety-net, if it existed, would be adequate to obviate the need either to borrow or to send children out as hired labourers. If the safety-net was of the 'workfare' type as under India's National Rural Employment Guarantee Scheme, this might serve, even in some cases for which the gap in household finances arose not from crop failure or unemployment but from an exceptional *expenditure* that seemed unavoidable, as for a wedding or a dowry.

But a special case, unfortunately not uncommon, is one in which a family is faced with *catastrophically high medical expenses* to prevent a tragedy such as the death or incapacity of a main income-earner or indeed the death or chronic illness of any family member. A safety-net such as we have supposed for supporting *disposable income* may often be inadequate in itself for dealing with this kind of contingency. And borrowing the large sums involved may so easily be the route to irredeemable disaster. Faced with the risk of such extraordinary, and for practical purposes unavoidable, expenditure, any disposable-income guarantee would need to be supplemented by some form of medical insurance. Banerjee and Duflo (2011, pp. 144ff.) go into the question, and give reasons, with evidence, for thinking that informal networks that may support their members in other forms of misfortune will quite often be inadequate in major health emergencies.

So preventing extreme impoverishment in such cases may require specific health insurance, contributory or not. If it is to cover most of the catastrophic health expenses, it will probably need at least a considerable state subsidy. The ILO's suggested safety-net scheme (ILO 2008a), discussed below in Chapter 4, includes comprehensive health coverage as an additional costed element, and the UN aspiration of an income floor includes defence against 'impoverishing' medical expenses. (More discussion and evidence is given in Chapter 10 below.)

3.2 Objections to a safety-net considered

3.2.1 Why not rely on economic growth?

The question arises whether it is desirable, as well as possible, *to use personal transfers* (free grants) as a necessary element among the means for – fairly promptly – achieving the objective of a minimally acceptable disposable income for all.

Our answer here on the desirability of personal transfers for the purpose is a definite yes. Personal transfers are potentially a more direct and quick and reliable method *for raising the disposable income of the extremely poor* than depending on any version of the main alternative broad strategy commonly advanced. That strategy is to encourage, by whatever means, what is in many countries the slow and uncertain process of general economic growth, and to hope for a consequent 'trickling down' of benefits to the poorest. Our knowledge of how to generate, or to speed, sustainable economic growth is highly imperfect, as is our knowledge of how at the same time to influence its character toward a pro-poor bias. All experience suggests that *sole* reliance on market mechanisms – that is without some deliberate socially generated redistribution of income flows or wealth – will leave *some* people in any society completely destitute on that society's own understanding, and in the poorer countries leave many more seriously deprived by even the most frugal standards.

This truth should always have been obvious but has not always been in the forefront of public discourse in and about that large part of the world that has been officially focused on 'development' for much of the last two-thirds of a century. This truth was prodded into wider recognition as a result of the exploration begun by Amartya Sen (1981) of famines, and extended by him and others into the conditions leading to chronic under-nourishment. By concentrating on the need of people for what he called their '*entitlements*' to food, he has directed attention away from *a too exclusive* concern with aggregate output and productivity. If the world's people are to be adequately fed, there must not only be enough food produced but also *appropriately distributed claims* upon it.

The fact that there have recently been *well over a billion* people with disposable income *below* the extreme-poverty line (an estimated 1.3–1.4 billion in 2005) and apparently surviving, at best, in a deprivation almost unimaginable to most citizens of the rich world, must surely throw doubt on the case for a strategy of simply removing policy obstacles to output growth, and waiting for the consequent benefits to trickle down. The waiting-room is still uncomfortably full. Though recent output growth in certain countries (notably China and the East Asian 'tigers' and parts of South East Asia) has been accompanied by big shifts out of the ranks of the destitute or near-destitute, huge residues of extreme poverty clearly remain, not only in Sub-Saharan Africa but also in South Asia, with large numbers of people quite often driven far below the line by adverse seasons or abnormally high prices of food staples. Also there are at all times some people who, because of disability or social ostracism or simply bad luck in one of its many forms, have to rely, if they are not to starve, on some form of begging or crime.

If the savants and leaders of the world-community knew the secret of *generating enough growth*, and, *without personal transfers, having some of the proceeds of that growth distributed*, so that the basic needs of all would be satisfied within say ten years, leaving only a small body of the extremely disabled to survive on the charity of the rest, there might seem to be a case for asking the destitute or near-destitute to wait patiently for life to improve. Yet hardly anyone surely expects that to happen.

However, there is a dubious assumption implied in the argument so far. This is that eliminating extreme poverty in disposable income through personal transfers is *an alternative* to promoting economic growth, or at least removing policy obstacles to it: that it is either one or the other. We argue here, and try to show, that no such agonizing choice has to be made. This is for three reasons.

First, the annual cost in actual convertible currencies of simply providing the disposable income to raise *all those people currently below the extreme-poverty line* to just above it turns out to be *so small* as to be virtually trivial by world standards: of the order of 0.2 per cent of world income,[2] as we have mentioned in Chapter 1. Admittedly the practical task of 'filling the gap' is by no means as easy as that might make it appear. There are unavoidable questions of administrative costs, and of administrative devices for transferring the cash or goods to those who need it most without undue losses and misdirections on the way. Further, in all but the most bureaucratized countries, providing the targeted standard of disposable income for all would inevitably entail some 'over-provision', which would increase the cost. Also, the need to adjust the cash level of the 'safety-net' in any area as food and other prices fluctuate would be another necessary complication. And of course, though the costs may be small, *someone* will have to be prepared to pay them. We have not overlooked these potential stumbling-blocks, as we intend to show. But the account of the facts as we have stated it, and as they appear in the tables within Appendix 4.2, remains. If the figures for extreme disposable-income poverty as presented by the international institutions (notably the World Bank) mean what they purport to mean and are even approximately correct, simply providing enough US dollars or equivalent to fill the gap *is not a large hurdle to surmount.*

Second, and following from the previous point, raising the funds for making the transfers *need not put such a large burden on the countries that might reasonably be expected to pay* – middle-income countries providing for their own poor, rich countries helping those of low income to fill the gaps – *as to reduce significantly their own growth rates.*

Third, as we have submitted above, there are good reasons why the transfers constituting a safety-net in any country may, if reliably and credibly established, actually promote economic growth. This is because they may reduce the risks, perceived and real, faced by very poor people when they have choices to make over whether to save, invest, borrow for productive purposes, or adopt new techniques. Hence there are reasons to hope that *increased outlays and changed practices that have the risks of novelty but also offer positive 'expected' returns will be encouraged.* Appropriate institutions will no doubt be needed to realize these responses. Discussion above in Section 3.1, however, gives ground for hoping that a suitably defined and securely established safety-net could not only, through the 'assurance' that it would provide, support informal-sector investment and innovation, but also improve the quality of the workforce through facilitating household outlays on nutrition, health and schooling, and on all these grounds *be a positive contributor to economic growth.*

3.2.2 It would encourage consumption at the expense of investment

No doubt at least the first part of this assertion is largely true: transfers of cash to very poor people would be likely to increase their consumption. But it by no means follows that the effects supposed are wasteful or harmful – or indeed that the second part of the statement (that this will reduce the resources for investment) follows even over the very short term and even in the absence of inward capital movements and of institutional credit. Extra cash will allow a household *both* to consume more *and* to invest more. Moreover much that counts as consumption in the national accounts, such as spending on schooling and vaccination and de-worming and water-chlorination and extra nutrients, deserves as well or better to be regarded as human-capital investment.

The slippery term 'development', as an expression of what the people of the poorer countries are supposed to need, or to aspire to do, has helped encourage the judgement that may be parodied as 'investment good, consumption bad'.

This is an aberration not confined to distant observers from rich countries. Governments, elites, the relatively well-off, in poorer countries themselves, may, for reasons of national prestige or influence, be concerned that there should be high rates of economic growth, regardless of the current welfare costs. Amartya Sen (1995) has expounded how in India there had long been a strain of official aversion to any emphasis on current welfare (in the form of health services, schooling and nutrition), which had been regarded as a distraction from what were seen as the higher-priority requirements of investment for economic growth.

Any idea that people, actual people, in 'developing countries' value only outlays that are classified in the national accounts as extra investment, not extra consumption, defies all experience. The idea that they *should do so*, or that authorities *should act as if they did so*, is a paternalistic value-judgment in the worst sense, one indeed that suggests that the person judging has, and admits to having, motives *other than* to maintain the welfare of the people concerned. Indeed, where there is competition for resources between consumption and investment, it may be argued that a humane-utilitarian view of policy values investment *only for the sake of* (someone's) future consumption. In that case, deciding between consumption and investment is a matter of balancing values of future against present consumption at the margin. Where the future beneficiaries are not the same people as those who make the present sacrifices, the choice involves balancing the claims of one group against those of the other. On the other hand, if the same people are presumed to be involved now as in the future, then, the more highly those taking decisions on behalf of the poor value investment against consumption, the *lower* by definition (to put it technically) is the rate of discounting the future they are applying – whereas in fact experience suggests that the poorer people are the *more highly* they tend to discount the future, in other words the *less* future-oriented they are. There may be, and are, a number of good reasons for actively encouraging investment among the poor, even the very poor, with real (time-discounted) gains to be made in appropriate circumstances – as many of the recipients of microfinance loans testify, by coming back for more. But first people must eat. Supplementing the consumption of the very poor *is in itself good, in some cases an urgently necessary good*, though of course all the more so when it is done in a way that does not discourage desirable effort or enterprise.

Added to this, certain marketable goods and services that bring immediate consumer benefits may also result in improved nutrition, health and knowledge; and these, as we have implied, may, individually or collectively, represent human investments that increase production.

Difficult as it may be, with complete consistency and fairness, to raise those below the extreme-poverty line by means of transfers to them – that is, to do what is meant here by providing a social safety-net – there should be no prior presumption against the attempt as if it were necessarily inferior, as a use of public resources, to 'directly productive investment'.

3.2.3 Free hand-outs discourage effort and enterprise

Against this assertion it should be recognized that transfers designed primarily to raise the incomes of the very poor are not necessarily given without conditions. India's National Rural Employment Guarantee Scheme, supposed since 2008 to cover the whole country's rural population, and guaranteeing a certain amount of low-paid work in each year for any household that desires it, was emphatically not framed for administering free hand-outs, except when the state or local government had no productive work that it could make available. The Brazilian and Mexican schemes (*Bolsa Familia* and *Oportunidades*), and similar ventures in Nicaragua, Honduras, Bolivia and Ecuador, make small periodic payments to poor families, but only on condition that their children attend school or accept certain vaccinations, or both. So it is quite possible to give payments to the poor that are *conditional*: received either in exchange for work or in consideration of some other socially useful behaviour. Admittedly payments to households for the old and infirm or handicapped, and for children (as proposed in the ILO's 2008 scheme, discussed below in Chapter 4), may be given without requiring as a condition some social contribution, but for these classes of people, with the possible exception of some of the mildly handicapped, it *will not in many cases be desirable* that they should be subject to strong incentives to find remunerative work. In particular, it is surely extremely important that households with children (say under 14) should *not* be subject to the incentive, or the perceived necessity, to put the children to full-time paid work.

3.3 Advantage of transfers in cash as against those in kind

There is always a risk that cash benefits may be, in the eyes of those that provide them, 'misused'; but, whatever is taken to constitute misuse, this risk is not plainly any greater with the transfer element in disposable income than with the earned element. Cash allows people to choose, within their budget constraints, the goods and services that they want, whereas bureaucratic decisions on the nature of benefits to be given in kind may arbitrarily leave the recipients, for example, with unfamiliar and unwelcome foods. Giving any income supplements in cash form accepts the autonomy of the recipients.

Certainly there are instances, especially for children or pregnant or nursing women at risk of under-nourishment, where the case for the state or civil society (voluntary groups or charities) to provide regular healthy meals, or fortified food supplements, in forms that are widely acceptable locally, or particular health-directed outlays, as on water purification or de-worming, may be considered overwhelming. If on the other hand people's entitlements to essentials such as food are in cash form, the authorities may need to ensure that there is enough food within the local markets to keep its prices within the ranges that had been supposed when the amounts of the cash transfers had been fixed. Failing success in this, quantitative rationing of staples may be needed, but it should be treated in these circumstances as decidedly a second-best.

There is currently controversy in India over whether benefits given hitherto in the form of free or subsidized food or fuel would be better given in cash. (See *The Economist* 2012c; London School of Economics 2012.) Apart from issues of the recipients' choice, there are questions over the reliability and cost of delivery and over which form can be made more resilient against theft or other loss en route. If all transfers take the form of electronic messages, often to specified individuals, as is being contemplated in India (see Chapter 6), physical pilfering is presumably out of the question, but internet security for half a billion or so bank accounts can be no small matter.

3.4 Interpretation of 'a dollar a day'; its pragmatic justification

The first of the Millennium Development Goals (MDGs) is to halve, between 1990 and 2015, the proportion of people whose income is less than one dollar a day. That sounds simple enough until we start asking the meaning of 'one dollar a day'. The most sensible practical answer seems to be to take it to mean the daily real amount that the World Bank treats as defining *the more severe of its two international poverty lines*. This, since a re-evaluation that followed from more satisfactory price estimates made for the year 2005, is *a consumption or income level of 1.25 PPP (purchasing-power parity) or 'international' dollars a day at 2005 prices.* It represents a slight modification[3] of an attempt to reflect in real terms what the one dollar a day had earlier been taken to mean. The PPP dollar in any country in any year is now defined so as to be equal in value to the number of units of that country's currency in that year that would buy in that country the equivalent of what one US dollar would buy in 2005, *not in that country but in the United States.*

The inevitable 'index-number problems' mean that there is no uniquely right answer to the question how many units of a country's currency at any time constitute a PPP dollar – and therefore to the question how many of those PPP dollars are the *equivalents, in purchasing-power within the country, to an actual US dollar in foreign exchange* – but best estimates of equivalences are calculated each year for each country,[4] and the resulting numbers of each country's PPP dollars equivalent to one US dollar are widely used in statistical publications entailing international comparisons of value. Each of these equivalences is in effect an exchange-rate, particular to the specific country/currency and year, showing the relationship in purchasing-power between actual US dollars and the 'shadow-currency' which is the country's PPP or international dollar in that year.

Defining poverty by some measure of purchasing-power as determined by household surveys has definite limitations. It will refer to access only to goods that *can normally be* bought and sold: will refer in other words only to *disposable income*. So goods such as staple foods that are produced by the household itself will be included as well as those bought from outside. But the surveys do not take account of the households' access to services provided free of charge by nature, by civil society, or by government. Differences in these latter conditions and provisions may of course make big differences, as we have said, to material well-being.

But in fact the results of the household-purchasing-power surveys will inevitably point largely to differences in capacity to acquire food, though, as already mentioned, recent evidence (Banerjee and Duflo 2011, pp. 22ff.) shows that even very poor people do spend significant proportions of their incomes on non-food goods and services. (Some attempts indeed have been made to express household purchasing-power in calories per day rather than in PPP dollars per day.) The *World Development Indicators 2008* (*WDI 2008*) 'Poverty data' supplement indicates that the *national* poverty lines that are used, as mentioned in footnote 1, to fix the *international* line (as an approximation to *the lowest* of them)

> are typically set with some version of the 'cost of basic needs' method. First, a food-poverty line is established by pricing a food bundle that provides a minimum desirable calorie intake. To this is added an allowance for non-food spending, typically obtained from data on the non-food spending of people near the food poverty line.
>
> (*WDI 2008*, 'Poverty data' supplement, p. 2)

The source goes on to point out that there may be considerable differences from country to country in the quality of food and the levels of non-food spending considered essential. These are among the reasons for the differences among national poverty lines. But the point to be made here is that minimal calorie requirements generally form the core of the assessments. So it is very likely that many households *below* the international line will not, by the most meagre standard, have enough to eat. Food or food-and-water is of course not enough in itself. Being above the line for access to food and a few other marketable goods can be taken, as we have implied above, as *a necessary, but not a sufficient, condition* for avoiding extreme poverty. The implied 'official' judgement of the world, as expressed in the first MDG, is that there is *at least* a level of nutrition (together with other commodities rated by the customers as either necessary complements or equivalent substitutes) that *no one should on any account be denied.*

So the international extreme-poverty line may be regarded as a boundary (arbitrary but reasonable, for want of something more bountiful) of extreme absolute poverty *in this limited sense*: those *above* the line *are not necessarily free* of extreme poverty. They may have no access, or access only with difficulty, to clean water; they may lack basic health care (on some reasonable definition of 'basic') or reasonable protection against endemic and epidemic diseases; they may have no opportunity for schooling and literacy. But those *below* the line *are* extremely poor: probably malnourished in some degree, quite possibly, we may presume, chronically hungry for at least some part of the year. (For reasons given above and elaborated in Chapter 10, the UN and other international organizations have added a further requirement to this basic level of disposable income: that there should be a means of meeting medical costs without risking impoverishment as a result. Hence there is an understanding tacked on to the idea of a safety-net against extreme poverty in disposable income that it should include effective medical insurance geared to the circumstances of those needing the protection.)

The international poverty lines (for 'poverty' and 'extreme poverty' respectively) are about absolute, not relative, poverty – a condition that is poverty or extreme poverty by anyone's definition, not as defined in relation to the expectations of a particular nation or community. The 1.25 PPP dollars a day used since the 2005 recalculation was fixed as *some approximation to a consensus among the lowest* of the national poverty lines (*WDI 2008*, 'Poverty data' supplement, pp. 1–3). Households *above* it may still stand *below* the poverty lines of their own nations. If 'the world at large' – shorthand for those sections of its population rich and/or generous enough to feel any responsibility of human solidarity or morality for sharing their good fortune – has any obligation to provide a systematic opportunity for certain people to rise out of poverty, that obligation applies *at least* to the rescue of people whose incomes (in cash and kind combined) imply that they are severely deprived, even quite possibly of basic food, *by the standards of the poorest countries. Their* (the poorest people's) needs must have a high priority for the world, as the statement of the first MDG implies. Guaranteeing the continued provision of enough disposable income to afford a reasonable, if very basic, level of nutrition for the billion or so people who would otherwise be below the line surely has an extremely high claim on human concern and compassion.

It would be gratifying if the business of providing a safety-net universally could be treated not just as a world *aspiration* but also as a world *project* to be undertaken jointly. Yet we recognize that that response is so improbable as to be scarcely worth consideration. The most we can reasonably hope is that each of the individual nations – its government and civil society – takes the prime initiative and responsibility over filling the gap for its own poor and in its own way, but with the rich nations also offering serious material support to the efforts made by those of the lowest incomes. What has begun to be recognized, as we elaborate in Chapter 12, is that the middle-income countries can, without extraordinary sacrifice on the part of any section of their populations, provide a safety-net for disposable income no lower than the extreme-poverty borderline.

It is of course strongly to be hoped that, once the essentials of a safety-net are established in any country, the level of income supported will gradually be raised – probably as the country becomes more wealthy and its poor more politically demanding.

We go on to consider in Chapter 4 the size in dollars of the gap to be filled and how that size might be reflected in the actual cost of filling it.

Conclusion

Maintaining a target level of income is necessary to ensure that everyone can be fed at a tolerable level and can have other essentials provided – however 'tolerable' and 'essential' are understood for the purpose. The extreme-poverty borderline serves as a target for want of something more ambitious. There is little dispute that anything lower is intolerable. Providing reliably and credibly against falling below it has immediate consumer benefits, including the relief of anxiety at the possibility of destitution, and it also encourages investment, physical and human, on the part of the very poor by reducing their downside risks.

Without social intervention, by the state or civil society, remaining above that borderline cannot be guaranteed, as over a billion people could bear witness. Leaving it to economic growth to raise the floor is too slow, too unreliable and even at its best incomplete. On the other hand, maintaining a safety-net above the borderline is so sparing in the demands it needs to make on resources that at worst it is not inconsistent with economic growth in the countries that take responsibility for it within their own domains. There may very well be synergy between the two.

So there are very strong grounds – both of people's current welfare and of their future growth prospects – for each country not so far covered to make a commitment to a safety-net – a floor to disposable income at a level suited to its own conditions but no lower than the extreme-poverty borderline – for all its citizens; and for liberal support, on the part of high-income countries and international institutions, of all manifestly serious efforts, at least by low-income countries, to meet these commitments.

Notes

1 On the returns to de-worming as assessed in one study, see the figures in Banerjee and Duflo (2011, pp. 31, 39).
2 If world incomes are translated into US dollars at current exchange-rates.
3 A slight modification, apparently because of the attempt, mentioned below, to set the international line so as to reflect some kind of approximation to consensus among the *lowest* of the *national* extreme-poverty lines.
4 See, e.g. World Bank, *WDI 2008*, pp. 8–10; and its 'Poverty data' supplement, pp. 23–5. For example, the 2005 figure for India in the column 'Ratio of PPP conversion factor to market exchange rate' in both these publications was given as 0.33. This means that in 2005 one Indian PPP ('international') dollar would represent in India the purchasing-power of 0.33 actual US dollars in foreign exchange. Or, to put it another way, if you had taken one actual US dollar to India and changed it in the market into Indian rupees, the proceeds would buy 3.0 times as much in India as the single dollar would have bought in the USA. The corresponding 'exchange-rate' in the 2011 *WDI* was 0.4, implying that the US dollar would then be equivalent in purchasing-power to 2.5 PPP dollars in India.

4 Size of the extreme-poverty gap

This chapter aims to measure the size of the extreme-poverty gap in low and lower-middle-income countries, thus necessitating some extensive estimates shown in Appendix 4.2, preceded by Appendix 4.1 which explains the method of calculating them. Indeed, the discussions that follow will depend heavily on these tables.

4.1 Transfers required to fill the gap

4.1.1 Magnitude in dollars of the world's extreme-poverty gap

The question to be addressed here is this. If, purely hypothetically, there was a world desire to provide – for every household whose consumption (or disposable income) per person was *below* 1.25 PPP dollars a day – cash just sufficient to raise its consumption to that level, how many actual US dollars per year would be required? We suppose first, for the sake of the exercise, that these supplementary dollars fall from heaven in just the right amounts and into exactly the hands where they are needed to fulfil the objective. In other words we ignore initially the costs of administration and wastage and the 'overkill' that would almost certainly be necessary, in a scheme administered, however honestly and cleverly, by and for human beings, to ensure that no household that needed the extra cash to meet the requirement would be left out.

Another way of putting this is to say that we aim to show the apparent cost, in dollars of foreign exchange, that would have been required to fill the estimated *total extreme-poverty gap* for a particular year, which we take for simplicity's sake as 2005, the year for which so much of the world poverty map was redrawn. The total poverty gap (TPG), in relation to any particular poverty line, is the total amount that would have to be added to the purchasing-power of those people below the line to bring them up to it. The intention here is to calculate each country's *total extreme-poverty gap* (per year) and to convert it into an annual sum in dollars of foreign exchange. Estimates of TPG figures are given in Appendix 4.2, Tables 4A.1–4A.3. How they are calculated is set out in Appendix 4.1. Columns (3) of Tables 4A.1 and 4A.2 show the TPG for the various countries in millions of PPP ('international') dollars. Columns (5) show the same gap for each country but expressed in millions of actual US dollars. Column (5) of Table 4A.3 gives the sum of the Column (5) totals of Tables 4A.1 and 4A.2, showing the TPG estimate for the low-income and low-middle-income countries combined.

As a further simplification, we are supposing for purposes of the discussion here, that the only people below the line are those identified in *low-income* and *lower-middle-income* countries. At least we consider their needs alone, on the supposition that the needs of those in high- and upper-middle-income countries should be dealt with entirely by their own states. But for completeness we also give in Table 4A.4 upper and lower estimates of the comparatively small annual amount[1] that the very poor in the upper-middle-income countries would add to the size of the gap: to judge by the figures in Table 4A.4, somewhere between US$2.0 and 2.5 billion per year.

We then for the present simply mention (Section 4.1.3) the need for administrative devices for getting the amounts needed into the right hands. These will be further considered in the course of Chapters 5–10.

We compare below the total-poverty-gap estimates (Appendix 4.2, Tables 4A.1–4A.3) with the estimated costs, for seven African and five Asian low-income countries, of a particular practical model of basic social security proposed from within the International Labour Organization (ILO 2008a) and discussed further in this chapter. (See Appendix 4.2, Tables 4A.5 and 4A.6.)

The countries *covered by poverty-gap estimates* here comprise all the low-income and lower-middle-income countries *for which the World Bank gave 2005 poverty figures.* With a few others that are included in Appendix 4.2, Tables 4A.1 and 4A.2, they appear to include all low-income and lower-middle-income countries except for some tiny states with less than half a million people each. The 2007 *WDR* gives the total population in these two income categories in 2005 as 4,828 million (World Bank 2007). This is 1.06 times the 4,552 million in the two categories of countries for which we do have poverty data here. To raise by that multiple, 1.06, the US$66,833.3 million (which as indicated is a *maximum* needed for filling the TPGs quantified in these calculations) would require $70,843.3 million. To allow arbitrarily an addition of 15 per cent for the administrative costs[2] and wastage of any scheme designed actually to fill the gap (counting this for the time being as including any such over-filling as would inevitably be required in practice in order to go reasonably close to filling the TPG completely) would bring it altogether to around $81.5 billion in 2005 (US) prices. This total happens to be well *within the range of high-income OECD donors' aid* in some recent years (including 2005 and 2006), and, even added to existing aid, would still be *well within the range of what these donors would be giving annually if they fulfilled the pledge to transfer in aid 0.7 per cent of their own incomes.* (They, the donor countries, would in that case have been giving about $224.5 billion in 2005 at the prices of that year, when actual aid given was $106.8 billion). Measured by the scale of rich countries' incomes and budgets, these are far from astronomical figures.

As mentioned in Chapter 1, the $80 billion would represent about 0.2 per cent of world gross income (GNI) in 2005.

Making these calculations is not intended to imply that the most appropriate way of meeting these very elemental needs of the billion or so people estimated to be below the (1.25 PPP dollars-a-day) extreme-poverty line is for them all to be provided by the rich OECD countries. Both how they *should* be met and how realistically in the political context they *might* be met are further and separate questions; but estimating the sheer value in actual US dollars of the cash that would have to be handed over seems an important first step.

4.1.2 A reservation: impact of a universal safety-net on food prices

It is true that providing the means of buying more food for the billion or so people who fall below the line and are probably hungry or undernourished for at least some part of the time is likely to have the effect of raising basic-foodstuff prices. We take it that the poorest people will have a higher propensity to spend additional income on the more basic foods than will those richer people who will probably have had to be taxed at least a little more highly, and so suffered a slight reduction in their own disposable income, in order to cover the cost of the safety-net. If such a transfer of spending-power designed to raise the disposable incomes of a billion or so people were to be made on a particular day or within one year, the effect on prices might be drastic. But of course that is not at all likely to happen. The world for the time being – with present population numbers, incomes and tastes – has spare potential food-producing *capacity*. Any big transfer of spending-power from the richer to the poorest *that would not otherwise have occurred* will indeed very probably leave relative staple-food prices higher at first than they would otherwise have been and raise the cost (as measured in other goods and services) of the transfers that will be necessary to raise everyone above the poverty line, but, *given time for adjustment of production levels and no artificial obstacle to their doing so*, there will be more of the staple foods produced, so that the final alteration in relative prices will be much less than it would have been initially if all the transfers had been attempted at once.

This, however, should not be taken to justify an entirely *laissez-faire* approach to staple-food production and prices. If the *relative* prices of staple foodstuffs are on a consistent upward trend, the level of the safety-net in any country in relation to the price of a representative basket of consumer goods will also need to rise over time if it is to maintain its purchasing-power for the very poor consumer. To reduce the fluctuations in staple-foodstuff prices, which create particular difficulties for the poorest, international and national food stocks may need to be increased and their inflows and outflows actively managed. Moreover, to reduce any upward trend in their relative prices there will be an increasingly strong case for the very active propagation of knowledge relevant to increasing productivity and for the removal of artificial obstacles to it such as those prompted by pseudoscientific objections to GM crops.

4.1.3 Quest for devices for targeting transfers to the poorest

A crucial challenge with income-support schemes aimed at providing a social safety-net is to give help to those who meet the criterion of need without extending it to those who do not. Some test of need has to be met, but in most low- and lower-middle-income countries there are at least difficulties in making it depend upon a highly bureaucratized means test. The various approaches to meeting this difficulty are set out in Chapter 5.

4.2 How far can the extreme disposable-income poverty gap reasonably be filled *from domestic resources* in the countries concerned?

To answer that question, we first consider simply the size of the consumption (or disposable-income) gap in cash (or equivalent in kind) and suppose, for the sake of argument, that the test in each country of whether the gap might reasonably be filled from domestic resources is whether that would cost less than 10 per cent of the consumption (or disposable income) of the highest-consuming (or highest-earning) quintile (i.e. fifth) of the population. This is explored in Appendix 4.2's Tables 4A.7 and 4A.8 for low-income and lower-middle-income countries respectively.

Figures in column (2) of Tables 4A.7 and 4A.8 are those for 'household final consumption expenditure' in 2005 as reported in the Poverty Supplement of the *WDI 2008*, Table S3. Those in column (3) represent in most cases the percentage share in total consumption of the top 20 per cent of *consumers* (but in the cases marked ^{Y} they are percentage shares in – presumably disposable – *income* of the top 20 per cent *of income-receivers*), as assessed in the most recent surveys, as given in *WDI 2008*, pp. 68–70. Column (5) reproduces the TPG figures as presented (in PPP dollars) in column (3) of Tables 4A.1 and 4A.2.

Column (6) thus gives the percentage of the total consumption (or of household disposable income) received by the top quintile that is equal to the TPG of the country concerned.

By the test suggested above, those countries with values less than 10 per cent on column (6) of Tables 4A.7 and 4A.8 might be able 'in principle' to fill the extreme TPG from domestic resources (with no account taken for the moment of administrative costs of doing so or of the excess costs involved because of the practical difficulties of fitting safety-net payments precisely to the gap).

With those qualifications, it would seem that, from the *low-income-country* list, India,[3] Pakistan, Vietnam, the Kyrgyz Republic, Tajikistan, Mongolia, Côte d'Ivoire, Kenya and Mauritania – but no others – could reasonably have been expected to fill the gap on their own in 2005. But *all* on the *lower-middle-income-country* list, with the exception (by a small margin) of Lesotho, could be expected to do so (though with Swaziland, Namibia and Cameroon near the 10-per-cent margin).

It is also of interest that, of the 12 countries for which projected affordability calculations were reported in the ILO (2008a) study cited below (though in that case for a particular benefit package, one that included an allowance for administrative expenses and a medical service, and on a different criterion of affordability from the one we are using), India, Pakistan and Vietnam (but also Guinea though *not* Kenya) came out as able to afford the safety-net projected by the ILO's scheme in each of the years 2010, 2020 and 2030.

4.3 The 2008 ILO model of a social safety-net

The ILO (2008a) outlined a model of a social safety-net programme for low-income countries consisting of (a) non-means-tested payments to aged people (65 years and over) and to disabled people of working age, and (b) non-means-tested payments for children under 14 years old (but for no more in any household than two children per woman who has given birth[4]); together with (c) unemployment ('social-assistance') support consisting of a right for people who choose to claim it, but no more than one per household at any time, of 100 days per year of low-paid work. The third of these elements follows closely in general structure the National Rural Employment Guarantee Scheme started in 2006 and since then applied right across rural India. (It was assumed for the ILO's purposes of calculating costs of the programme that an able-bodied working-age adult from one household in ten would claim the 100 days of low-paid work in any year; and also that disabled people of working age would make up 1 per cent of the working-age population.)

An attraction of such a safety-net scheme is that it, if its implementation were perfect, it would require *no assessment of the individual incomes* of those applying for its benefits. Benefits under (a) and (b) would require judgements only of age and disability. Benefits under (c) would go only to those who chose to work for them: so-called self-targeting. By choosing to apply for work, say at or just below the prevailing wage in their respective localities, the workers themselves would be applying the means test.

The level of age and disability benefit would in the proposal be set at 30 per cent of GDP per head with a maximum of 1 PPP dollar a day. The level of child benefit per child would be set at 15 per cent of GDP per head with a maximum of 0.5 of a PPP dollar a day. Payment in the unemployment (social-assistance) scheme would be set at a daily rate equivalent to 30 per cent of GDP per head with a maximum of 1 PPP dollar a day. These details were used by the proponents for costing the scheme but, with some others mentioned above and some that we have not retailed here and that were probably not important to the estimated costing of the scheme,[5] they could of course be varied by any authority introducing a scheme along these lines.

In addition there would be (d) a scheme of designedly universal provision of basic health care, modelled apparently for its level of provision largely on an actual system implemented in Thailand since 2001 and employing health-service staff at 300 per 100,000 population, which is said to be approximately 40 per cent of the number per 100,000 of population employed by the UK National Health Service. Where no actual wages in the health sector were available, the assumption was that health-service staff would be paid the same average wages as teachers in the country concerned, with a minimum of three times GDP per capita. Non-staff health costs were assumed to be 67 per cent of health-service wage costs. Simulated costs of the health-service provisions were those of the whole costs of providing the services, as if the state were to be the 'single provider', without any assumption of a contribution in the form of fees from patients. In this respect the cost simulation would differ from the actual net costs to the state of the Thai scheme (see Chapter 10 below), which were reduced by mandatory insurance premiums from one part of the population and small fees per unit of service from another part.

A fifth element in the estimated costs would be (e) an amount to cover administration of the system equal to 15 per cent of the first three elements (the direct transfers to persons).

The term 'social safety-net' (SSN) is used here, simply for convenience in the calculations, to cover the first three elements (age and disability benefits, child benefits and unemployment social-assistance), without the cost of the health service and the administrative add-on.

For 12 countries, seven in Africa and five in Asia, ILO staff calculated the costs of the five elements in the scheme and expressed these as percentages of GDP in each case. The 12 countries were all among those classed by the World Bank as being of 'low income' until around 2006, although one of them, India, had come by the end of the decade to rank as a 'lower-middle-income' country.

4.4 Comparison between projected costs of the 2008 ILO scheme for the countries to which its application is simulated and the estimated size of the extreme poverty gap for each of those countries

In what follows a comparison is made, for each of the 12 countries, between (1) the estimated cost of the SSN element (that is, all except the health service and the administrative add-on) in the ILO scheme and (2) the (1.25 PPP dollar-a-day) total poverty gap as estimated from the World Bank figures in Tables 4A.1–4A.3. The point of this investigation was to see whether there seemed to be a close, or at least detectable, consistent relationship between the total-poverty-gap figure for a country, as it was estimated in Tables 4A.1 and 4A.2, and the cost of the direct payments to persons projected under the ILO scheme. If there turned out to be a consistent relationship, this would strengthen the presumption that the estimated magnitude of a country's TPG might serve, either as it stood or as systematically modified, as an indicator of the actual cost of the direct transfers (the 'social safety-net', SSN) under a defined and apparently workable scheme of basic income support such as that projected by the ILO in 2008.

All the statistics in the tables relating to the ILO scheme refer in principle to 2005, but the percentages of GDP used to calculate the cash costs of the ILO programme are those estimated for 2008 (ILO 2008a, pp. 23–4). In effect it is supposed that the ILO programme, if applied in 2005, would have cost the same *proportions* of the various countries' GDPs as in 2008.

In Table 4A.5, each of the aggregate-cost figures is expressed first in PPP$ billions per year, with (in square brackets underneath) the corresponding figure in US$ billions per year. Each of the latter figures is equal to the corresponding figure in PPP$ billions multiplied by the US$: PPP$ exchange-rate as given for the country concerned in column (4) of Tables 4A.1 and 4A.2.

At first sight, column (11) in Table 4A.5, showing the ratio for each of the 12 countries in the ILO's sample between (i) the cost of the SSN element in the ILO scheme and (ii) the total poverty gap as given in Tables 4A.1 and 4A.2, is not at all encouraging to the idea that the TPG, as estimated from World Bank figures, might be used as an indicator, for each country and across the low-income countries, and possibly also the lower-middle-income countries, of the cost of the direct transfers under a scheme such as the ILO's. The ratios range from 0.17 for Guinea to 2.54 for Vietnam.

It would not be at all surprising if there were considerable inaccuracies in the poverty percentages, based on sample field surveys, on which the TPG estimates depend. However, if the differences between the two sets of figures do misrepresent what would in reality be greater similarity (or a greater country consistency in the cross-country differences or ratios), the discrepancy seems quite likely to be explained in part by the inevitable simplifying assumptions made in the calculations of the ILO scheme's costs.

A major purpose of the ILO paper's simulations was to gain some idea of how far the low-income countries considered might reasonably be expected to be able to finance a comprehensive basic social-security scheme *out of their own resources* and how far the 'donor community' would be required to help. In the cases of 4 of the 12 countries examined (India, Guinea, Pakistan and Vietnam), the ILO authors found, on their criterion of affordability,[6] that the costs projected could be fully met out of domestic resources in each of the years 2010, 2020 and 2030, and that in Senegal they could be met at least in 2030. But in attempting realistic projections of the actual costs that would need to be borne by or for individual low-income countries they have, as we have seen, been obliged to take some short-cuts in order to reach quantitative answers.

In the ILO scheme, the child and old-age benefits projected are not means tested and so conveniently can be supposed to go to all in the relevant demographic categories, as has presumably been done in the simulations; but, for purposes of calculating prospective costs, estimates from country to country of the numbers receiving disablement benefits and of those taking part in the basic-pay-for-work scheme are apparently based entirely on uniform fractions of the numbers of people of working age. So, while the demographic data used (including those for numbers in each country of children aged under 14 and of people aged over 65) may well be reasonably reliable and so may give reasonably good estimates of the costs of the child and old-age benefits, there is of necessity no equally simple way of reliably estimating, in advance of actual experience under the scheme, the costs of the unemployment social assistance or the disablement benefits. Indeed, as we have seen, the proportions (a) of working-age people who are poor enough to wish to take advantage of the unemployment social assistance, and (b) of those of working age disabled from work, are taken for purposes of the calculation to be *uniform* across the country sample (with proportions of 10 per cent and 1 per cent respectively of the working-age population at any time). This means that there are no close surrogates used in these calculations to take account of *differences in the extent and depth of poverty* from one country to another.

These approximations may well play at least some part in explaining the size, and particularly the variety, of the ratios in column (11) of Table 4A.5.

However, when the figures for the 12 sample countries are aggregated, the ratio in the 'total' row of column (11), at 0.92, comes very close to 1. This is doubtless connected with the fact that India's ratio in the same column, 0.95, is also very close to 1 – given that India, with a much bigger population than the other eleven combined, must have a very large weight in the 12-country aggregate.

Comparison in Table 4A.6 between columns (1) and (2), or alternatively between columns (6) and (7), shows that, for *the 7 African countries* in aggregate, the ILO's estimated costs of the SSN part of its scheme fall quite a long way short of the estimates of the total extreme-poverty gap. But, for *the 5 Asian countries together*, or (because of their relative weights, especially the weight of India) for *the 12 countries together*, the two sets' aggregates in total are remarkably similar.

Knowledge of how the ILO estimates were made cautions us against generalizing from this similarity to expect it very confidently to be repeated in a wider sample or with more detailed knowledge. But presumably there is at least *some* mutual support from these figures, covering between them quite a large slice of the combined low-income and lower-middle-income *population* (with India on the cusp between the two classes), for the idea that either of these approaches gives a definite pointer to the *order of magnitude* into which the costs of an actual comprehensive system of *basic* social support[7] across the whole range of low-income and lower-middle-income countries are likely to fall. So *it might well be possible* to construct an *operational* social safety-net of cash payments to households, perhaps on the broad lines of the ILO model, that serves to fill the extreme total poverty gap across the low-income and lower-middle-income countries at costs in US dollars *of the same order* as those that can be estimated from the size of the gap.

If, taking the last row of Table 4A.6 (B) as a further rough indicator, we supposed that the health-service and administrative costs of a comprehensive scheme on ILO lines would on average bear the same proportion to the SSN costs as was estimated by the ILO writers, we could multiply the figure for filling the extreme total poverty gap by the ratio of the column (10) to the column (7) figure in the last row of Table 4A.6 (B), that is by 48.12/26.37, namely by 1.825. This ratio, multiplied by the $70,843.3 million (derived by raising the $66,883.3 million in the second-last row of column (5) of Table 4A.3 by

4,828/4,552 to take account of the 'missing' population) gives a total annual cost estimate of $129,275 million, in round numbers *$130 billion.* This figure, *added to the actual overseas development assistance (ODA) (from OECD countries) of the year concerned,* would have been *above, but only by $12 billion or so,* the 0.7-per-cent-of-GNI aid target accepted on paper by OECD countries. But note that part of the point of the ILO authors' estimates is to establish what fraction of the cost might quite reasonably be raised *internally* (and the answer on their criterion is 'all of it' in the case of several of the largest of the 12 low-income countries considered).

If so, in spite of all the simplifying assumptions made in order to reach it, this figure has the encouraging implication that, whatever the political and administrative obstacles, the actual costs of the transfers required, with a reasonable allowance for administration, combined with those of the projected health-service provision, and hence of doing *a large part* of the insurance-plus-redistribution job of protecting people across substantially more[8] than the poorest sixth of the world's population from the *actuality or fear* of extreme destitution, *including the deprivation of food, to which they would otherwise at least be at risk,* need not be outside the realm of financial possibility.

And note that, by using 2005 poverty figures, these estimates ignore the further moves toward enhancing internal safety-net provision already made since that year by countries as important in the picture as India, Mexico and Brazil.

Admittedly (to repeat) even convincingly eliminating extreme 'disposable-income-poverty' (and hence the subjective risk of falling into it), and providing clinical health services on affordable terms, would address only a part of the subject matter of the Millennium Development Goals and the sources of extreme deprivation. Without readily accessible clean water and some form of sanitation, plus protection against the prevalent endemic diseases (vaccinations, deworming, mosquito nets, and the rest), life will remain materially pretty wretched and precarious for many, even before we get into questions of schooling. And, in the face of continuing population growth, especially in Africa, rising consumer expectations, especially in East, South East and South Asia, and the climate change already latent in the system, huge public works may well be needed in a number of countries either to get extra fresh water to where it is needed or to keep the salt water out, as well as a great deal of development and transfer of agricultural technology penetrating to the grass-roots rural population. Without these provisions, the conditions of life for many millions will simply get worse. The UK's Stern Report on climate change envisages a need across the world from 2020 for something like $100 billion a year *each* for 'mitigation' of climate change and for 'adaptation' to it, much of both mitigation and adaptation inevitably directed to developing countries (Stern 2009, p. 9). But, as proportions of world income, or even of the income of the rich world, or as measured against military spending, even these, *added to existing aid (ODA) and a substantial contribution to a world social and clinical safety-net,* are not immense amounts.

Conclusion

These comparisons are still on balance encouraging to the hope that a social safety-net at the extreme-poverty limit need entail only manageable costs for the world in general. If anything the two estimates tend, through their very broad agreement with each other, to confirm the estimate that the actual costs of transfers in say US dollars for filling the world's extreme-poverty gap in disposable income could, with sensible administrative arrangements in each country, be of the same order as the size of the gap calculated from World Bank figures in Columns (5) of Tables 4A.1 to 4A.4 of Appendix 4.2 of this book, namely in the region of $80 billion a year, a minute proportion of world income.

Notes

1 Figures in Table 4A.4 suggest it is somewhere between $2.0 and 2.5 billion a year.
2 The ILO publication (brought into the discussion in this chapter as ILO 2008a) adds, for administrative costs of the income safety-net alone, 15 per cent of the direct amounts of transfers to persons under the scheme it puts forward.
3 India, as mentioned above, was classified as a low-income country in 2005 but 'promoted' later in the decade.
4 This proposed limitation to two children per household strikes the present writers as unreasonable, based as it apparently is on the doubtful presumption that it will be necessary to limit population growth.
5 An example is a proposal, whose rationale is hard to discern, that *no* household that had any member receiving age, disability or child benefit should *also* be able to claim the 100 days per year of paid work. These benefits deal with separate needs. Unemployed working-age adults are no less unemployed and in need of subsistence because they have aged or child dependants.
6 Related to the size of the government's budget.
7 Broadly geared to a floor based on the extreme-disposable-income-poverty margin.
8 'More' because it includes those likely to be troubled by the fear, as well as by the reality at any one time, of destitution.
9 http://siteresources.worldbank.org/DATASTATISTICS/Resources/WDI08supplement1216.pdf.
10 The main reason is that the prices of non-tradables (which tend to have a relatively high domestic-low-skilled-labour input) are generally lower with respect to the prices of tradables in lower-income than in higher-income countries.

Appendix 4.1: Note on the sources and the meanings of the data used for poverty gaps

The data used in our first step of estimating the total poverty gap (TPG) are entirely World Bank figures published in issues of the World Bank's *World Development Report (WDR)* and *World Development Indicators (WDI)*, together with the 'Poverty data' supplement to *WDI 2008.*[9]

There was recently a major revision of World Bank national-income and poverty figures for developing countries. This was based on price surveys in 2005 that had been greatly improved and expanded in scope. The results of the revision are embodied in the 2008 edition of *WDI* and its 'Poverty data' supplement. There were quite big differences for a number of developing countries between the poverty figures reported then and those that had been published earlier, and correspondingly different estimates of PPP equivalences of currencies.

Though the calculations are related to the year 2005, the figures used to indicate the distribution of consumption or income in various countries are based on surveys conducted at various times. Where there is a choice we use those from surveys conducted as close to 2005 as possible.

The 2008 *WDI* and its 'Poverty data' supplement give, for each country, implied 'exchange-rates' between US dollars of foreign exchange and that country's PPP dollars. For almost all of the developing countries these figures imply that each actual US dollar will buy goods and services equal in that country to considerably more than one PPP dollar (generally between two and four PPP dollars).[10] It seems perfectly legitimate to treat these figures as exchange-rates. They have been used here to convert *total poverty gaps* expressed in PPP dollars into US dollars of foreign exchange.

The 'poverty gap' figures given as percentages in *WDI* and *WDR* statistics are what are called *normalized poverty gaps (NPGs).* In relation to a particular poverty line such as 1.25 PPP dollars a day, a country's NPG expresses the percentage that its *total poverty gap (TPG)* – the aggregate amount by which some of its residents fall short of the poverty-line income – bears *to what the population's total income would be if everyone received exactly the poverty-line income.*

So: $NPG = TPG_{PPP\$}/N.y_a$
where N is the total population,
y_a is the income per head at poverty-line a in PPP dollars p.a.,
$TPG_{PPP\$}$ is the total poverty gap in PPP dollars p.a., and
NPG is the normalized poverty gap, a fraction usually expressed as a percentage
Hence $TPG_{PPP\$} = NPG.N.y_a$
and $TPG_{US\$} = NPG.N.y_a.\ E_{US\$/PPP}$
where $TPG_{US\$}$ is the total poverty gap in US\$ p.a.
$E_{US\$/PPP}$ is the exchange-rate US\$ per PPP dollar (i.e. number or fraction of US dollars exchanging for the value of one PPP dollar in the country concerned)

Where the poverty-line used is 1.25 PPP dollars a day, $y_a = 1.25x365.2425 = 456.553$
Where it is 2.00 PPP dollars a day, $y_a = 2.00x365.2425 = 730.485$
This is because there are 365.2425 days on average in a year in the Gregorian Calendar.

Appendix 4.2: Estimated costs of filling the poverty gap

Table 4A.1 Total extreme-poverty gaps: low-income countries (absolute values in US$ millions, per year)

Country name	*(1)*	*(2)*	*(3)*	*(4)*	*(5)*
	Population (mil., 2005)	*NPG (%, 2005)*	$TPG_{PPP\$}$ *(mil., 2005)* $= (1) \times \left(\frac{2}{100}\right) \times 456.553$	$E_{US\$/PPP}$ *(2005)*	$TPG_{US\$}$ *(mil., 2005)* $= (3) \times (4)$
Afghanistan	n.a.				n.a.
Bangladesh	142	13.1	8,492.8	0.37	3,142.3
Benin	8	15.7	573.4	0.42	240.8
Bhutan	0.918	7.0	109.8	0.36	39.5
Burkina Faso	13	20.3	1,204.8	0.38	457.8
Burundi	8	36.4	1,329.5	0.32	425.4
Cambodia	14	11.3	722.3	0.31	223.9
Central African Republic	4	28.3	516.8	0.50	258.4
Chad	10	25.6	1,168.8	0.39	455.8
Comoros	0.6	20.8	57.0	0.57	32.5
Congo Democratic Republic	58	25.3	6,699.5	0.45	3,014.8
Côte d'Ivoire	18	6.8	558.8	0.55	307.3
Eritrea	4				n.a.
Ethiopia	71	9.6	3,111.9	0.26	809.1
Gambia	1.5	12.1	82.9	0.26	21.5
Ghana	22	10.5	1,054.6	0.41	432.4
Guinea	9	32.2	1,323.1	0.33	436.6
Guinea-Bissau	1.6	16.5	120.5	0.41	49.4
Haiti	9	28.2	1,158.7	n.a.	n.a.
India	1,095	10.8	53,992.0	0.33	17,817.4

continued

Table 4A.1 Continued

Country name	*(1)*	*(2)*	*(3)*	*(4)*	*(5)*
	Population (mil., 2005)	*NPG (%, 2005)*	$TPG_{PPP\$}$ *(mil., 2005)* $= (1) \times \left(\frac{2}{100}\right) \times 456.553$	$E_{US\$/PPP}$ *(2005)*	$TPG_{US\$}$ *(mil., 2005)* $= (3) \times (4)$
Kenya	34	6.1	946.9	0.39	369.3
Korea Democratic Republic	22				n.a.
Kyrgyz Republic	5	4.4	100.4	0.28	28.1
Laos	6	12.1	331.5	0.28	92.8
Liberia	3	40.8	558.8	0.49	273.8
Madagascar	19	26.5	2,298.7	0.32	735.6
Malawi	13	32.3	1,917.1	0.33	632.6
Mali	14	18.8	1,201.7	0.46	552.8
Mauritania	3	5.7	78.1	0.37	28.9
Mongolia	3	3.6	49.3	0.35	17.3
Mozambique	20	35.4	3,232.4	0.37	1,196.0
Myanmar	51				n.a.
Nepal	27	19.7	2,428.4	0.31	752.8
Niger	14	28.1	1,796.1	0.43	772.3
Nigeria	132	29.6	17,838.4	0.46	8,205.7
Pakistan	156	4.4	3,133.8	0.32	1,002.8
Papua New Guinea	6				n.a.
Rwanda	9	38.2	1,569.6	0.33	518.0

Sao Tome & Principe	0.2			0.53	n.a.
Senegal	12	10.8	591.7	0.48	284.0
Sierra Leone	6	20.3	556.1	0.37	205.8
Solomon Islands	0.5				n.a.
Somalia	8				n.a.
Sudan	36				n.a.
Tajikistan	7	5.1	163.0	0.24	39.1
Tanzania	38	46.8	8,119.3	0.35	2,841.8
Timor Leste	1.0	19.1	87.2		n.a.
Togo	6	11.4	312.3	0.46	143.6
Uganda	29	19.1	2,528.8	0.36	910.4
Uzbekistan	27	15.0	1,849.0		n.a.
Vietnam	83	4.6	1,743.1	0.30	522.9
Yemen Republic	21	4.2	402.7	0.36	145.0
Zambia	12	32.8	1,797.0	0.54	970.4
Zimbabwe	13			1.48	n.a.
Totals with full data	**2,149**				**49,406.7**
Totals with population data (all except Afghanistan)	**2,326**				

Sources: World Bank (2008a and 2008b).

Note
In the top row of each of these tables in Appendix 4.2, figures in round brackets represent column numbers and their contents, so that, e.g., '(3)=(1)×(2)' means that the column (3) figure equals the product of the column (1) and column (2) figures.

Table 4A.2 Total extreme-poverty gaps: lower-middle-income countries (absolute values in US$ millions, per year)

Country name	*(1)*	*(2)*	*(3)*	*(4)*	*(5)*
	Population (mil., 2005)	*NPG (%, 2005)*	$TPG_{PPP\$}$ *(mil., 2005)* $= (1) \times \left(\frac{2}{100}\right) \times 456.553$	$E_{US\$/PPP}$ *(2005)*	$TPG_{US\$}$ *(mil., 2005)* $= (3) \times (4)$
Albania	3	<0.5	<6.8	0.49	<3.4
Algeria	33	1.4	210.9	0.43	90.7
Angola	16	29.9	2,184.1	0.51	1,113.9
Armenia	3	1.9	26.0	0.39	10.1
Azerbaijan	8	<0.5	<18.3	0.35	<6.4
Belarus	10	<0.5	<22.8	0.36	<8.2
Bolivia	9	9.7	398.6	0.28	111.6
Bosnia & Herzegovina	4	<0.5	<9.1	0.46	<4.2
Brazil	186	1.6	1,358.7	0.56	760.9
Bulgaria	8	<0.5	18.3	0.38	6.9
Cameroon	16	10.2	745.1	0.48	357.6
Cape Verde	0.507	5.9	13.7	0.78	10.7
China	1,305	4.0	23,832.1	0.42	10,009.5
Colombia	46	6.1	1,281.1	0.47	602.1
Congo Republic	4	22.8	416.4	0.51	212.4
Cuba	11				n.a.
Djibouti	0.793	5.3	19.2	0.48	9.2
Dominican Republic	9	0.9	37.0	0.57	21.1
Ecuador	13	3.2	189.9	0.42	79.8
Egypt	74	<0.5	<168.9	0.27	<45.6
El Salvador	7	6.7	214.1	0.50	107.1
Georgia	4	4.4	80.4	0.41	32.9
Guatemala	13	3.8	225.5	0.53	119.5
Guyana	0.751	3.9	13.4	0.44	5.9

Honduras	7	10.2	326.0	0.43	140.2
Indonesia	221	4.6	4,641.3	0.41	1,902.9
Iran	68	<0.5	<155.2	0.30	<46.6
Iraq	n.a.				n.a.
Jamaica	3	<0.5	<6.8	0.60	<4.1
Jordan	5	<0.5	<11.4	0.54	<6.2
Kazakhstan	15	<0.5	<34.2	0.43	<14.7
Lesotho	1.795	20.8	170.5	0.55	93.8
Macedonia	2	<0.5	<4.6	0.39	<1.8
Moldova	4	1.7	31.0	0.35	10.9
Morocco	30	0.5	68.5	0.55	37.7
Namibia	2	24.6	224.6	0.67	150.5
Nicaragua	5	5.2	118.7	0.38	45.1
Paraguay	6	3.4	93.1	0.32	29.8
Peru	28	2.0	255.7	0.45	115.1
Philippines	83	5.5	2,084.2	0.39	812.8
Sri Lanka	20	2.6	237.4	0.35	83.1
Suriname	0.449	5.9	12.1	0.59	7.1
Swaziland	1.131	29.4	151.8	0.52	78.9
Thailand	64	<0.5	<146.1	0.40	<58.4
Trinidad	1.305	1.1	6.6	0.61	4.0
Tunisia	10	<0.5	<22.8	0.45	10.3
Turkmenistan	5	7.0	159.8	0.36	57.5
Ukraine	47	<0.5	<107.3	0.33	35.4
Total with full data (all except Cuba and Iraq)	**2,403**				**<17,476.6**
Total with population figures (all except Iraq)	**2,414**				

Sources and Notes: Same as Table 4A.1.

Table 4A.3 Sum of total extreme-poverty gaps: low-income and lower-middle-income countries combined (absolute values in US$ millions, per year)

Country name	*Population (mil., 2005)*	*$TPG_{US\$}$ (mil., 2005) = sum of cols (5) from Tables 4A.1 and 4A.2*
Total with full data	2,149+2,403=**4,552**	49,406.7+<17,476.6=**<66,883.3**
Total with population figures (all except Iraq and Afghanistan)	2,326+2,414=**4,740**	

Sources and Notes: Same as Table 4A.1.

Table 4A.4 Total extreme-poverty gaps: upper-middle-income countries (absolute values in US$ millions, per year)

Country name	*(1)*	*(2)*	*(3)*	*(4)*	*(5)*
	Population (mil., 2005)	*NPG (%, 2005)*	$TPG_{PPP\$}$ *(mil., 2005)* $= (1) \times \left(\frac{2}{100}\right) \times 456.553$	$E_{US\$/PPP}$ *(2005)*	$TPG_{US\$}$ *(mil., 2005)* $= (3) \times (4)$
Argentina	39	1.0	178.07	0.44	78.35
Botswana	1.765	11.0	88.65	0.47	41.67
Chile	16	<0.5	<36.53	0.60	<21.92
Costa Rica	4	<0.5	<9.13	0.51	<4.66
Croatia	4	<0.5	<9.13	0.66	<6.03
Czech Republic	10	<0.5	<22.83	0.60	<13.70
Estonia	1.345	<0.5	<3.07	0.62	<1.90
Gabon	1.384	0.9	5.69	0.49	2.79
Hungary	10	<0.5	<22.83	0.64	<14.61
Latvia	2	<0.5	<4.57	0.53	<2.42
Lithuania	3	<0.5	<6.85	0.53	<3.63
Malaysia	25	<0.5	<57.08	0.46	<26.26
Mexico	103	<0.5	<235.15	0.65	<152.85
Panama	3	2.7	36.98	0.52	19.23
Poland	38	<0.5	<86.75	0.56	<48.58
Romania	22	<0.5	<50.23	0.49	<24.61
Russian Federation	143	<0.5	<326.47	0.45	<146.91
Slovak Republic	5	<0.5	<11.42	0.55	<6.28
South Africa	45	8.2	1,684.85	0.61	1,027.76
St Lucia	0.166	7.2	5.46	0.60	3.28
Turkey	73	0.9	299.99	0.65	194.99
Uruguay	3	<0.5	<6.85	0.54	<3.70
Venezuela	27	8.8	1,084.88	0.55	596.68
Totals (in US$ millions p.a.)					
			Maximum		**2,442.81**
			Minimum		**1,964.75**

Sources and Notes: Same for as Table 4A.1.

Table 4A.5 Estimated annual costs of ILO's proposed (2008) social-security programme, as applied to GDP of 2005: 12 selected African and Asian countries*

Country name	*(1)*	*(2)*	*(3)*	*(4)*	*(5)*	*(6)*	*(7)*	*(8)*	*(9)*	*(10)*	*(10)*
	GDP 2005 (bil. PPP$)	*SSN cost (% of GDP)*	*Health cost (% of GDP)*	*Admin. cost (% of GDP)*	*Total cost (% of GDP)*	*TPG 2005 (bil. PPP$) as in Table 4A.1 col. (3)*	*SSN cost (bil. PPP$)* $(1)\times\left(\frac{2}{100}\right)$	*Health cost (bil. PPP$)* $(1)\times\left(\frac{3}{100}\right)$	*Admin. cost (bil. PPP$)* $(1)\times\left(\frac{4}{100}\right)$	*Total programme cost (bil. PPP$)* $(1)\times\left(\frac{5}{100}\right)$	*Ratio* = (7)/(6)
(A) In PPP$ billions											
Burkina Faso	14.3	4.5	5.5	0.7	*10.7*	1.20	0.64	0.79	0.10	1.53	0.53
Cameroon	34.9	3.0	2.6	0.4	6.0	0.75	1.05	0.91	0.14	2.09	1.40
Ethiopia	47.2	4.4	3.6	0.7	8.7	3.11	2.08	1.70	0.33	4.11	0.67
Guinea	9.7	2.4	1.5	0.4	4.3	1.32	0.23	0.15	0.04	0.42	0.17
Kenya	47.9	4.5	3.0	0.7	8.2	0.95	2.16	1.44	0.34	3.93	2.27
Senegal	18.2	3.6	2.5	0.5	6.6	0.59	0.66	0.46	0.09	1.20	1.12
Tanzania	40.4	4.8	2.4	0.7	7.9	8.12	1.94	0.97	0.28	3.19	0.24
Bangladesh	163.7	3.9	1.5	0.6	6.0	8.49	6.38	2.46	0.98	9.82	0.75
India	2,440.8	2.1	1.5	0.3	3.9	53.99	51.26	36.61	7.32	95.19	0.95
Nepal	26.0	4.8	1.5	0.7	7.0	2.43	1.25	0.39	0.18	1.82	0.51
Pakistan	340.3	2.0	1.5	0.3	3.8	3.13	6.81	5.10	1.02	12.93	2.18
Vietnam	178.1	2.5	1.5	0.4	4.4	1.74	4.45	2.67	0.71	7.84	2.54

Sources: Col. (1) from World Bank (2008a and 2008b); and cols (2) to (4) from ILO (2008a).

Note

* Based on 2005 GDPs and ILO estimates of proportions of GDP required in 2008.

Table 4A.5 Estimated annual costs of ILO's proposed (2008) social-security programme, as applied to GDP of 2005: 12 selected African and Asian countries*

Country name	*(1)*	*(2)*	*(3)*	*(4)*	*(5)*	*(6)*	*(7)*	*(8)*	*(9)*	*(10)*	*(10)*
	GDP 2005 (bil. PPP$)	*SSN cost (% of GDP)*	*Health cost (% of GDP)*	*Admin. cost (% of GDP)*	*Total cost (% of GDP)*	*TPG 2005 (bil. PPP$) as in Table 4A.1 col. (3)*	*SSN cost (bil. PPP$)* $(1)\times\left(\frac{2}{100}\right)$	*Health cost (bil. PPP$)* $(1)\times\left(\frac{3}{100}\right)$	*Admin. cost (bil. PPP$)* $(1)\times\left(\frac{4}{100}\right)$	*Total programme cost (bil. PPP$)* $(1)\times\left(\frac{5}{100}\right)$	*Ratio* = (7)/(6)
(B) In US$ billions											
Burkina Faso	5.43	4.5	5.5	0.7	*10.7*	0.46	0.24	0.30	0.04	0.58	0.52
Cameroon	16.75	3.0	2.6	0.4	6.0	0.36	0.50	0.44	0.07	1.01	1.39
Ethiopia	12.27	4.4	3.6	0.7	8.7	0.81	0.54	0.44	0.09	1.07	0.67
Guinea	3.20	2.4	1.5	0.4	4.3	0.44	0.08	0.05	0.01	0.14	0.18
Kenya	18.68	4.5	3.0	0.7	8.2	0.37	0.84	0.56	0.13	1.53	2.27
Senegal	8.74	3.6	2.5	0.5	6.6	0.28	0.31	0.22	0.04	0.58	1.11
Tanzania	14.14	4.8	2.4	0.7	7.9	2.84	0.68	0.34	0.10	1.12	0.24
Bangladesh	60.57	3.9	1.5	0.6	6.0	3.14	2.36	0.9	0.36	3.63	0.75
India	805.46	2.1	1.5	0.3	3.9	17.82	16.91	12.08	2.42	31.41	0.95
Nepal	8.06	4.8	1.5	0.7	7.0	0.75	0.39	0.12	0.06	0.56	0.52
Pakistan	108.9	2.0	1.5	0.3	3.8	1.00	2.18	1.63	0.33	4.14	2.18
Vietnam	53.43	2.5	1.5	0.4	4.4	0.52	1.34	0.80	0.21	2.35	2.58

Sources: Col. (1) from World Bank (2008a and 2008b); cols (2) to (4) from ILO (2008a).

Note

* Based on 2005 GDPs and ILO estimates of proportions of GDP required for the programme in 2008.

Table 4A.6 Total extreme-poverty gap and estimated costs of ILO scheme elements: aggregates across the seven African, and across the five Asian, sample countries (in PPP$ billions and in US$ billions, 2005)

	(2)	*(3)*	*(4)*	*(5)*	*(6)*
	Total extreme-poverty gap	*ILO scheme SSN cost*	*ILO scheme health cost*	*ILO scheme admin. cost*	*ILO scheme total cost*
(A) In PPP$ billions					
7 African countries	16.04	8.76	*6.42*	*1.32*	*16.50*
5 Asian countries	69.78	70.15	*47.23*	*10.21*	*127.59*
Total 12 countries	85.82	78.91	*53.65*	*11.53*	*144.09*
	(6)	*(7)*	*(8)*	*(9)*	*(10)*
	Total extreme-poverty gap	*ILO scheme SSN cost*	*ILO scheme health cost*	*ILO scheme admin. cost*	*ILO scheme total cost*
(B) In US$ billions					
7 African countries	5.56	3.19	*2.35*	*0.48*	*6.03*
5 Asian countries	23.23	23.18	*15.54*	*3.38*	*42.09*
Total 12 countries	28.79	26.37	*17.89*	*3.86*	*48.12*

Sources: World Bank (2008a and 2008b); and ILO (2008a).

Table 4A.7 An indicator of domestic capacity for filling the extreme poverty gap: low-income countries

(1)	*(2)*	*(3)*	*(4)*	*(5)*	*(6)*
Country	*Household final cons'n expenditure (bil. PPP\$, 2005*	*Consumption share of top quintile (%)*	*Consumption of top quintile (bil. PPP, 2005)* $= \frac{(2) \times (3)}{100}$	$PG_{PPP\$}$ *2005, bn.*	$= \frac{(5)}{(4)} \times 100\%$
Afghanistan	n.a.				
Bangladesh	108.3	42.5	46.0	8.4928	18.5
Benin	6.4	44.5	2.8	0.5734	20.5
Bhutan	0.8	n.a.			
Burkina Faso	9.0	47.2	4.2	1.2048	28.7
Burundi	1.9	48.0	0.9	1.3295	147.7
Cambodia	13.4	49.6	6.6	0.7223	10.9
Central African Republic	2.0	65.0	1.3	0.5168	39.8
Chad	5.7	n.a.			
Comoros	0.5	n.a.			
Congo Democratic Republic	9.1	n.a.			
Côte d'Ivoire	19.6	50.7	9.9	0.5588	5.6*
Eritrea	1.8	n.a.			
Ethiopia	32.8	39.4	12.9	3.1119	24.1
Gambia	n.a.	52.9		0.0829	
Ghana	18.4	n.a.			
Guinea	6.7	46.1	3.1	1.3231	42.7
Guinea-Bissau	0.4	53.4	0.2	0.1205	60.3
Haiti	8.4	63.4[¥]	5.3	1.1587	21.9
India	1,321.8	45.3	598.8	53.9920	9.0*
Kenya	33.0	49.1	16.2	0.9469	5.8*
Korea Democratic Republic	n.a.				
Kyrgyz Republic	6.6	39.4	2.6	0.1004	3.9*
Laos	6.0	43.3	2.6	0.3315	12.8
Liberia	0.9	n.a.			
Madagascar	11.1	53.5	5.9	2.2987	39.0
Malawi	4.0	46.6	1.9	1.9171	100.9
Mali	7.6	46.6	3.5	1.2017	34.3

continued

Table 4A.7 Continued

(1)	(2)	(3)	(4)	(5)	(6)
Country	*Household final cons'n expenditure (bil. PPP$, 2005*	*Consumption share of top quintile (%)*	*Consumption of top quintile (bil. PPP, 2005)* $= \frac{(2) \times (3)}{100}$	$PG_{PPP\$}$ *2005, bn.*	$= \frac{(5)}{(4)} \times 100\%$
Mauritania	3.7	45.7	1.7	0.0781	4.6*
Mongolia	3.0	40.5	1.2	0.0493	4.1*
Mozambique	10.5	53.6	5.6	3.2324	57.7
Myanmar	n.a.				
Nepal	17.4	54.6	9.5	2.4284	25.6
Niger	5.3	53.3	2.8	1.7961	64.1
Nigeria	n.a.	49.2		17.8384	
Pakistan	241.5	40.8	98.5	3.1338	3.2*
Papua New Guinea	5.0	56.5	2.8	n.a.	
Rwanda	4.7	53.0	2.5	1.5696	62.8
Sao Tome & Principe	n.a.	n.a.		n.a.	
Senegal	11.7	48.4	5.7	0.5917	10.4
Sierra Leone	2.2	47.3	1.0	0.5561	55.6
Solomon Islands	n.a.				
Somalia	n.a.				
Sudan	38.2	n.a.			
Tajikistan	6.2	41.9	2.6	0.1630	6.3*
Tanzania	22.0	42.4	9.3	8.1193	87.3
Timor Leste	n.a.				
Togo	3.5	n.a.			
Uganda	15.9	52.5	8.3	2.5288	30.5
Uzbekistan	21.6	44.7	9.7	1.8490	19.1
Vietnam	90.1	44.8	40.4	1.7431	4.3*
Yemen Republic	n.a.	45.3			
Zambia	8.0	55.1	4.4	1.7970	40.8
Zimbabwe	n.a.	55.7			

Sources: World Bank (2008a and 2008b).

Notes

¥ indicates that for this country it is the *income*-share of the top quintile that is given in col. (3) and used to calculate the figure in col. (4).

* indicates cases with figures below 10% in col. (6).

Table 4A.8 An indicator of domestic capacity for filling the extreme poverty gap: lower-middle-income countries

(1)	*(2)*	*(3)*	*(4)*	*(5)*	*(6)*
Country	*Household final cons'n expenditure (bil. PPP$, 2005*	*Consumption share of top quintile (%)*	*Consumption of top quintile (bil. PPP, 2005)* $= \frac{(2) \times (3)}{100}$	$PG_{PPP\$}$ *2005, bn.*	$= \frac{(5)}{(4)} \times 100\%$
Albania	12.5	39.5	4.9	<0.0068	<0.14
Algeria	65.4	42.6	27.9	0.2109	0.76
Angola	n.a.			2.1841	
Armenia	8.6	42.8	3.7	0.0260	0.70
Azerbaijan	14.9	44.5	6.6	<0.0183	<0.28
Belarus	44.5	36.8	16.4	<0.0228	0.14
Bolivia	19.7	63.0[¥]	12.4	0.3986	3.21
Bosnia-Hercegovina	18.2	43.2	7.9	<0.0091	<0.12
Brazil	825.1	60.8[¥]	501.7	1.3587	0.27
Bulgaria	39.2	38.3	15.0	0.0183	0.12
Cameroon	21.4	50.9	10.9	0.7451	6.84[#]
Cape Verde	0.9	n.a.		0.0137	
China	1742.6	51.9[¥]	904.4	23.8321	2.64
Colombia	98.7	60.9[¥]	60.1	1.2811	2.13
Congo Republic	2.4	n.a.		0.4164	
Cuba	n.a.				
Djibouti	0.8	n.a.		0.0192	
Dominican Republic	32.1	55.3[¥]	17.8	0.0370	0.21
Ecuador	49.0	58.0	28.4	0.1899	0.67
Egypt	190.5	41.5	79.1	<0.1689	<0.21
El Salvador.	29.0	55.9[¥]	16.2	0.2141	1.32
Georgia	9.9	46.7	4.6	0.0804	1.75
Guatemala	40.1	54.1[¥]	21.7	0.2255	1.04
Guyana	1.2	n.a.		0.0134	
Honduras	14.3	58.3[¥]	8.3	0.3260	3.93
Indonesia	425.9	47.3	201.5	4.6413	2.30

continued

Table 4A.8 Continued

(1)	(2)	(3)	(4)	(5)	(6)
Country	*Household final cons'n expenditure (bil. PPP$, 2005*	*Consumption share of top quintile (%)*	*Consumption of top quintile (bil. PPP, 2005)* $= \frac{(2) \times (3)}{100}$	$PG_{PPP\$}$ *2005, bn.*	$= \frac{(5)}{(4)} \times 100\%$
Iran	282.0	45.1	127.2	<0.1552	<0.12
Iraq	n.a.	n.a.			
Jamaica	10.2	51.6	5.3	<0.0068	<0.13
Jordan	17.5	46.3	8.1	<0.0114	0.14
Kazakhstan	58.3	41.5	24.2	<0.0342	<0.14
Lesotho	2.6	66.5	1.7	0.1705	10.03#
Macedonia	9.4	45.5	4.3	<0.0046	<0.11
Moldova	7.3	41.4	3.0	0.0310	1.03
Morocco	53.7	46.6	25.0	0.0685	0.27
Namibia	4.1	78.7¥	3.2	0.2246	7.02#
Nicaragua	9.9	49.3	4.9	0.1187	2.42
Paraguay	16.3	61.9¥	10.1	0.0931	0.92
Peru	104.2	56.7¥	59.1	0.2557	0.43
Philippines	156.0	50.6	78.9	2.0842	2.64
Sri Lanka	42.3	48.0	20.3	0.2374	1.17
Suriname	1.1	n.a.		0.0121	
Swaziland	3.1	56.3¥	1.7	0.1518	8.93#
Thailand	231.8	49.0	113.6	<0.1461	<0.13
Trinidad	10.5	44.9¥	4.7	0.0066	0.14
Tunisia	34.1	47.3	16.1	<0.0228	<0.14
Turkmenistan	8.7	47.5	4.1	0.1598	3.90
Ukraine	143.1	37.4	53.5	<0.1073	<0.20

Sources: World Bank (2008a and 2208b).

Notes

¥ indicates that for these countries it is the *income*-share of the top quintile that is given in col. (3) and used to calculate the figure in col. (4).

# indicates cases with figures *above* 5% in col. (6).

Part II

Ways and means

5 Targeting the poor and fixing rates

Those who doubt the feasibility of a social safety-net for the general run of low- and middle-income countries commonly refer to one or more of three supposed difficulties:

1 Difficulty of estimating the incomes of individual people or households and hence which of them face poverty gaps and the sizes of the gaps that would have to be filled in each case;
2 Difficulty of filling the gaps without deterring effort or enterprise;
3 Difficulty of avoiding widespread leakage of benefit funds through misappropriation.

The third of these challenges we consider in Chapter 6. Here we address the other two, making considerable use of Grosh *et al.* (2008), the volume entitled *For Protection and Promotion*, in which the authors offer what is virtually a detailed working manual of the range of ways in which the requirements – of identifying the people who would have to be paid, fixing the amounts that should be given to them and managing the transfers – might be met. For our present purpose what is important to convey is that there are several possible approaches to filling the gaps, with various advantages and limitations; that making choices among them frequently involves trade-offs between partly-rival 'goods'; that an ideal solution is likely to be elusive, but that the trade-offs can often be improved by changes in the design of the methods adopted, which will sometimes include a combination of approaches. Much in the Grosh *et al.* book that relates to good practice in matters that are *not specific* to the task of providing a safety-net or income floor we shall here overlook, and confine ourselves to what has a direct bearing on meeting the first two of the three difficulties.

5.1 Methods of targeting

People from highish-income social-democracies contemplating the possible extension of a disposable-income safety-net to the people of a low-income or lower-middle-income country naturally try to imagine a social-security system such as is common in much of Europe. There quite a high proportion of the population are regularly drawing cash benefits for which they are classed as eligible on grounds of age or infirmity or family responsibilities or simply because their other sources of income are considered inadequate. For this purpose records are needed that can be used to register the claims of each individual who may be eligible for benefit, and where relevant giving that person's income and other circumstances. Records also have to be kept up to date, to which end the people concerned need to keep on providing the information.

Translating a system such as that to a 'developing country' presents obvious difficulties. If payments are to be made subject to a 'means test', and especially if the amount of any payment *varies* with the recipients' income or wealth, this bureaucratic model would make excessive demands. It supposes that the potential beneficiaries have the means and the habit of communicating with officialdom, which is unlikely especially for those who are not functionally literate or are working in 'the informal sector'. It is all the more difficult for migrant workers who have no fixed residential address or for people, like many in towns and cities today, who are in technically illegal settlements. Reporting net earnings accurately is well-nigh impossible for the high proportion of earners in the poorer countries who are in the 'informal sector': that is, they are not on regular wages but earn what they can from season to season or day to day, and any income-earning expenses that might be set against their receipts are likewise highly variable. Moreover it is probable that many earners in the informal sector are quite unaccustomed to estimating their net income or wealth, let alone reporting it.

These are genuine obstacles, and they do probably mean that the highly bureaucratic model of the way to provide a safety-net will be unworkable in a number of countries and situations, and also that we may often have to be satisfied with a less-than-perfect solution. The ideal in provision of a safety-net is to make payments to all who satisfy the agreed criterion of need but not to any of those who do not, and to ensure that payments made are just enough to meet the target level of disposable income for each person or household. That would be an efficient solution in the sense that it would mean that whatever was given in benefits would do as much 'work' as possible in relieving poverty.

However, on the evidence of recent experience, there are ways of getting around these difficulties and performing much at least of the essential function of a safety-net, provided the system is adjusted to circumstances and that compromises with the ideal are accepted.

The key tasks that would have to be performed by the system are two: *identifying the peopl*e who need to be supported, and *determining the amount* of benefit to be paid.

Targeting is the term used for identifying individuals from a population for whom some particular treatment or investigation is intended. In the present context it will be mainly people who are in poverty of whatever degree is of interest. Ideally, if costs and other sources of difficulty could be ignored, this could mean direct and accurate assessment of each individual's or household's income or wealth or both. But there are several 'second-best' approaches. Choice of any method of targeting for poverty involves a trade-off between accuracy and cost (in the widest sense: not only financial cost to the administering authorities but also cost, in for example time or inconvenience, to those who might hope to benefit from complying with any conditions imposed). Accuracy is likely to be costly.

There is also a trade-off between propensities to 'errors of inclusion' (some of the non-poor included as beneficiaries) and propensities to 'errors of exclusion' (some of the eligible poor denied benefits). More rigour in preventing the one will tend to mean increased proneness to the other. For example, rigorous action taken to make sure that no one of the very poor is wrongly left out of the benefit list is quite likely to mean that some who are not very poor are (wrongly) included. And the converse also applies. Success in targeting for poverty – a matter of degree – would be reflected in the avoidance of errors of exclusion and inclusion.

It would seem that errors of inclusion are generally easier to identify than errors of exclusion. Grosh *et al.* guess (2008, p. 92) that the three main causes of exclusion errors are, in descending order, inadequate financing, inadequate outreach (itself possibly a result of inadequate financial provision) and, much less important, misclassification of eligible claimants as ineligible.

But first there is the question of the case for targeting as against universal benefits in the reduction of extreme poverty. If funds are available for reducing the poverty of a poor population, why not spread them around equally? Briefly the reason, obvious once stated, is that, given any limited budget for household-poverty reduction, the more the benefits can be concentrated on the most needy, the more on average each very poor beneficiary can receive. Targeting for poverty implies concentrating the benefits in this way. It will of course have its costs, and the strength of the case for it will depend on how those costs compare with the benefits of the reduction in poverty that the targeting makes possible.

Here we set out the various approaches to targeting, with their advantages and drawbacks, so as to fill the gap for each of the extremely poor.

5.1.1 Self-targeting through paid work on public projects

There is one solution extremely simple in principle and often, it seems, applicable in practice. This is so-called 'self-targeting', in which members of households deemed to be in or at risk of extreme poverty are given the opportunity of (usually unskilled) work paid at rates at or just below those locally prevailing, work which they may take or not at their discretion. The American term *workfare* is commonly used for such arrangements. This obviates the necessity of assessing any particular household's means. The workers themselves reveal their needs by their readiness to accept the work at the wage on offer. The big difficulty for self-targeting is the complex administrative task – most striking over a rural population the size of India's – of arranging and supervising useful public work, over hundreds of thousands of individual sites, for a workforce whose numbers of members active at any time cannot be known far in advance and presumably may vary from day to day. Experience suggests that self-targeting works most readily in rural areas where there is ample occasion for public works carried out through labour-intensive techniques by unskilled labourers. However, many people with strong grounds for supplementation of their means by transfers in cash or in kind cannot or do not fit these circumstances. So there remain situations in which, and individuals or groups for whom, some actual assessment of means, however crude, will be necessary.

5.1.2 Means testing

This involves in principle assessing either the wealth or the income (or some combination of the two) of all the people who apply for benefits or appear from a survey as if through outward signs of poverty they may be eligible. A household's up-to-date income – in the sense of its *regular* net receipts per year, say – will be strictly unknowable if, like so many of the very poor, the household's main earners do not have formal-sector jobs but are small entrepreneurs, with receipts and business expenses that vary unpredictably from day to day, without detectable regularity, and are probably unrecorded. The household's net wealth, the other indicator of the level of its 'means', will probably amount to the value of livestock and a few household objects, minus any debts; will be difficult to compute objectively; and will quite often be negative. Grosh *et al.* say with reason that it is this method of targeting *if any* that may introduce work-disincentives.

5.1.3 Proxy means testing

This involves observers in making rough overall assessments of each household's level of prosperity or want, through such visible indicators as standard of accommodation, livestock numbers, household composition, water supply. By comparison with attempts at precise quantitative means tests, proxy means tests would not need such frequent updating, but, with a range of types of potential indicators, they would inevitably have a more subjective element in the judgements made, which would lay them open to dispute.

5.1.4 Nutritional-status targeting

Grosh *et al.* (2008, p. 85) mention this as a possibility. (Other 'risk factors', such as membership of deprived ethnic minorities, might also be used as criteria.) There are simple tests, apparently objective, that can quickly and non-disruptively be applied to children in order to test for certain forms of malnutrition that may result from either inadequate quantity and quality of food or parasite infestation. Applying these tests may not only reveal a presumption of severe poverty but also give important danger signals, indicating what needs to be done to open possible avenues of escape. But, applied alone and only to children, they may miss the poverty of childless households.

5.1.5 Demographic targeting

This will generally mean identifying *by age* the people to be helped: most probably children and the elderly, together probably with pregnant women (and also with lactating women, at least if they are not simultaneously given allowances for the children who are being breast-fed). It is probably convenient to treat disabled adults of working age on terms similar to those for elderly people. Demographic criteria are generally simple and easy to apply. They may either be the only ones used (so that all individuals within certain age-groups receive benefits without being subjected to any form of means test in addition) or simply be used as the first stage in a two-stage or multi-stage process, with some form of means test or proxy to follow. Used alone to select for some level of poverty, they will of course entail errors either of exclusion or of inclusion.

5.1.6 Geographic targeting

This refers to selecting needy people by the areas in which they live. Again this may be done either as the sole test of eligibility or as a first stage to sort out those with most likelihood of severe poverty before some approach to a means test is applied in addition. As with demographic targeting for poverty, geographic targeting will be open to errors of inclusion if it is the sole hurdle to be passed, and to errors of exclusion if it means selecting only part of the population of interest.

5.1.7 Community-aided targeting

Here there might be, for each locality over which there is likely to be a fair amount of mutual acquaintance, a small group of respected citizens drawn upon to help make judgements on which households are in extreme poverty. The very durable English Poor Law of 1601, mentioned in Chapter 9 below, fairly clearly depended in part on such use of local knowledge. It might be useful to include in any advisory group one or more people such as schoolteachers, living in the vicinity but originating outside it, and also to see that all known local factions and castes or equivalent are represented. Such community aid in targeting might be used in conjunction with other methods and could quite possibly play a vital part in proxy means testing.

As implied above, two or more of these methods may advantageously be used together in targeting for the one programme. Coady *et al.* (2003, p. 5) conclude from their review of targeting studies that generally ‘using more targeting methods produced better targeting’.

5.2 Anti-work incentives

On general reasoning from human behaviour it is of course possible that grants received free of reciprocal obligations may discourage effort or risk-taking, either (i) because they reduce the urgency of earning activity (an *income effect*) or, if the amount of grant received is known to be inversely related to the amount of earned income, (ii) because they reduce the net rate of reward for additional productive activity (a *substitution effect* or *price effect*). It would seem that this possibility, a perennial worry in rich-country welfare states that aspire through grants to provide standard minimum levels of disposable income, does not, for several reasons, need to be much cause for concern in very poor countries that are aiming at *income floors* near to international extreme-poverty lines.

First, if the floor is set by self-targeting ('workfare') methods that rely on paying for work done at or near prevailing wage rates, this can hardly act as a disincentive to work. (Grosh *et al.* 2008, p. 96, say that self-targeting labour on public works may reduce time spent on other forms of labour, but, if that matters, it can presumably be prevented by altering wages on the workfare project.)

Second, where benefits are received by or for *people not expected to work* (children, old people and the incapacitated), any disincentive to work that may come about as an income effect at worst does not matter, and at best (as in the case of children) is even desirable.

Third, unless the amount received as a benefit is substantial in relation to the recipients' accustomed levels of income, the *income effect* of the receipt is unlikely to reduce the pressure to earn in any important degree.

Fourth, unless the amounts received as benefits are predictably and closely related (inversely) to earned income (which entails adjusting the levels of benefit as earned income fluctuates), there is no ground for a *substitution effect* of the benefit to reduce earning activity. In fact, many of the very poor – often the majority of them – derive their income from the informal sector, in which daily, monthly and annual amounts earned by each individual will often vary widely and unpredictably over time. To reflect these movements at all closely in the benefits given to individuals will be simply out of the question. It is partly because of difficulties in relating benefits closely to actual earnings that 'proxy means tests', rather than attempts at precise means tests, are likely to be used. If the proxy tests based on outward signs of poverty are applied, they will tend to give a less sensitive short-term account of variations in households' levels of prosperity than would ideally be supplied by accurate and up-to-date means tests; but the point here is that they *will not be expected* to give a precise and sensitive measure of income, and hence benefits based (inversely) upon them seem very unlikely to discourage earning activity. This is even more true of any form of geographic or demographic targeting applied on its own, which would by definition not be at all sensitive to fluctuations in income.

Grosh *et al.* (2008, p. 138) summarize the limitations of the theoretical case for expecting work disincentives on three grounds. First, not all the beneficiaries (children, the old, invalid, handicapped) are expected to work. Second 'the typical beneficiary from a low-income country' will probably be 'a poor, credit-constrained entrepreneur', who may well use the extra cash for a small investment and as a result work more rather than less. Third, the worry clearly does not apply where work is the condition for being paid.

All this summarizes or supports *a priori grounds* for believing that, in many or most cases, anti-work incentives of safety-net measures in developing countries do not exist, do not matter, or can be avoided. Further, Grosh *et al.* (2008, pp. 140ff.) summarize some *empirical evidence* from Armenia (Family Poverty Benefits Program), Brazil (school grants), Zambia (Kalomo District Pilot Social Transfer Scheme), rural Ethiopia (food aid), Mexico (PROGRESA conditional cash transfers), Romania (Guaranteed Minimum Income Program) and Sri Lanka (rice subsidy). In none of these cases except that in Sri Lanka was there any clear evidence of work reduction as a result of the transfers, and indeed in Ethiopia the programme appeared to have had the effect of *increasing* labour supply. The authors (ibid.) explain some of these results and give four general reasons why (as they believe) work disincentives are smaller in developing countries than in richer countries: in the former, many programmes are targeted to households without able-bodied adults; programmes are less generous; verified means-tested programmes with frequent recertification of household income are rare; and *regularity* of transfers in developing countries (i.e. *insensitivity* to income fluctuations) is often, rightly, preferred by administrators because it '[helps] households make productive investments in their futures'. (Further evidence – in that case relating to the effects of *conditional* cash transfers and tending in the same direction – is given in Chapter 8 below.)

5.3 Costs of targeting

Grosh *et al.* (2008, p. 87) distinguish five types of targeting cost: administrative cost, private cost (transaction costs – in time and trouble – to recipients and potential recipients of applying for benefits and complying with any requirements), incentive costs (induced changes in behaviour, which indeed may sometimes be beneficial as is the intention with conditional cash transfers), social costs (stigmatization of recipients) and political costs (possible envy of beneficiaries and adverse reactions of holders of power to programmes discriminating in favour of the less influential, though again there may be favourable public reactions as well).

Studies summarized by Grosh *et al.* (2008, pp. 93–5) imply a distinction, among the total *administrative* costs of an anti-poverty programme, of those that are attributable to targeting (the proportions due to targeting in one set of eight studies are given as varying between 24 and 88 per cent). The authors emphasize that, even if benefits are universal (in the sense presumably of *either* going literally to everyone in a national or regional population *or else* being confined to a very easily identified class of the population, such as children below working age), so that targeting costs can be regarded as minimal, there may still be substantial administrative costs, as for registration and organizing payment of beneficiaries.

In these eight studies (from Latin America, Central Asia and Eastern Europe) administrative costs of targeting are given as varying between 0.6 and 6.3 per cent of total programme costs, but the authors stress that the scale and general character of programmes can lead to big differences in the relative importance of these costs within the total programme. This is a cue to look for ways in which the proportions of administrative costs of programmes may be cut by the sharing of facilities and services across programmes and agencies.

Private costs of anti-poverty programmes (costs in time and inconvenience to beneficiaries and would-be beneficiaries) may also be important (the authors mention particularly those of workfare-type ventures), and may at worst deter eligible claimants, but they may be reduced by reshaping the arrangements with consideration for the users. Having 'one-stop shops' for several programmes or agencies may serve this purpose as well as reducing administrators' own costs.

5.4 Success of poverty targeting

One possible measure of success is the proportion of beneficiaries falling in the lowest income quintile (fifth) of the population. A figure (Grosh *et al.* 2008, p. 90) shows, for various conditional-cash-transfer (CCT) and other poverty-directed programmes in Europe, Central Asia and the Americas, the proportions of recipients in the lowest quintile of the population in each case. This shows proportions from 70 to 80 per cent for the 'last-resort' transfer programmes of the USA, Romania, Bulgaria and Lithuania, and for Brazil's CCT *Bolsa Familia*; and at the other extreme proportions in the region of 20–30 per cent (not much different from the rates expected by chance) for some last-resort schemes in the Caucasus, the Balkans and Central Asia.

Other studies summarized (Grosh *et al.* 2008, p. 92) give the average proportion of the lowest quintile benefited in one set of Latin American programmes as 19 per cent; and in another set as 42 per cent.

Such figures are, without further knowledge, only in the loosest sense indicators of success in poverty targeting. This is because the 'poverty' to be targeted need not be coterminous with the lowest income quintile in whatever country is concerned. The 'extremely poor' by international standards will extend well beyond the lowest income quintile in Bangladesh or Mozambique but be much fewer in Romania or Uzbekistan. So the criterion for extreme poverty used in a particular study will determine what share of the population at its poorest end we should 'expect' to identify as extremely poor.

However, Coady *et al.* (2003, pp. 4ff.) give as the first core message from an extensive study of targeted programmes that '*Targeting can work*'...

> The best programs we found were able to concentrate a high level of resources on poor individuals and households. Argentina's *Trabajar* public works programme, the best programme in this regard, was able to transfer 80 per cent of programme benefits to the poorest quintile. The best ten performers deliver to the poor two to four times the share of benefits they would get with random allocations. Progressive allocations were possible in all country settings, in countries at markedly different income levels and in most types of programmes.

They add that '*[targeting] doesn't always work*'; that '*there is no clearly preferred method for all types of programmes and all country contexts*' (in their sample of programmes '80 per cent of the variability in targeting performance was due to differences *within* targeting methods and only 20 per cent to the differences *across* methods'); that '*a weak ranking of outcomes achieved by different mechanisms was possible*' (with favourable mention of 'means testing, geographic targeting, and self-selection based on a work requirement', and somewhat more qualified mention of 'proxy means testing, community-based selection of individuals and demographic targeting to children'); and finally that '*Implementation matters tremendously to outcomes*' (emphasis added).

5.5 Fixing levels and durations of benefits

On *levels* of benefit Grosh *et al.* (2008, p. 128) start from the axiom that the benefit should be 'the smallest transfer necessary to achieve the desired impact on intended outcomes (consumption, income, earnings, school enrolment, or use of nutritional or health services)'.

5.5.1 Impacts that may be desired

On the subject of *duration* of any benefit payments, we consider as impacts that may possibly be desired:

- Relieving severe deprivation;
- Providing a sense of security against future destitution;
- Offering a firm platform to diminish the risks of entrepreneurship…
- …or of losses due to educational and health investments;
- Providing cash that might be devoted to education and health outlays;
- Encouraging households to move towards economic independence.

Clearly any benefit payments that have depended on the presence of children or other members of the household who have left through death or otherwise or, in the case of children, have ceased to be children, should be ended. However, where benefits paid have not depended, for example, on the presence of a certain number of children, the question arises whether there should there be a sunset clause or time limit after which the payments decrease or disappear.

5.5.2 Case for and against a time-limit

The last of the six possible objectives listed as bullet-points above might seem to dictate a time-limit, or some other terminating arrangement, on assistance. Numbers two, three and four, however, offer a contrary case, suggesting that any arrangement for termination under certain conditions should not be imposed as part of the initial bargain, and not brought into effect until the beneficiary had become securely prosperous by local standards. In other words security might be given a high priority, for reasons of supporting both consumption benefits, including a measure of confidence itself, and investment.

5.5.3 Factors bearing on levels of payments

The *size* of any benefit or stipend might be influenced by the following considerations:

- If it is to be closely related inversely to earned income, it might be kept small enough to avoid any *serious* risk of *undesirable* work disincentives (the italics are used here to emphasize that not all such risks need be serious and not all such disincentives undesirable);
- If it is designed as pay in a self-targeting public-works scheme, it should be close to, but not above, the prevailing unskilled manual wage rate (possibly the male rate, if that seems the more relevant to the self-targeting purpose in the local labour market);
- If an important purpose of the benefit (as either a conditional or an unconditional cash transfer) is to encourage health or education investments in children, the amount paid might be related to the costs of those investments, possibly including the opportunity costs of the children's time, as in Honduras (Grosh *et al.* 2008, p. 129);
- If the primary purpose is to meet current consumption needs, the stipend might come at several levels (for example, the 'poor' and the 'very poor' as in Brazil's *Bolsa Familia)* and also be related not only to household size and age-composition but also to any special disadvantages such as lack of an able-bodied earner, as well as to the current cost of living in the area.

Conclusion

Though a precise floor to disposable income at a national or international poverty line, consistently maintained, may not be attainable, especially in low-income and low-middle-income countries, without some 'overkill' (that is, a larger volume of transfers than is 'theoretically' necessary to fill the gap), there is a variety of devices that, singly or in combination, may be used to obtain an approximation to the objective, with reasonable economy, and with confidence that the approximation can be maintained in such a way as to convey a sense of security to the recipients. There is also little reason to fear that safety-net devices in developing countries will, to any significant extent or in any undesirable way, discourage effort or enterprise; and, insofar as there are concerns on this score, there are choices from among the safety-net approaches that, for sound and obvious reasons and on good empirical evidence, can avoid or neutralize any feared ill-effects.

6 Difficulties and obstacles

6.1 Governmental weakness and corruption

Any society considering the provision of a safety-net has to face the possibility that the funds allotted for the purpose may fail to reach those for whom they are intended. This may be because failure in the political mechanism means that they are not actually paid at all, or because of slackness or incompetence or various forms and degrees of dishonesty: nepotism and favouritism in public appointments (which help to explain the incompetence); giving and demanding of bribes to influence official decisions; and sheer theft of public funds. Though there is no close relationship between countries' incomes and their degrees of corruption, with quite large variation both across high-income and across middle- and low-income states, figures collected by Transparency International show that on the whole the poorer counties are worse. And it is of course the poorest countries for whose people an effective safety-net is most urgently needed.

Corruption and incompetence present handicaps not only for attempts at a safety-net but for any programme involving the expenditure of public funds. That is of course no ground for complacency – corruption in many countries has enormous social costs in inefficiency and inequity – but there is no obvious reason why it should be more of an obstacle and source of excess cost to safety-net programmes than to any other. It provides no more argument for ending attempts at a safety-net than for, say, ending altogether public-works contracts for providing transport and communication infrastructure, which are essential in spite of being a notorious source of peculation, bribery and improper influence.

6.1.1 Remedies: consistent pressure from the centre

There are many ways in which attempts may be made, and are being made, to control corruption and the slackness and incompetence that give scope to it or have similar effects. These include severe penalties, publicity about rights and means of asserting them, obligations for various elements of transparency in public and private accounts, legal protection and other support for whistle-blowers, independent auditing of accounts of public bodies and programmes, rights of appeal against official decisions, call centres for reporting complaints.

Much experience has been taken to suggest that many attempts seriously to limit corruption may fail more or less in the absence of consistent pressure from the top, the centre of power. Recent examples had led to the hope that in any state there might be serious improvement if there was a competent and committed independent official equipped with full inquisitorial powers, under strong personal protection and possessing the consistent support of the head of government. (Nigeria and Kenya are fairly recent examples in which some, but it seems in the upshot not quite enough, of these conditions were fulfilled.[1])

6.1.2 Remedies: incremental approach

However, in a fascinating and quite compelling chapter, Banerjee and Duflo (2011, pp. 235ff.) argue that hope of seriously reducing the effects of the corruption, slackness and group prejudice in the public services and local decision-making that critically affect poor people's welfare and life chances lies not so much in revolutionary changes in major institutions (what they call 'INSTITUTIONS') as in a multitude of manageable acts to improve the rules under which everyday services and selections of representatives are designed to work, and to check that they are actually working as intended. They give (2011, pp. 243ff.) a number of examples, backed by controlled investigations, of how apparently small changes, sometimes introduced experimentally and sometimes for real, may lead to quite large *reductions* in failings and malpractices – specifically in the theft of public funds; in the non-recording by police of notified crimes; and in voting according to ethnic or caste group – and may also lead to *increases* in such tendencies as a readiness to vote for local-government candidates according to audited evidence of their integrity; the assertiveness of, and trust in, women in local politics; and the tendency of poorer and less educated candidates to be chosen in national elections, a case of this last being accompanied by an apparently resulting 'increase in public health expenditures and a reduction in the number of low-birth-weight babies among less educated mothers' (2011, p. 247).

Much of the task is to find out what is actually happening on the ground and to make it public, in order to avoid the impression that plunder, bias and dereliction of duty can always go unpunished or even unnoticed.

This discussion may seem a diversion from the issue that this section of the chapter is considering: the challenge posed by corruption and theft of public funds, or by simple negligence and incompetence, to the effective provision of a safety-net. But it suggests that these deficiencies do not simply have to be accepted. They are part of a major world problem, widely recognized certainly in the large, but needing to be combated in detail wherever it arises.

So, if we follow the evidence and reasoning offered by Banerjee and Duflo, well-wishers of a safety-net should react to awareness of the existence of negligence and plunder in attempts to introduce a safety-net *not* by simply regarding these failings as part of the way of the world and turning to other matters, *not or not only* by searching for ever more plausible political and administrative concepts and devices by which corruption in national or world life may be progressively eliminated, *but rather* by looking in detail at some actual attempts at safety-net-like ventures (of which the Indian and Latin American programmes should provide plenty of examples), following up some allegations or suspicions of deficiencies and malpractices, testing the evidence, seeking for opportunities of various kinds of nudge (publicity, confrontation, tweaking the rules) by which these particular abuses in this particular venture and place may be at least reduced, and, where the attempt is successful, making the result more widely known.

The *Economist* (2012d) article, comparing the workings of India's Public Distribution System and Employment Guarantee between two villages in adjacent states, provides a persuasive example of the difference that can be made, both between villages and between the states in which they lie, apparently by differences in the zeal, integrity and ingenuity with which 'welfare' is administered.

6.1.3 Accountability through modern communication technology

However, in contrast to this approach through small things are the beginnings of some striking attempts to use modern communication technology in order to make government more consistently accountable. Most ambitiously, the Indian government is in the process of introducing a 'unique identity' (UID) scheme begun in 2010 and projected eventually to cover the whole population. This would provide for each person a biometric record of identity (*The Economist* 2012e). It is intended particularly to ensure that welfare payments and subsidies reach their intended beneficiaries, probably through the use of individual bank accounts. The idea would apparently be that cash could be transferred directly from the federal or state government to an identified individual. Clearly this would offer no absolute guarantee that funds voted would be delivered to the right people, but it could be used to eliminate a number of stages in the process that would otherwise be open to misuse. It would be possible for a central authority, or potentially any individual with a legitimate interest, to check whether an authorized transfer had occurred: a striking form of accountability. An example cited of its usefulness already (ibid., p. 52) is that the government of Karnataka state has claimed to have been enabled by virtue of UIDs to eliminate 2 million non-existent workers from its payroll in a rural public-works project. If the Karnataka evidence is typical and other favourable judgements (ibid.) on the financial implications are found to be justified, the net gains for the public finances or for the purposes to which they are directed may quell the recent controversy over the UID project in India and lead it to be widely copied elsewhere. A total of 215 million people were said to be enrolled in the scheme and provided with identification by late 2012, with numbers expected to rise to 600 million by the end of 2014 (*The Economist* 2012c). Controversially, but consistently with this recipe for security and accountability in the transfer process, reforms announced to the Indian parliament for their introduction to begin on the first day of 2013 would gradually convert welfare benefits in kind and consumer subsidies to cash equivalents, with 'all India's 629 districts ... covered' by the end of 2013 (*The Economist* 2012f).

6.2 Delivery under political instability

Clearly this may be difficult or impossible in some extreme cases, but that should not be a pretext for assuming a general moral exemption from any attempt at a shelter from extreme destitution. Use of modern communication systems of the type being attempted in India may eventually achieve the secure transfer of cash to individuals even when much of the more traditional infrastructure of communication is disturbed.

6.3 Levels and understandings of 'cost' of a safety-net

The cost of providing a safety-net may be seen as involving various components or aspects.

First there are the straightforward financial costs of the transfers of the cash or the goods and services made over to the use of the extremely poor beneficiaries.

Then there are the costs of the administrative organization, including transport and communication and where relevant the arrangement and supervision of productive work, that may be required for bringing the transfers or other payments in cash or in kind to those for whom they are designed.

Third there are political costs in the form of negotiating time and energy, together with moral debts and claims, that need to be expended by those championing the cause of the relevant safety-net toward politicians in the initiator country and potential donors including the multilaterals.

Conclusion

There are strong prospects that – through some combination of zealous administration in the field, ambitious use of modern communication technology and exercise of reforming will at the highest political level – corruption and misappropriation of public funds can be greatly reduced as obstacles to the effective realization of a social safety-net. There are grounds for hope that, with much more, and more readily accessible, information about cash transfers, poor people who are the intended beneficiaries of welfare payments will increasingly be prepared to mobilize for the purpose of securing their rights.

Note

1 See the cases of John Githongo in Kenya and Nuhu Ribadu in Nigeria, two zealous scourges of corruption who at crucial points lacked enough high-level support (*The Economist* 2005, 2006, 2008).

7 Financing social safety-nets

There are at least five possible methods of recruiting funds to pay for the cost of providing a social safety-net: reallocation of existing expenditure, additional taxes, foreign aid, borrowing and money-creation. (Foreign aid and borrowing are not mutually exclusive: what can be counted as 'aid' can run from free grants to concessional loans with varying degrees of grant-equivalence or 'softness'. So the act of lending and borrowing may be anything from a purely commercial transaction on market terms to an act of gratuitous international assistance.)

7.1 Methods available

7.1.1 Reallocation

If funds can be redirected from lower-priority purposes, without the need to raise extra revenue and therefore quite probably without increasing the current-account deficit, that may provide an easy source of spending-power for devising a safety-net. The first place to look for spending that might be redirected is at any general subsidies on such essential commodities as foodgrains and fuel. The benefit from these subsidies, such as it is, goes to rich and poor alike, while all but those who rely entirely on 'in-house' production for acquiring goods otherwise subject to taxation will very probably have made through indirect taxes some contribution to the revenue used to pay for the subsidies. Moreover the more anyone spends on these commodities the more he or she will gain from the subsidies on them. So on the whole it is definitely the richer who will gain more.

Under the heading 'Redistribution to the rich versus redistribution to the poor', Grosh *et al.* (2008, pp. 32–3) give an idea of how much income in a number of countries is regularly directed by the government in various forms to the 'non-poor': as one among many examples, that Egypt in 2004 'spent 8 per cent of its GDP on energy subsidies'. They mention also very expensive state bailouts to financial institutions (Indonesia, for example, paying 50 per cent of its GDP to its banks after the late-1990s financial crisis), and large sums paid to subsidize or rescue pension funds catering largely for the relatively privileged; and they note how small by comparison are safety-net programmes, and pro-poor and social-welfare programmes generally in the same countries.

Hence clearly redirecting funds from general subsidies to transfers targeted at the very poor will represent a thoroughly equitable redistribution. The change is all the better if, as seems more than likely, the effect of the commodity subsidies would have been 'inefficient' in channelling demand differentially to consumption of the commodities subsidized, encouraging for example the wasteful use of fuel oil, while if, instead of subsidies on goods purchased, the poor receive transfers in cash they can spend them as they choose without imposed incentives to spend on some goods rather than others.

Unfortunately removing any form of assistance to special interests is politically difficult. And the difficulty is especially great with general subsidies on food or fuel. Any move to reduce or abolish them will be felt immediately as a blow to almost everyone, regardless of the benefits that their abolition might make possible, and, unless the change is very closely and immediately tied to other, manifestly pro-poor, measures, it can readily be represented as a move *against* the poor. So any such change would probably need to be extremely cautious and gradual, with the subsidies reduced in stages as safety-net-type payments are increased.

Subsidies to the rich, often masquerading as bonuses to everyone, are like a vein of valuable ore waiting to be mined for the general good, but extracting the precious metal may be no easy task. However, the process outlined below in Chapter 12, for exposing gaps in the income floor as a preliminary to progressively closing them, may allow changes such as this to be seriously considered.

7.1.2 Taxation

If income and expenditure are increasing, there should be a 'fiscal bonus': a progressive rise in the amount of revenue collected without the need to increase tax *rates*. Demands on the revenue will of course be increasing at the same time, maintaining or increasing the flow of public goods and merit goods. But measures toward completing the safety-net, supporting the *disposable incomes* of the poorest, can also put in a claim. There is abundant evidence that comparatively small additions to poor households' disposable incomes – such as are now offered by a number of countries in the form of conditional cash transfers (CCTs) – can lead to better child nutrition, higher school attendance and greater uptake of health measures. (See examples in Chapter 8 below.) Public spending on health and education is needed not only to provide the buildings and staff and equipment and information but also to ensure that there is a basic level of disposable income to pay any charges made for the services and of course the food and other supplies.

If taxes are introduced or increased in order to pay for safety-net-type outlays, what form of taxes should they be? A first requirement, it would seem, for the purpose in hand is that they should be progressive rather than regressive, that is that the average rate of any additional taxes as a proportion of any taxpayer's income should increase as the taxpayer's income rises: the proportion should be higher for the richer taxpayers, and lower, probably often zero, for the poorer.

This rule would tell in favour of *income taxes*, where progressiveness can be written into the tax schedule, rather than *general* indirect taxes such as VAT which all but the completely destitute must pay. There is also the possibility of *indirect taxes on particular classes of goods* that are essentially luxuries, outside the normal expenditure of those on low incomes. These indirect taxes on luxuries will probably be easy to justify politically but may not be thought to raise enough revenue to justify the extra administrative cost, and there may be objections in principle to starting or continuing a process of complicating the tax system with a number of special cases. A payroll tax (a tax on the wage bill of employers, probably only those in the formal sector) may also be politically attractive, but it has the big drawback, especially from the viewpoint of the poorest, that it differentially discourages employment. Taxes on income *including company profit* (or on wealth in aggregate, or any particular class of assets such as land, where the structures for collecting such taxes exist), are perhaps least open to objection unless their *marginal* rates become so high as seriously to discourage effort or enterprise. Taxes on corporate profit, which will normally cover equally the earnings of both domestic and incoming-foreign enterprise, may need to moderate their rates with a view to international comparisons.

Any change in tax rates or structure is almost sure to have its additional transaction costs as well as any straight transfer costs – for the taxpayers as well as the government. If the need for additional funds can be met by reallocating existing expenditure, that is surely devoutly to be wished.

7.1.3 Aid from external donors

It probably has to be accepted that, at least in a number of low-income countries, some financial help from the rich world will be needed if they are to close their extreme-poverty gap in disposable income. Chapter 4 of this book carries in the figures it presents the implication that it would be no very extraordinary burden for the 'rich world' to finance entirely the filling of the gap. But, regardless of whether this would or would not be a good thing, we can be reasonably sure that it is not going to happen, certainly not in that simple, straightforward form. What we can hope for is that gradually, one by one, the governments and societies of each of the countries housing significant numbers of the extremely poor should themselves each *take the initiative* in setting out a projected safety-net for its own people: that doing no less than this should come to be recognized as a mark of a humane and civilized polity with concern for its members.

Estimates given in Chapter 4 and Appendix 4.2 (see Tables 4A.7 and 4A.8), and also those made by the ILO (2008a) authors, suggest that a number even of the lower-middle-income countries might be expected to be able to finance an extreme-poverty safety-net for their peoples without external help. However, we are here suggesting as an aspiration and target *neither* that the whole burden should be borne by the rich world *nor* that it should be carried *entirely* by each of the 'developing countries' for its own people, certainly not those among them classed as of low-income. That is where help from the rich OECD countries will need to be concentrated. The aim should be an *initiative* entailing the commitment of *at least some* financial contribution from every country toward providing safety-net shelter for the extremely poor of its own, together with *measured support* from the countries of high income to those of (more-or-less) low income. Without the home-bred initiative, support from the rich countries would probably seem to themselves unreasonable and in any case would be liable to the mistakes that are inclined to follow from the introduction by foreigners of foreign priorities. On the other hand the figures in Appendix 4.2, Table 4A.7, suggest that, without the expectation of significant foreign support, a number of the poorest countries cannot be expected to make a serious attempt to project consistent safety-nets of their own. We proceed to consider some of the difficulties in the path of reliance on external aid. Grosh *et al.* (2008, p. 54) argue that such aid is often inflexible, unreliable and volatile and tends to have high transaction costs.

7.3.1 Inflexibility, unreliability and volatility of external aid

Each donor country generally has its own programme of aid, in the generation of which its own perceived interests and the climate of its own public opinion naturally play a part. Ministers in charge frequently change, and a new minister will want to put a new stamp on the programme. If the donor seeks a wide spread of recipients, each of its recipient-country programmes is likely to be small, and there is a presentational attraction in conceiving each programme as a number of projects each of which can be completed in the lifespan of the donor country's ministry or parliament. The net effect may well be that a low-income-country, seeking a *reliable and long-lasting commitment* of foreign support for an unglamorous programme (not just a collection of projects), such as a vital cash component in a disposable-income safety-net, may seek in vain.

Of course conscientious donor governments and their aid ministers may resist these tendencies, as some do. But there seems to be something intrinsic in the aid relationship that typically favours inflexibility and volatility.

7.3.2 Transaction costs: need for coordination with and among donors

One potential drawback of an initiator country's reliance on foreign donors is the transaction costs involved in coordination with them, especially if there is more than one significant donor and the donors differ among themselves in their priorities. This suggests the desirability of arrangements among potential donors and potential recipients under which they affirm together a general commitment to support the principle of safety-nets against extreme poverty and maybe seek the good offices of one of the multilaterals to help negotiate the broad general lines of a 'division of labour' among themselves, with some form of indicative guidelines on how far low-income and lower-middle-income countries at various income levels should take responsibility for their own extremely poor and how far they should reasonably expect help from the rich world.

As already implied it should be made clear that the government of the country planning to make provision for its own poor will be in the driver's seat. Nevertheless it is inevitable that any significant external donor will be able to exercise influence. Hypothetically this raises the question whether it would be generally better for the 'initiator' to deal with one donor or with several. In favour of having *one* donor that will accept some significant responsibility for helping to fill the gap for one or more initiator countries, it can be said that this might favour the development of a 'special relationship' between the donor and each of the initiators involved and perhaps make the donor more likely to be flexible with its help when the initiator country faces difficulties in fulfilling the commitment to its safety-net. It also arguably limits the transaction cost of having a number of donors with whom to negotiate in order to maintain the flow of support on which it may be relying.

A counter-case might be made for supposing that the initiator will be in a stronger position if it depends on the relatively small individual contributions of a number of donors. A withdrawal or reduction in the contribution of any one donor is likely in that case to be less disturbing.

Certainly the task of achieving coordination with and between external donors will not necessarily be an easy one. The suggestion that one of the multilaterals might be drawn in as facilitator of coordination seems to be an entirely reasonable one and fits with the process described in Chapter 12 below.

7.3.3 Ensuring external support is consistent and adaptable to need

This is closely related to the previous two difficulties, and the following merely suggests a general approach to dealing with all three.

Securing consistency of external support is one aspect of the problem of keeping the provisions of a safety-net up to date as conditions (notably, for example, food prices) change.

We have been supposing that the 'home' government of the lowish-income country for which the safety-net is to be provided (the 'initiator') must take the lead, propose the structure of the income-support scheme at which it is aiming and give a projected outline of its budget for a few years into the future, with any gap that is to be filled by donor aid specified. Then it might ideally try to get medium-term commitments from one or more potential donors, possibly on a (three-year, say) rolling system, preferably of course with the projected amounts of aid automatically adjusted by some relevant price index, and with the hope that the three-year commitment might be continually renewed. This could go along with, and be coordinated with, the procedure outlined in Chapter 12 below for each country that wishes to participate in the UN's Social Protection Floor (SPF) initiative.

For these purposes, the safety-net provision should possibly be separate in the accounts of the initiator government from its other expenditure.

7.4 Borrowing

As a general rule financing expenditure by borrowing can be justified if *either* there is an emergency that is expected to be over fairly soon *or* the expenditure financed is an investment considered likely to generate enough return to pay for itself at an appropriate interest rate. It may well be that transfers contributing to a safety-net in a particular case would meet the second of those tests on a social-cost-benefit calculation, but, unless the benefits can be converted into hard negotiable cash, accepting that justification alone as sufficient may be risky for government finances. Any concessional element in the loan should of course be taken into account and added to what would otherwise be the 'present value' of its returns. A foreign concessional loan can properly be considered as if it were a combination of (i) a commercial loan of the same nominal amount and (ii) a grant in aid amounting in value to the 'grant-equivalent' of the loan.

7.5 Money-creation

Money-creation by a lowish-income country's central bank need not be ruled out in all circumstances. If there was a generalized shortage of effective demand which commercial loans were unlikely to fill, and to which a failure of money supply to grow fast enough seemed to be contributing, and any public-sector (central-bank or equivalent) money-creation could be kept within strict limits of extent and timing so that any resulting price-inflation could also be limited, then it might be justified. But monetary authorities and governments generally are right to be wary because of the temptation to what is in effect financing expenditures by inflation, which can then be hard and painful to stabilize, let alone reduce.

7.6 Quest for 'countercyclicality' (leaning against the wind)

If sustaining the real value of the safety-net is given a high enough priority, then the upgrading of the nominal amounts of any payments may need to be done regularly and automatically by formula, establishing an 'entitlement'. This may well be regarded by fiscal authorities as risky in that it may initiate a process with some of the character of a wage-price spiral, and more generally it may create budgetary difficulties for the government that would be due to make the payments and may quite possibly increase those payments frequently in unpredictable ways.

To see the issue more generally, extreme falls in a country's real income are among the pressing hazards of life for many developing countries, especially those heavily dependent on primary-commodity exports or food harvests. Of those of their people who are already poor many will almost inevitably be especially hard-hit by adverse movements in national income. A safety-net policy that aspires to set a reliable floor to household incomes will be all the more urgently required to make additional payments out when the capacity to pay is already low. Societies, and especially the poorest among them, will in other words need to act countercyclically, that is against the prevailing 'winds'.

There are three possible ways of reducing or limiting such difficulties, none of them necessarily easy. One is by short-term borrowing, which in some circumstances may extend to money-creation.

Another is to find a foreign donor country that on certain conditions will backstop the recipient's safety-net. At most times the rich OECD countries are not nearly as subject to national-income fluctuations as are many developing countries, and the timing of their fluctuations may be different in any period from those of some at least of the developing countries. Relatively speaking, they may be in a good position to help when help is needed, and may be willing to stand ready to backstop, especially if the country to be helped shows a convincing commitment to a safety-net policy.

A third way, as a more general approach to support for a country's countercyclical policy against fluctuations of external origin over which the country itself has no control, is for the building up in favourable times of a reserve fund that can be drawn down in time of need. The conditions under which contributions to the fund *must* be made might be laid down in law, as well as the circumstances in which payments out of it *may* be made. There are international precedents for such legally binding fiscal rules over reserve funds, for example in Papua New Guinea, which adopted them near the time of its independence in the mid-1970s.

7.7 Allocation of financing functions among levels of government

Grosh *et al.* (2008, pp. 68ff.) examine the question of how the functions involved in creating an income floor might be spread across tiers of authority from the central to the very local in accordance with comparative advantage. One criterion is whether or not the activity concerned is subject to significant economies of scale, and another is how far its execution needs to be influenced by (or perhaps in some cases insulated from) local knowledge and local politics. They register the common view that the major decisions about distribution of disposable income should be taken by central government, with the detailed implementation passed to various points down the line, but they recognize that even this broad rule need not be rigidly observed.

As an example of a subordinate government that generated a major system of redistribution on its own initiative, the Indian State of Maharashtra, one of the largest in population, itself initiated in 1979, as a device for famine relief, a guarantee of a limited amount of paid employment at the expense of the State government, the concept that became the model for the all-India employment guarantee that began to be introduced in 2006. As another example, Mexico City instituted its own social pension (Grosh *et al.* 2008, p. 76). On the other hand the authors mention the fact that Mexico's conditional cash transfers, PROGRESA, later Oportunidades, which they take as well targeted and successful in pursuing its objectives, has been highly centralized in its administration, while Argentina's Trabajar, a scheme of 'workfare', also well targeted and at the same time useful in the infrastructure created, has been largely devolved to municipalities (ibid., p. 77).

The lesson seems to be that the assignment of functions to administrative levels needs to be decided case by case, partly influenced of course by the levels that exist. A table (Grosh *et al.* 2008, p. 78) displaying the assignment of tasks in the Indian employment-guarantee scheme shows that there are six levels, from the federal government through state, district, block and village council, to the village meeting, all of which have responsibilities.

Conclusion

No less than five methods of financing state expenses such as safety-nets are listed here, each of which may be appropriate in certain circumstances.

The most important proposal made in this chapter for safety-net financing in the immediate future is to use every opportunity for *reallocating* funds that are currently directed to general subsidies on items of consumption or to supplementing public-sector pensions and engaging in other forms of *disguised redistribution to the relatively rich*, (which are often also socially inefficient in their effects on patterns of spending). Increasing rates of taxation, the next most eligible method, need only be considered when opportunities for pro-poor reallocation have been exhausted.

On a longer perspective, small groups of lowish-income countries might each covenant, among themselves and with one or more richer states: the low-income countries to observe disciplines for stabilizing their own economies, probably through building and managing reserve funds, as well as working explicitly toward their own safety-nets; and the high-income partners to make medium-term aid commitments in support of both the stabilization and the income-floor projects of their lower-income partners.

8 Conditional cash transfers (CCTs)

In 1997 the government of Mexico, prompted by Santiago Levy, then a deputy Finance Minister, pioneered a device designed 'to kill two birds with one stone' in the fight against poverty (Banerjee and Duflo 2011, pp. 78ff.). This was to make regular cash payments to poor families with children on condition that their children attended school regularly and went through certain procedures such as immunization for protecting their health. The scheme, called originally PROGRESA and later Oportunidades, had first been introduced, as Banerjee and Duflo have emphasized, in a randomized trial, under which some villages, a random sample, received the treatment and others did not. Comparing school-enrolment rates between the two groups made it possible to determine with a high degree of confidence whether the treatment was consistently followed by increased rates, which on the evidence it was. The success of the trial application was such that the procedure became firmly established in Mexico, and it has since been widely copied in a number of countries, especially in Latin America.

8.1 Nature and purpose of CCTs

The term 'conditional cash transfer' (CCT) is used now to cover all devices with these two components: payments to a household with children, but on condition that certain actions conducive to the children's education, and commonly also health, are performed.

The basic purpose is thus twofold: to contribute to the household's present well-being, and to enlarge the future income of its members as a result of the human-capital investment so encouraged. But there may of course also be considerable present consumer benefits for the children themselves in learning to read and write and calculate and much that follows therefrom, and in protection against pathological infections and infestations. The case for making the cash transfers *conditional* is enhanced insofar as it is believed that the parents will *undervalue* either the present and future consumption benefits for the children or the future-income gains to be expected for the household from the health and education investment. The case for cash transfers in general, insofar as they can be expected to increase the health and education investments, is enhanced by any belief that higher educational and health status *for the society as a whole* will increase its income-earning capacity and opportunities for enjoyment over and above the sum of the gains that would be made by each of the members of the society individually in the absence of comparable investment by others, in other words that there are positive externalities in individuals' advances in education and health.

The commitments imposed as conditions vary in detail from country to country, some of them involving only schooling. Virtually all those in Latin America, but a lower proportion elsewhere, also have health obligations, at least for families with children under the age of six; some also cover conditions relating to the health of pregnant or lactating women, and a few to the health of other adults. For children of the relevant school age, 'almost all CCTs require enrolment and attendance on 80 or 85 per cent of school days…' (Grosh *et al.* 2008, pp. 313–14). Variants may make payments in food rather than cash, as in the Bangladesh Food for Education Programme, which ran from 1993 to 2002. Scholarships and fee waivers for poor families and school feeding programmes, though they may be similar in purpose to CCTs, are one step away from the standard form, in that in those cases the transfer in cash or in kind and the human investment are inextricably tied together.

8.2 Conditional or unconditional?

Insofar as a CCT does increase the education and health investment of the family receiving it (and there is plenty of evidence that it often does), this may be because of one or both of two effects. There is a so-called '*income effect*': the family values health and education and comes to spend more (in cash or time) on these goods because the transfer payment it receives *makes it richer*. And there is a '*substitution effect*': health and education outlays (in money or time) are increased *in relation to* spending on other objects because the conditional character of the payments makes the health and education outlays *cheaper relatively in comparison with those other objects*.

The possibility of income- and substitution-effects leads to the question whether one or both of these effects is operating when the CCT increases the health and education investments. On the verdict given to that question hangs the answer to another: is the conditionality important, or would the recipients spend (or sacrifice) just as much extra on health and education if they were given the payments unconditionally?

Banerjee and Duflo (2011, p. 80) report an experiment designed to find out. The families of a sample of school-age girls in Malawi were randomly divided into three groups. Members of two of these groups received a monthly stipend: in one case on condition that the children remained in school, in the other case unconditionally. The third group received no stipend. That third (control) group had a dropout rate of 11 per cent, while the other two had rates in both cases of 6 per cent, a difference between the third group and the others that in the circumstances was strongly significant, but there was no difference between the responses of the other two. So it seemed that the stipend did indeed have the effect of encouraging enrolment, presumably by defraying its cost, but that the effect was independent of whether the payment was or was not conditional. It seems that it was the extra income alone, not the condition attached to it, that led to the higher enrolment. The same authors report a similar result from a study in Morocco (ibid.).

These findings seem consistent with the view that even very poor families value schooling and do not need to be bribed to invest in it, and that it may need only a rise *in their income* to induce them to make the necessary sacrifices. Banerjee and Duflo report the more general observation that the share of poor families' spending that goes on education rises faster than their income as that income increases from below the extreme-poverty line to around $6–10 per head per day, and that this implies that spending on schooling *per child* rises still faster because the average number of children per family falls over this same range of income.

However, it might well be a mistake to conclude that the conditional element in what would otherwise be CCTs should simply be dropped, so eliminating the administrative costs associated with monitoring the fulfilment of the conditions. For one thing, the conditionality seems to be politically useful in removing any pretext for disparaging the transfers by alleging that the recipients of stipends to relieve poverty are getting something for nothing. But second, granted that in the case of school enrolment and attendance the parents may commonly be willing enough to make any necessary sacrifices, monitoring may also be valuable, if not essential, for checking that the children themselves attend regularly and that the teachers are present and teach. Similar considerations probably apply to the conditions relating to health. Banerjee and Duflo give plenty of examples and statistics (e.g. 2011, pp. 54, 74) of cases in which those paid to staff schools and health centres are simply not present in classrooms and clinics when they should be, and evidence that some of this slackness can be corrected if it is clear that the performance of the people involved is being checked, even in the absence of disciplinary sanctions: clear in other words that someone else is at least interested in whether the nurses and teachers fulfil their obligations.

8.3 Administration of CCTs

Administration of CCTs involves first, targeting to ensure that eligible households – those with children and the required level of poverty or vulnerability – are, as far as possible, included; second, monitoring to establish that families targeted are still eligible and to check on the fulfilment of conditions; third, assessing payments due; and fourth, making the payments. The impression given by Grosh *et al.* (2008, pp. 313ff.) is that the standard of administration, at least on the longer-running examples, is high, better than the usual practice in anti-poverty programmes before the advent of PROGRESA and Bolsa Familia: 'The designers of the first wave of CCT programmes paid a great deal of attention to targeting, compliance verification methods, and payment methods.' Targeting methods to select individual households have usually involved 'poverty maps, proxy means tests, and sometimes community targeting' (ibid., p. 313). 'In the first wave of programmes, administration has been of a high calibre. Though neither unique nor inherent in CCT programmes, they have generally had higher than average targeting, monitoring, evaluation, administration, and trouble-shooting systems' (ibid., p. 319).

Administrative costs are given as '6 per cent of total costs for Mexico's Oportunidades and about 12 per cent for Brazil's Bolsa Familia' (Grosh *et al.* 2008, p. 318), but may be higher in certain circumstances.

8.4 Income-distribution effects

Estimates for a small assortment of CCT schemes and years (for Brazil, Mexico and Chile, with one of a more restricted scope for Cambodia) show 40–60 per cent of the cash benefit going to the decile (tenth) of the population with the lowest *per-capita* consumption (Grosh *et al.* 2008, pp. 319–20), but the few other cases given appear to be less progressive in their effect on distribution.

8.5 Behavioural impacts

To summarize the impacts of CCTs on the behaviour of the recipients, we draw entirely, except where otherwise indicated, on Grosh *et al.* (2008, pp. 312–24, mainly pp. 320–1), where sources for the evidence drawn upon are of course cited. (References to page numbers will be to pages in that work, except where another is specified.) Beside any education and health conditions, the grants received as CCTs are necessarily means tested, as is the case with most benefits in cash or kind directed against current poverty. This raises unavoidably the question whether the means testing leads to a reduction in inputs of labour. If it does, this may be regarded in some cases as a defect, but in the present context a reduction in labour supplied by children counts as favourable, and it may of course often go with increased use of schooling.

Fundamental to evaluation of CCTs are their impacts on the consumption of the poor, on child labour, on education, and on nutrition and health. But any effects on adult-labour inputs and on fertility are also of interest. The judgements on these matters in the work cited are based on studies of CCT programmes in 'Brazil, Colombia, Mexico, Nicaragua, and a few other countries' (p. 320).

On *consumption and poverty alleviation*, the overall judgement is that the impact of the programmes has been substantial and beneficial. Examples were that communities in Mexico participating in PROGRESA had a 17 per cent reduction in poverty and consumed 7 per cent more calories. Substantial proportions of respondents from these communities reported that they were eating better (48 per cent) or eating more (19 per cent). A programme in Colombia increased household consumption by 19 per cent in rural areas and 9 per cent in urban, and led to a better diet. 'Evidence from Nicaragua [suggested] a 17 per cent increase in consumption' (ibid., p. 320).

There was evidence from Nicaragua, Bangladesh, Brazil, Colombia and Mexico that, where there were CCT programmes, the prevalence of *child labour* fell. Nicaraguan evidence cited referred specifically to a group of children of primary-school age.

On *education*, 'virtually all the many evaluations of the impact of CCT programmes on education have shown [positive] impacts on enrolment and/or attendance' (ibid., p. 320). Evidence is cited from Mexico (increases in both primary and secondary enrolment, stronger for secondary and for girls), Colombia, Nicaragua (evidence from the lower-primary-school range, with stronger positive effects the poorer the group considered), Bangladesh (elementary) and Chile (preschool and lower primary).

On *health and nutrition* (ibid., p. 321), evidence not only shows increased participation in protective measures such as immunization and health monitoring but also in some cases points to actual health improvements including 'a lower overall incidence of severe illness', increasing children's growth and reducing the incidence of stunting (Mexico), and reducing the incidence of acute diarrhoea in children under six (Colombia),

As to *labour disincentives*, 'so far studies have shown no decrease in adult labour effort' (ibid., p. 321).

The only evidence cited on a possible *increase* in human *fertility* as a result of CCTs comes from Honduras. No similar effect appeared in Mexico or Nicaragua, and in Turkey a programme seemed actually to reduce the probability of pregnancy (ibid.).

8.6 CCTs and a social-protection floor

Fundamental to the idea of a safety-net or social-protection floor for disposable income is the guarantee that no one should fall through it. This, if believable and believed, removes at least the worst extremes of economic insecurity under which so many of the world's people live. The general form of a CCT that is now, or seems in process of becoming, virtually standard in Latin America is not designed to give that guarantee. It covers only families with children from birth up to school age, plus sometimes pregnant women. And even the most generous examples, such as Bolsa Familia in Brazil, are not geared to providing subsistence-level benefits for households that are completely without other means of support.

To take as an example Bolsa Familia transfers as they stood at the end of 2007 (Grosh *et al.* 2008, pp. 134–5), it would appear that, for the higher of the two benefit categories (the 'extremely poor'), the benefit for a family of five containing one or more eligible children (and/or pregnant women) would come to roughly PPP$ 2 a day, that is a daily PPP$ 0.4 per head (with the amounts in Brazilian Reais converted to PPP$ at the 2009 PPP$-Real exchange-rate as given in World Bank, *WDI 2011*, p. 254). It would appear from the figures cited in the source that at that time those receiving the higher level of benefit would roughly correspond to those who, in the absence of the benefit, would be either roughly at or else below the extreme-poverty line (assumed still at the time concerned to approximate to PPP$ 1.25 per head per day). So those whose earnings without the benefit would have put them *close enough below the line* could by virtue of the benefit be raised above it if they had an appropriate household composition and also fulfilled the health and schooling conditions; but clearly those *without any other earnings* would not. And households, however poor, without children in the relevant age range (or pregnant women) would receive no benefit, whatever other conditions they might fulfil.

Conclusion

There is abundant evidence that conditional cash transfers can play a highly important role for many of the extremely poor and the poor in mitigating present, and probably also future, poverty, with strongly positive impacts on a number of aspects of present welfare. Reports also indicate that they are popular – with politicians as well as with the general public. Yet it would seem that they cannot by themselves minister the highly important assurance element for households of various sizes and compositions conveyed by a reliable income floor. To go closer to achieving this, additional or modified provisions would be needed.

9 Employment guarantees

This chapter considers in general the arrangements known in America as 'workfare' that might on the face of it make possible an important part of the task of providing a consistent floor to disposable income. But inevitably it concentrates on the most ambitious recent venture of this kind, India's scheme set up under the National Rural Employment Guarantee Act of 2005, and with it briefly other recent Indian moves toward an effective income floor.

9.1 Self-targeting and workfare: the context

Self-targeting with employment guarantees entails paying people enough to keep them from extreme poverty on condition that they earn the benefits through productive work. The work obligation appears to overcome in principle, for able-bodied people, the main difficulty in targeting benefits to those who most need them. The beneficiaries in effect *decide for themselves* whether it is worth their while to accept work on the terms offered: thus determining whether they are poor enough to qualify. But, if this self-targeting mechanism is to work, the authority providing the benefits *must also provide the work opportunities*. Making free payments *in the absence of the work* would invalidate the self-targeting mechanism. Ideal self-targeting requires that the pay, the benefits, should be not too low and not too high: not so low that the potential beneficiaries are not interested in offering for work, and also not so high that they attract some of the not-so-poor from other work, which would mean allowing them, if there is a fiscal constraint rather than unlimited funds, to usurp the benefits designed for those in extreme poverty, and possibly leaving labour shortages elsewhere.

Of course in practice the human requirements of a self-targeting system of relief from destitution are not as easily met as this account suggests. The self-targeted benefits must be large enough, given any other stipends assumed to be coming into the same households (say for children and the aged and infirm), to afford whatever are taken in the context as basic needs. Furthermore providing, when and where they are needed, work opportunities adapted as far as possible to the capacities of the potential workers, and at the same time generating socially useful output, must often be far from simple.

'Public works' have been widely used, in conditions of extensive unemployment or famine, to relieve destitution. For obvious reasons these are often highly localized or temporary or both. Zepeda and Alarcón (n.d., p. 3) list a number of reviews, from 1989 on, of studies of 'the theory and practice of public work programmes'. Not all have explicitly aspired to combine self-targeting with an employment guarantee. However, Jean Drèze (1995) gives an account of the experience of Cape Verde in the crop failures of the 1980s, where arrangements for self-targeting worked, apparently with success, through guaranteed employment on public works. Also the Indian State of Maharashtra pioneered from 1979, under the stimulus of famine, a scheme on which the present all-Indian one is based.

In this chapter we concentrate on the scheme set up under India's National Rural Employment Guarantee Act of 2005, which from 2009 had 'Mahatma Gandhi' prefixed to its title (hereafter 'MGNREGA' or simply 'NREGA'). This is truly exceptional in its intended scope, covering in principle the whole rural population (about 70 per cent of the total population) of a country that had 1.155 billion people in 2009.

Under the Act one able-bodied adult in each rural household must be given on demand up to 100 days of unskilled manual work paid at no less than the legal minimum wage for agricultural labourers in the state concerned. The wage cost, plus 75 per cent of the associated material cost and a part of the administrative cost, is to be borne by the central government. The relevant state government pays the rest of the material cost and apparently also of the administrative cost. It is also responsible for paying an unemployment allowance, presumably for those who have offered for the employment due to them but have not received it. The unemployment allowance is to be at the rate of no less than 25 per cent of the legal minimum wage for the first 30 days and 50 per cent thereafter. It has been pointed out that, since the state governments have to pay the unemployment allowance, while the central government pays the wage, the states – provided they expect the unemployment-allowance obligation to be enforced – have a strong fiscal incentive to keep their eligible workers employed. Wages paid under the scheme are to be the same for women as for men; no less than a third of those employed are to be women; and certain provisions laid down for work conditions have probably or certainly been devised with women workers particularly in mind.

One source (*Wikipedia*, 2012a) gives the central government fiscal cost of the scheme in FY2010–11 as 400 billion rupees or a little short of US$8 billion at the official exchange rate, and the total fiscal outlay as just under nine billion dollars in the same year, which would be of the order of 0.6 per cent of gross national income. Zepeda and Alarcón (n.d., p. 16) estimate 'total programme expenses' at 'about one per cent of GDP'.

As might have been expected with such an enormously ambitious project facing huge logistic problems – problems all the more serious for being dispersed over 26 states and about 600 districts – some of the detailed provisions of the Act have not been consistently fulfilled. There are divergences in official statements about the numbers of households that have been granted work under the scheme. And, again not surprisingly, there have been numerous public allegations of impropriety and corruption. We shall consider later what probably can be known with reasonable confidence about implementation and performance of the scheme.

9.1.1 An example from pre-industrial Europe

It may be instructive to consider for comparison an earlier attempt – in a largely 'pre-industrial' society – to provide a nation with a consistent disposable-income floor. A combination of 'workfare' with a rough means test implied by 'community-based targeting' is what constituted the English Poor Law of the year 1601, which remained in effect until it was replaced more than two centuries later by the much less humane Poor Law of 1834 (the poor law of the workhouses, made familiar by *Oliver Twist*, which were more or less on principle made as unpleasant as possible in order to discourage people from relying on them except in extreme necessity). By contrast, the 1601 poor law, instead of herding the destitute into workhouses, had provided 'outdoor relief': support which people without other adequate means of subsistence could receive while continuing to live in their own homes. This involved paid work for the able-bodied, arranging apprenticeships for young people and regular payments to the aged and infirm. The relief was administered in each parish by local residents appointed as 'Overseers of the Poor' operating under the supervision of Justices of the Peace, who were unpaid landowners or others of comparable local standing, responsible to the officers of the crown in the county concerned. The Overseers of the Poor in each parish were charged with raising a 'rate', a local tax on those considered able to pay, in order to finance the work of protecting the poor from destitution. Rural parishes were small enough for reasonable acquaintance to be possible between the Overseers of the Poor and those for whose relief they were responsible. So there was plenty of opportunity for any household's state of need to be judged, without necessarily going into precise figures. In the latter years of the system conventions developed over the scales of relief to be paid. (For the text of the act of 1601, see Bland *et al.* 1914, pp. 380–1.)

By the early nineteenth century the 1601 system had come to seem too costly to many in the propertied classes, and at the same time inadequate to meet current welfare needs. Its dependence in part on what we would now call civil-society institutions, based largely as it was on small and fairly settled rural parishes in which everybody was likely after a fashion to know everybody else, came up against industrialization and the accompanying urbanization. These changes help to explain its abandonment in England in 1834.

So it is possible that the apparent success of this system, which lasted over 200 years, depended on characteristics of rural society in England at the time that cannot be fully replicated elsewhere today. Any approach to a successful replica might have to be confined, like India's Employment Guarantee scheme, to rural areas. But there may be somewhat different ways of exploiting the same ingredients: work for those of the able-bodied who will accept it at basic rates; small stipends for the aged and infirm (subject possibly to a crude means test); some contribution to the cost from everyone with ostensible means; oversight including some judgement of need by a small number of trusted neighbours who will have enough personal knowledge of the people involved; *their* responsibility to officials at a higher level who, it might be hoped, will not be unduly influenced by any personal or factional attachment or hostility to the people immediately concerned.

It is evident that there is a lot that might go wrong with an arrangement of this sort if it is tainted by faction, favouritism or corruption.

Law and practice in Scotland from the late sixteenth century, in which there were attempts at first to follow this English model, then in course of development itself, failed to provide consistent support for the poor along English lines (Mitchison 2000, ch. 1 *et passim*), and responsibility passed effectively to the institutions of the Scottish Church, in which the individual kirk sessions and their 'heritors' – landowners with powers of supervision – acted, in varying degrees of harmony and tension between themselves, with more independence of central authority than any comparable local institutions in England. So we can say that the relevant power in Scotland after the Reformation was more decentralized. This probably was a major factor in explaining why the Scottish attempt at a safety-net was less successful than the English in the seventeenth and eighteenth centuries. It may or may not also be relevant that Scotland before the industrial revolution was distinctly poorer than England.

It is clear that the objectives and devices of the highly durable English Poor Law of 1601 have a lot in common with those of the great Indian experiment of 2005–6.

9.2 Characteristics of the MGNREGA scheme

Sudarshan (2011) emphasizes the scheme's aspiration for complete national coverage; its inbuilt mechanisms favourable to accountability; and its elements – not by any means all of them dead letters – of gender-sensitivity (the rule, though widely ignored apparently, that crèches are to be provided close to worksites; the stipulation that no less than a third of beneficiaries are to be women; equal pay for men and women on the scheme's worksites; and roles for women in supervision and management.

The fundamental purposes of the system, as mentioned by various writers, are of course first to transfer disposable income to the very poor (specifically to spread a safety-net for filling the extreme disposable-income poverty gap among able-bodied adults); second, in support of this, to minimize leakages of income from the scheme to the non-poor and not-so-poor (which either deprive the intended beneficiaries of some of the benefits due to them or increase the cost of providing those benefits); third, to check the painful and wasteful practice of 'distress migration' – migration enforced by want – through removing its motivation; and fourth, to create productive assets as contributors to local development.

There are two further benefits to be expected from the presence of a *reliable and trusted* social safety-net. The first of these is *assurance* as we have emphasized earlier: the confidence arising from belief that no one can fall below a certain level of destitution. The second is *empowerment*: not just of the poor generally but particularly of women and also of all those groups that are inclined to suffer prejudice and discrimination (despised castes and tribes as well as the rural landless and near-landless). The knowledge and belief that people in these groups have a certain level of income guaranteed puts them in a stronger position in bargaining with the richer and more powerful. These powers may admittedly remain potential rather than actual unless those afforded an income floor decide in sufficient concentrations to use them.

But there is another important proviso to both the assurance and the empowerment advantages. Half-measures are of dubious value for these purposes. So long as a significant number of those that have legal rights to so many hours of employment and wish to use them *nevertheless are not actually offered the work*, we cannot expect those in this position or others aware of it to feel either assured or empowered. There is no safety in an attempted safety-net that is plainly full of holes.

9.3 Basic tasks in setting up the system of employment on demand

The first task is to make the employment guarantee and its conditions known and accessible to the target population and to those who will have to implement it. (Reports suggest that the fact of the offer of 100 hours of paid work a year is known, but often little else about it.)

The second is to set out guidance for the fixing of the wage in each area and for moving it in response to changes in local conditions.

The third is to provide the basic administrative arrangements for a village or group of villages under which people can be mobilized for work and paid for work done, with a supervisor, records of attendance, simple book-keeping and channels for payment.

The fourth is to build up a 'shelf' of projects for each area, projects that fit into a local plan (possibly modifying or indeed framing it), that require only simple tools, and are susceptible to being interrupted and resumed as varying numbers of workers offer their services; and to procure the necessary tools and stocks of materials. Doing this efficiently – that is, with minimum waste – must undoubtedly be a serious challenge. It suggests the need for a small cadre of technical-and-business-advice staff to serve each significant segment of a district.

9.4 Administrative cost

The aim is to employ unskilled manual labour, without the use of machinery or private contractors. A ratio of wage costs to material costs of 60 : 40 is supposed to be maintained (Zepeda and Alarcón n.d., p. 16) This fortifies other provisions tending to ensure that the works are highly unskilled-labour-intensive, which of course, even with the best management, is not necessarily the least fiscally costly choice of techniques. The same authors (ibid.) cite 'NREGA data' as indicating that 'the programme is transferring income at a cost of one dollar per dollar transferred, with most of the [non-wage] cost accounted [for] by construction materials'. In other words each dollar received by the MGNREGA workers costs the public purse two dollars. But against this cost must be set the value of the improvements produced.

Total programme expenditures per head of population for the year 2010/11 (which we presume include state as well as central outlays) are given (Dutta *et al.* 2012, p. 26) as 477 rupees, but with huge variation across states, from 896 in Andhra Pradesh and 884 in Chhattisgarh down to 98 in Punjab and 60 in Maharashtra.

9.5 Criteria of success

The first criterion must clearly be how far the people who want work at current Employment Guarantee scheme (MGNREGA) rates *are able to get it.*

Second is how far jobs created are *concentrated* in their uptake on the poor or the otherwise disadvantaged: in other words, how far leakage to the less-poor is contained.

Third, for each dollar transferred to the targeted poor, what is *the cost in administrative and other inputs.*

Fourth, how *useful*, per dollar of its cost, is the infrastructure created by the NREGA labour.

From recent empirical work we can give answers in what follows below in Section 9.9, at least on the substance of the first point and tentatively on the second.

9.6 Empowerment of women

Sudarshan (2011, *passim*) gives quantitative information that at least provides some background on the importance *of women in NREGA employment*, together with anecdotal evidence suggesting the importance *of NREGA employment to women.* On the first point we can say that women have comprised recently a little less than half the workers on NREGA sites – 43 per cent in 2007 and 48 per cent in 2009/10 – but with huge variation in the proportions across states: in 2009/10, from 88 per cent in Kerala and 83 in Tamil Nadu, to 21.6 per cent in Uttar Pradesh, 17 in Arunachal Pradesh and 6.6 in Jammu and Kashmir.

Factors mentioned by Sudarshan that might play a part in explaining these vast differences across states in female participation rates included, first, wage-rate comparisons between 'casual' and NREGA work for women and between 'casual' and NREGA work for men, a matter of comparative advantage. According to the rules women and men are paid the same rates for NREGA work, but women are typically paid at lower rates than men for casual work. Where there was an effective choice over which member of the household should offer for work under the scheme, we would expect these comparisons, combined with considerations of convenience of time and place, especially for those with family responsibilities, to play a large part. Second, it was suggested that the nature of the landscape made a difference: hilly states such as Himachal and Arunachal were likely to depend more on household collection from the commons of such items as water, firewood and fodder, and hence on women's unpaid work, than states on the plains. For the rest, the extent to which women's paid work outside the home had been common and acceptable in the past was no doubt important in the present.

Sudarshan also mentioned special background circumstances and history bearing more or less on the ease of mobilization for the programme of women in the three States particularly studied by that author. Kerala, one of the three, is of particular interest because it was in 2009/10 the state with the highest proportion of women in the NREGA workforce. It also incidentally (2011., p. 19) had (in 2004) the highest minimum wage, and both the highest actual average male wage and highest average female wage in the 'casual' market, and notably also the highest 'gender gap' between them, the latter of which circumstances must in the context have made the 'equal pay' of NREGA work in the state differentially attractive for women. The author also gives some idea of the importance for Kerala of the Kudumbashree – described (2011, p. 10) as 'the state poverty eradication mission and a programme that has mobilized women into self-help groups for economic activity' – and of volunteer women supervisors. Sudarshan argues that drawing women into work beyond the home, which is likely to involve their making contact with a number of institutions in the wider world, is an important source of empowerment.

9.7 Number of households benefiting

Figures in Sudarshan (2011, p. 4) imply that the total number of person-days worked in the NREGA scheme in 2009/10 was 3,327 million. Zepeda and Alarcón (n.d.), citing the NREGA website, indicate that 52 million households provided the labour in 2009/10, and they say that the number of person-days was 'almost 3 billion'. If we take both numbers (the 52 million and the three billion) as roughly accurate, they appear to imply that there were in that year somewhere around 58 person-days of work per participant household, half to three-fifths of the annual number supposed to be available on request. The figure of 58, however, is hard to square with a much smaller one of 37.4 for 'mean person days amongst participating households' given by Dutta *et al.* (2012, p. 26), also for 2009/10. Whether it is rightly 58 or 37, that figure raises the question: why not more? Why not closer to 100?

To ignore that question for the moment and consider the positive side, we can say that, at an average of five people per household, the 52 million households would appear to mean that about 260 million individuals had their household income increased by the scheme, which would therefore in a sense 'cover' about a quarter of the population of India and something like a third of the rural population. But a question remains as to whether they were indeed more or less the poorest third, as the intention of the scheme would have demanded.

9.8 Why not an unconditional hand-out?

A fundamental question about a workfare scheme such as the NREGA is whether there are equally good or better (that is, equally or more cost-effective) ways of meeting the essential aim of poverty reduction, and specifically poverty-gap filling. The main competitor, considered for example by Zepeda and Alarcón (*op. cit.*), is simply making a transfer payment at uniform rates to all the extremely poor without any input condition. The main advantages of this are that that there would be no cost of materials and equipment and also much less administrative cost because there would be no call for the extremely complex work of project creation and appraisal and no need for supervision of work.

On the other side of the argument could be set the fact that the uniform rates of transfer would allow for no variation in need across households of a given demographic composition. To target more or less effectively for poverty, it would have to rely on 'proxy means tests', such as geographic or ethnic targeting. It would inevitably be either under-filling or over-filling poverty gaps. In itself it would be creating no capital assets, though the importance of that deficiency would depend on how useful the assets that would have been created by the workfare scheme would have been, and how their usefulness would have compared with that of the *alternative* potential uses of the funds.

Zepeda and Alarcón (n.d.) report the results of several studies bearing on this question, but the answers are inevitably inconclusive, depending on important unknowns such as the productive value of the public works undertaken, and also on controversial judgements of value, such as the priority to be given to creation of a genuine floor close to the agreed poverty line and whether the dependency associated with free hand-outs is itself a derogation from desired empowerment.

9.9 Answering key empirical questions

9.9.1 Does the 'employment guarantee' guarantee employment?

This simple but essential question is posed by Puja Dutta, Rinku Murgai, Martin Ravallion and Dominique van der Walle (2012). They have the advantage of being able to draw on the 66th Round of the National Sample Survey (NSS) for 2009/10. Questions on the Employment/Unemployment Survey allowed them to use evidence provided by people in their own homes about their desire for work on the MGNREGA scheme and whether it was in any degree met. The paper cited here was concerned only with whether the respondent household wanted work under the scheme and if so got some work, not with the number of days of work desired or realized. This was because the information available from the

NSS would not enable these further questions to be answered. (The authors of the paper offer reasons why the official 'administrative data' give a highly misleading picture of supply and demand for work, one which would have implied that 99.4 per cent of households that wanted MGNREGA work obtained it.)

The authors use the term 'demand rate' for the proportion of rural households that reported desiring work under the scheme; 'participation rate' for the proportion of those desiring work who obtained it; and 'rationing rate' for the percentage of the households that reported wanting work under the scheme who were unable to get the work. The 'poverty headcount' is the proportion of people who are below the relevant poverty line.

For India as a whole they find that 45 per cent of rural households wanted work under the scheme in 2009/10; 56 per cent of that 45 per cent obtained it. There was thus a rationing rate of 44 per cent. This varied by states from 16 per cent in Rajasthan to 84 per cent in Maharashtra. Only three states had rationing rates under 20 per cent. (Figures from table in Dutta *et al.* 2012, p. 25, covering 20 of the 26 states.) *So the answer to the question whether the employment guarantee guarantees employment is clearly 'no'.* 'There is', the authors conclude, a large excess demand for work' ... '*the employment guarantee is not in operation almost anywhere*' (emphasis added). Employment is by no means effectively guaranteed. 'Rationing is common, but far more so in some of the poorest states' (ibid., pp. 18, 19).

This means, as the authors of the paper point out, that, for reasons that we have explained, some of the important benefits to poor people from a reliable 'floor' – in the form of empowerment and assurance – are simply not realized.

The authors find, as expected, that the *demand for work* under the scheme is higher in the poorer states, but the actual *participation rates* are not consistently higher. This is possibly because various factors may work as counterweights to the greater desire for work (the '*demand effect*') within the poorer states: factors such as (Dutta *et al.* 2012, p. 6) weaker governance institutions, lower *per-capita* state budgets and less assertiveness and consequent political influence on the part of the poor (which together add up to a '*rationing effect*').

But participation rates in MGNREGA work are indeed higher in general for poor *people* than for others. A table (Dutta *et al.* 2012, p. 26) shows that for all rural India in 2009/10 demand rates for the work rise consistently as we move from richest to poorest quintile, and participation rates also rise but much less steeply. By implication the excess (i.e. unsatisfied) demand rate also rises. The proportions of households with a job card (which should indicate that a member of the household either has or desires work under the scheme) also rises as we move from higher to lower income quintiles, but paradoxically is consistently lower within each income quintile than the (self-reported) demand rate for the work.

That leads to a second major question with a less simple answer:

9.9.2 How far does the scheme favour the poor over others?

Or, as the authors put it: *Is rationing undermining the self-targeting mechanism?* The authors give what amounts to a qualified response. They *do not* find that the local processes determining who gets work are *generally* biased against the poor (Dutta *et al.* 2012, p. 18). Indeed 'participation rates in [the MGNREGA scheme] are higher for poor people than others', and this is very clearly so if the division is set at the official poverty line; but there is no sharp discontinuity at the line. Many households a little above the line participate, but the authors of the paper think that there may be quite a number of families apparently in that category *whose inclusion is justified* for reasons not expressed in the income or consumption figures.

The authors (Dutta *et al.* 2012, pp. 10, 11) use a metric, the *targeting differential (TD) rate*, which they apply to states, in order to compare the poor with the non-poor in the extent to which the selection for work under the scheme is concentrated on them. The targeting differential between the poor and the non-poor is normalized to vary between +1 and –1, with +1 meaning that all the poor and only the poor are selected, and –1 that it is all and only the non-poor that are selected. The departure of the TD rate from +1 therefore reflects together both any failure of the poor to be included and any 'leakage' of inclusion to the non-poor. For all-rural-India the authors decomposed this targeting difference into a 'self-targeting effect' (the part attributable to greater demand for work among the poor) and a 'rationing effect' (the extent to which this is counteracted by the way a limited amount of work has been allocated). The result of the decomposition is that *85.6 per cent of the targeting difference is due to the self-targeting effect and 13.7 per cent to the rationing effect*, with a negligible residual (ibid., p. 12).

Evidence they cite that 'targeting performance improves as the programme expands' (Dutta *et al.* 2012, p. 12) suggests that future increase in the scheme's participation rates (for example, because of more generous expenditure limits) will give greater scope to self-targeting. They also give reasons, based on experience in comparable situations (ibid., pp. 12, 13), for thinking that, in the early stages of a development programme with high start-up costs, there will be some tendency for the non-poor to receive initial advantages as part of the process of getting the scheme locally under way. This supports the expectation that in the present case targeting to the poor will also improve as the scheme becomes longer established. In the absence of radical change in the scheme or its administration, or of a fall in its share of the national cake, self-targeting under the MGNREGA is therefore likely to improve.

There is a further question of interest:

9.9.3 How far are those disadvantaged other than by sheer poverty – such as members of low-status castes and tribes – effectively targeted?

The *Wikipedia* (2012a, p. 2) reference mentions that of workers under the scheme 23 per cent have belonged to Scheduled Castes and 17 per cent to Scheduled Tribes.

Dutta *et al.* (2012, p. 28) show that there is a targeting differential rate of 0.155 for Scheduled and 'Other Backward' Castes and Scheduled Tribes taken together as a body against the rest. In other words the disadvantaged groups *are* differentially favoured in selection for work under the MGNREGA – but 'favoured' only in the same sense that the poor are favoured as against the non-poor: if they want work under the scheme, they have a higher empirical probability of getting it,

9.10 Additional note to Chapter 9: other incipient contributors to an income floor in India

9.10.1 Public distribution system

This presently consists mainly of subsidized supplies of food and fuel, to which poor individuals are supposed to gain greater or lesser access according to their levels of need. Claims on the system are indicated by the possession of a card mainly designed to show whether the holder is above or below the poverty line. There have been numerous complaints about weaknesses and abuses of the system, such as that the level of the poverty line has not been agreed, that there is no guarantee of availability of the subsidized supplies, and that cards are widely traded. Legislative proposals presented to the Indian parliament in late 2012 by the Finance Minister, Palaniappan Chidambaram, would apparently replace all claims on subsidized supplies by cash payments (*The Economist* 2012f). (This now, early 2013, appears to be in train.) There is an apparently strong case for this change, on grounds of transparency, accountability, security and transport and distribution costs; but it has been highly controversial. (See, e.g. London School of Economics 2012; *Wikipedia* 2012b).

9.10.2 Free medical treatment for the poorest

Economist (2012g) mentions in passing that domestic servants were added in 2011 to those covered by a free medical service. Nandi (2013) gives an estimate of 33 million families enrolled as of early 2013 in the medical insurance service known as 'RSBY', which, on a nominal enrolment fee per family amounting to the exchange-equivalent of $0.60, admits families recognized as below the poverty line to 'more than 700 medical treatments and procedures'. Those enrolled pay for procedures received up to a certain limit with a card. Public costs of the scheme are met 75 per cent by the central government and 25 per cent by the states. Nandi, the source of this information (ibid.), records doubts expressed by investigators over whether finance has been adequate for the objectives of the scheme to be met, and specifically about whether the enrolled population's out-of-pocket expenses are decreased or even increased.

Conclusion

Any judgement now of the effectiveness of this amazingly ambitious Indian venture has to be based on information relating to the first four years of its operation: from its very beginning early in 2006 to the end of the fiscal year 2009/10, the latest year for which much of the body of data to which reference is made here is derived. The interim report is mixed.

Evidence so far is that a little more than half of the households that have wanted work under the scheme have obtained it, with no clarity yet on how far the desire for hours desired by those who have got some work has been satisfied.

It does seem that the poorer or otherwise disadvantaged people are, the more likely they are to get work under the scheme. Hence to a considerable extent the self-targeting mechanism appears to be working.

The scheme's apparent impact on the empowerment of women varies hugely across states but seems considerable in some of them.

If the scheme eventually works more or less as it is intended to fill the gaps in a disposable-income floor for able-bodied workers, it will have met for reasonably fit rural people, what is probably the most difficult element of the challenge to provide a last-resort safety-net, one that in its fullness could play a major role in bringing basic assurance and consequent strands of empowerment for some 800 million people.

By 2009/10 about one-third of rural households across the country appear to have received some addition to their income as a result of the scheme.

There is every prospect that this number will increase; and that the specific role of the scheme in relieving poverty and disadvantage will be further advanced as experience accumulates, and as and if (i) the scheme comes to be more generously financed, and (ii) the leakage of value in transmission is decisively reduced through the ambitious electronic and other methods now in process of introduction.

10 Paying for health care

As in Chapter 4, here also we have tried to make some extensive calculations, this time focusing on health services and the relevant expenses, taking, as before, low- and lower-middle-income countries. These, shown in Appendix Tables 10A.1 and 10A.2, will feature prominently in our discussions.

10.1 Vital need for covering health risk

The UN's objective of a social-protection floor is interpreted as having four components. These are basic disposable-income requirements for elderly people, for children and for working-age adults, together with, as a fourth, comprehensive and non-impoverishing access to health care. Access to health care in a comprehensive sense has two components: that the health services are present and *physically accessible*; and that they are also *financially accessible*, namely that they can be paid for in a way that does not impoverish the users.

So a complete social-protection floor for a household involves not only amounts above certain minima in *disposable income* for (i) old people, (ii) children and (iii) working-age adults but also (iv) a limit to unavoidable household *expenditures* for health care.

There is a powerful case for including the covering of the expense of health care, an item of *expenditure*, alongside maintaining a floor to disposable *income*, as part of the necessary condition for avoiding extreme poverty. The reason is that it is only too easy for an illness or accident *not only* to put a household's main income-earner out of action *but also* to incur outlays for care and treatment that are very large in relation to the household's income. The incidence of medical expenses is quite unlike that of other items of expenditure. The need for most other items is *either* predictable like the need for food, *or* otherwise at least to some extent discretionary, avoidable, like the need for celebrations and festivals, alcohol and tobacco. By contrast medical expenses are unpredictable, highly variable across households at any one time, often immense in relation to normal levels of household income and expenditure, but at the same time often understandably regarded by the household as unavoidable.

There is plenty of evidence of the *impoverishment* that can readily come to any household as a result of 'catastrophic' medical expenses: at its worst the equivalent for consumption possibilities of being pushed below, or further below, the extreme-poverty borderline. In order, when the emergency arises, to maintain in the immediate present the essentials of the consumption of all members of the household, it may be necessary to sell productive assets such as livestock, so reducing the household's income potential, or to go into debt that before long comes to seem ineradicable and to become progressively deeper.

Because of these risks of drastic costs of treatment, there is a critical need for some form of risk-sharing over health expenses: one that through '*prepayment*' (by an insurance fund or the state) wholly or partly removes from users of the services the need for '*out-of-pocket*' (OOP) payments for individual items of medical expense as and when the services are used. Ideally the requirement for OOP charges might be completely removed, replaced by the proceeds of insurance contributions or general state revenue. The United Kingdom's National Health Service, for example, is one for which the great bulk of kinds of service require no OOP payment at all from the person using the service. The UN and ILO criterion for 'coverage' of medical expenses is not quite as demanding as this, but requires that any OOP payment (presumably within any year) should be 'affordable', which is taken to imply that it should not cost more than 40 per cent of the household's 'income' over the period, *'income' being taken for this purpose as the household's actual disposable income minus the cost of 'subsistence'*. OOP charges that exceed that limit for any household may be regarded as 'catastrophic' and *must* be so regarded if they entail the household's 'impoverishment', that is pushing it below 'subsistence' level, which we may take as synonymous with pushing it below the extreme-poverty borderline. It follows of course from that understanding of 'subsistence' that, for any household whose disposable income is already at or below the extreme-poverty threshold, *any* OOP charge at all will be 'catastrophic'.

10.2 Options and definition[1]

Where there is some form of health 'insurance' (in the broadest sense of risk-sharing), the prepayment of the cost may be *either* contributory, which means that the individual beneficiaries have paid into a fund – state or private – specifically set up to meet the projected expenses as they arise, *or* paid out of general state revenue ('taxation'). Or it may be a combination of the two. In any case the arrangements, if state-engendered, will almost certainly need to include an element of income-redistribution, as well as risk-sharing, if (i) the poorest at least are to be relieved entirely of the need for out-of-pocket charges, and at the same time (ii) any regular contributions that people are required to make in order to be covered will be themselves 'affordable'.

'Private health insurance', if it is made without any state contribution, is naturally assumed to be without any redistributive element. However, the term 'private' may be extended to schemes set up by community or non-governmental organizations (NGOs), which may have motivation that is not purely commercial. And in any case what is regarded as private health insurance may well have some state subsidy.

'Social health insurance' normally refers to schemes under state initiative that are contributory, commonly confined to particular groups of people such as civil servants, or employees in formal-sector enterprises, for whom membership in the schemes and the attendant contributions may well be mandatory. These schemes are quite likely to have at least some redistributive element, which will be the case if for example the contributions are graded according to ability to pay while the benefits are uniformly available to contributing members. (Health 'insurance' 'in the broadest sense', as we have used the expressions above, can be wider than this, referring to any form of cost-sharing device, even one in which the state bears all the health-service expense as a single payer.)

'Single-payer' schemes are those such as (with small exceptions) the UK National Health Service and at least the 'exempt' part of the Thai UC scheme outlined below. Here by definition the state meets – either out of general revenue or from a dedicated fund generally provided, in whole or in part, from previous contributions on the part of the beneficiaries – the whole of the expense of the services for the section of the population covered, without requiring any OOP payments from users of the services 'at the point of use', that is, as and when they use them.

Some arrangements for funding do not fall neatly into any one of these categories.

10.3 Two aspects of medical 'cover'

Groups of people or a nation's population at large may be 'covered' for medical services in one or both of two senses.

One is that the services of accepted quality, with the necessary trained staff, equipment and supplies, are physically, geographically, transport-wise accessible, independently of the cost of the services to the supplier and how that cost can be met. We may call this '*physical cover*' or *physical access.*[2] For much of the world, physical access to health services will be a matter of degree in the sense that some services and not others may be physically accessible to the people living in a particular area. It will also be a matter of degree in that physical access to health services for some potential patients may depend on their own mobility, and that mobility may depend on their income and assets and the cost of the relevant transport. So, because some individuals living in a particular area will be more mobile than others, some will have more physical access than others.

The other sense of cover is 'formal' *financial cover* – relevant in practice of course for those services for which there is also physical access. It will be financial cover that mainly concerns us here, though the extent of physical cover will clearly also be critically important for the people affected. We shall follow the ILO in treating financial cover as complete for populations or individuals for whom using the physically accessible medical services entails no 'catastrophic' OOP payments.

The ILO (2008b) tables mentioned use the term *formal coverage* to signify that financial arrangements are there to pay – without apparent risk of impoverishment – for services *wherever those services may be physically accessible.* On that understanding, physical cover *plus* 'formal' financial cover constitutes *effective access.*

But it seems inevitable that there will be some interaction between physical and financial cover. The cheaper a service such as birth attendance is to the user, the more use there is likely to be of the existing professionals and the more political or commercial pressure to increase their number and equipment.

10.4 Rating countries on extent of their physical cover

Rating the various countries for the extent of the *physical* cover of health services that they provide is by no means simple. Recent ILO publications use two rating systems that at least serve as pointers to the adequacy of the services provided (ILO 2008b, pp. 16–26, 77–82).

One of these, *the staff-related access (SRA) deficit*, is the percentage by which the 'density' of health professionals, taken to be the reciprocal of the number of the population per health professional, falls short of the density in Thailand, which is used as the standard. So Chad, which recently had 3,113 people per health professional while Thailand, the standard, had 313, had a density roughly 10 per cent that of Thailand and hence had an SRA deficit of 90 per cent. Indonesia at the same time had the high SRA deficit of 76 per cent, and Botswana one of only 4 per cent. Thailand's SRA deficit by definition was of course zero.

The other rating system used for physical access is *the birth-attendance access (BAA) deficit*, which is based on the proportion of live births in the country concerned that have been attended by a skilled health professional. The BAA deficit is the percentage by which that proportion falls short of 100 per cent. Thus Chad at the time concerned had a BBA deficit rating of 86 per cent, while Indonesia's deficit was 34 per cent, Botswana's 6 per cent and Thailand's 1 per cent. (See for examples Appendix 10.1, Tables 10A.1 and 10A.2, columns (8) and (9). See also explanations of the concepts in ILO 2008b, pp. 16–25.)

However, the adequacy of any given endowment of professionals in a country will depend in part on how evenly they are spread across the potential users. If they are inappropriately concentrated, say in the capital, the deficit figures will understate the real deficiencies.

10.5 Thailand: the gold standard for effective access?

Thailand was in 2008 a lower-middle-income country by the World Bank's definition: about two-thirds of the way up the range of countries in that category, with roughly the same income per head as China in that year, substantially below Brazil and Mexico, well above India and Vietnam. Yet it is regarded as having achieved close to 100 per cent formal health-insurance coverage. It reached that position in stages, with a variety of devices culminating in one exceptionally ambitious move in 2001 designed to provide at least formal financial coverage to the whole population with, by implication, minimal possibility of any impoverishment that might come about as a result of out-of-pocket health costs.

In addition it had a high standard of *physical* coverage at least on one of the two indicators used by the ILO for this purpose – the BBA deficit mentioned above – on which it rated a deficit of only 1 per cent. On the other indicator of physical cover, the staff-related access (SRA) deficit, Thailand was, as we have said, used by the ILO as the standard. Its own 'density' of professional health staff was about a fifth that of the UK and between a quarter and a third that of France. Hence on the same scale the UK and France would have negative SRA deficits.

The special interest of the case is not only that a country of Thailand's income level should have attained virtually universal 'formal' coverage but also in the diverse range of the financial devices used, described as a 'pluralistic' approach, and the stages through which the comprehensive cover had come about.

As in other countries, Thai state health insurance started with schemes to cover limited sections of the population, at first active and retired civil servants and their dependants (the Civil Servant Medical Benefit Scheme, CSMBS) and under a similar scheme employees of state enterprises (the State Enterprises Medical Benefit Scheme, SEMBS), one or both schemes initially providing services as 'fringe benefits' at the employing body's expense. To provide cover for private-sector employees as well, in 1991 the Social Security Health Insurance (SSO) was formed (apparently including or superseding the SEMBS) as a scheme funded by compulsory contributions *for employees of all enterprises with 20 or more workers*. It was extended in 2002 to cover all employed formal-sector workers. These two schemes between them would by around 2006–8 be covering about 14.4 million people (workers, dependants and retired former workers) who, together with another 5 million protected by voluntary private health insurance, would constitute 29 per cent of the 67 million population (ILO 2008b, pp. 65–7).

The big step was taken in 2001 to introduce the UC ('universal cover') or 30-Baht scheme. This was designed to cover all the people not covered by other forms of health insurance as well as extending the range of services included for those covered by some existing arrangements directed at those outside formal-sector employment. All these people would be given legal rights to receive the forms of treatment now provided.

> This extended the scope of coverage to 18 million people who were uninsured and to a further 29 million who were previously covered by less comprehensive schemes.... The new scheme offered comprehensive health care that included not just basics, such as free prescription drugs, outpatient care, hospitalization and disease prevention, but more expensive medical services, such as radiotherapy, surgery and critical care for accidents and emergencies.
>
> (WHO 2012a, p. 1)

Those given 'UC cards' formed two groups. One, numbering around 22.2 million in 2006, paid the very small 'co-payment' of 30 Baht (roughly US$1 at the then-current exchange rate) per item of treatment. The rest (24.3 million), the poorest, about 36 per cent of the population, were completely exempt from payment.

It was estimated that three million people in remote areas were not effectively covered for health services, though, since everyone has had a legal right to use the UC provisions, presumably those left out were excluded as a result of lacking physical access not from lacking official permission to obtain formal financial cover.[3]

A study (Prakongsal *et al.* 2007) found that the proportion of the population covered by 'the public health insurance system' increased from 71 per cent in 2001 to 95 per cent in 2003; that use of ambulatory services at sub-district health centres and of district and provincial hospitals was 'increasingly pro-poor' from 2003 (when the UC system came into effect); that the incidence of *catastrophic* health expenditures fell from 5.4 per cent (before the UC) in 2000 to 2.8 per cent in 2004; and that the headcounts of households *impoverished* by OOP payments dropped from 2.1 per cent before the UC to 0.5 per cent after its introduction.

On very limited information (ILO 2008b, pp. 65–7), it had been estimated that introducing the UC scheme added, in the early years of the 2001–10 decade, about 30 billion Baht a year (around a billion dollars at the then exchange-rate) to state health expenditure, and that it relieved households covered by the scheme, numbering about 45 million people, of 10–13 billion Baht a year (say 250 Baht on average per individual) that they would otherwise have paid out of pocket. Presumably the difference between the 30 billion and the 10–13 billion is at least partly explained by the fact that those covered by the UC scheme after 2001 were making, as might have been expected, more use of medical services than they would have done without it. The fact that the take-up of treatment under the UC scheme was stronger among the poorer strata of the eligible population was naturally taken as supporting the view that it differentially benefited the poor (Prakongsal *et al.* 2007).

The source for these observations noted that a number who took out UC cards did not use the UC provisions, and inferred from this that some of the more affluent people were either enrolled in private insurance or eligible for the SSO or CSMBS and used the UC as a backstop. This seems to imply that there were somewhat more or better benefits available under schemes other than the UC. The document cited implies that there are hospitals and primary-care units contracted to the UC that are separate and different from those contracted to the SSO. From the viewpoint of the government that has largely to finance the UC scheme, it would clearly be fiscally convenient if some of those eligible for the UC were to switch to private insurance or were rendered eligible to enrol in the SSO and found it attractive to do so.

Of the population around the middle of the decade in which the UC had been introduced, 97.7 per cent were held to be 'formally' covered financially, 75.3 per cent by the state (presumably one or other category of the UC) and 22.4 per cent by social health insurance, which was presumably taken to include both SSO and CSMBS. Though the numbers given do not precisely fit, the 2.3 per cent remaining uncovered presumably included, or were among, those in remote areas who had not been registered.

What is puzzling about the Thai case is that the remaining amount left to be paid out-of-pocket by the users (28.7 per cent of the nation's health expenditure according to column (6) of Table 10A.2) would appear to amount to well over one billion dollars. It is hard to see how the UC scheme co-payments of about one dollar per item of service for the 22 million or so people who would be the potential UC payers could amount to anything like this sum. This would suggest that those said to be covered by the social-health-insurance schemes or private insurance must still be paying out-of-pocket quite substantial sums. Recognition of this would add support to the view that treatment benefits offered by the insurance arrangements other than the UC, insofar as their use rather than the UC scheme was a matter on which service-users could choose, must be regarded as having a greater range or higher quality than those under the UC scheme. Otherwise there would be no incentive to choose the contributory schemes. A recent *WHO Bulletin* (WHO, 2012a) gives an example of a case in which this appears to be so: that the UC card-holders did not have access to renal dialysis, while those on the other medical social-security schemes (CSMBS and SSO) did have access to it. Provision of medical services wholly or partly at state expense will inevitably have limits set by cost; and politically it is always likely to be difficult to provide services of strictly identical range and quality for those who pay and those who do not.

It is also inevitable, even in the most comprehensive and egalitarian service, that there will be inequalities of physical access to services according to where people live and how mobile they are. There will be an unavoidable hierarchy of physical accessibility, probably from the capital through cities and towns large and small, to the most remote areas. Accounts of the Thai system suggest that attempts have been made at efficient and equitable provision of services through, among other things, emphasis on the full use of primary-care facilities. But some people will inevitably have greater physical accessibility than others. The existence of 'formal' financial cover of particular services in particular places presumably means that those services in those places will be financed to the extent necessary to avoid 'impoverishment' *if those services are available in those places.* However, despite this inevitable limitation, a WHO report on Thailand (WHO, 2012b, p. 2) mentioned, among much other, generally encouraging, information on rates of contagious diseases and of maternal and infant deaths, that about 98.8 per cent of pregnant women had received adequate health care from public-health personnel, and specifically that about 98 per cent of deliveries had been conducted under the care of public-health personnel.

10.6 Tables on physical and financial access

Tables 10A.1 and 10A.2 in Appendix 10.1, to which reference has been made, derived from those compiled by the ILO, give some indicators of the physical and financial accessibility of medical services. Apart from their columns (3), which give gross national income for 2008, they refer as mentioned to aggregates and relationships from a period slightly earlier in the decade, and columns (6) and (7) are in effect projections derived from applying the apparent ratios of 2003–5 to the GNI figure (taken as a surrogate for GDP) for 2008. As a matter of interest we have added the projected annual dollar amounts for 2008 of users' out-of-pocket health-service payments for 35 low-income and 38 lower-middle-income countries (comprising between them virtually all that were not either very small or at the time theatres of prolonged warfare). These amounted to $7 billion for the low-income, and $91 billion for the lower-middle-income, group.

These sums would not by any means have represented the full cost of the medical services, either to the whole societies or (if they had accepted the responsibility of paying them) to the governments, simply the part of the expense not paid for net by the governments and not covered by various other forms of contributory prepayment.

The idea of completely eliminating the need for OOP payments, at least for the low-income countries, is certainly attractive, and, where it is politically possible, it would presumably eliminate entirely the risk of impoverishment caused by medical expenses. But the Thai experience suggests that a 'pluralistic' approach – say, going as close as possible to eliminating OOP charges 'at the point of use', while at the same time making considerable use of the possibilities of contributory social insurance with the contributions graded by ability to pay – may often be the most promising way of ruling out the risk that people will be impoverished by medical bills. In addition, exacting, on the Thai UC pattern, some nominal co-payments for items of service from all but the poorest of those outside the contributory schemes could potentially be used, for example, to extend the range or reach or quality of services. Press accounts (e.g. in *The Economist* 2012a; and UHC Forward 2012) report that Indonesia plans to extend its 2008 scheme, *Jamkesmas*, which now as a single-payer provides a completely free service for about 30 per cent of the population's poorest. Though the reports in late 2012 suggested some lack of clarity on the budgeting of the extension, ostensibly *Jamkesmas* will be expanded by the start of 2014 so as to cover the whole country, still as a single-payer, prepayment system, in effect as a giant National Health Service on something like the UK pattern, but no longer apparently completely free of charges, which will apparently serve as insurance-type premiums. The state is referred to as collecting premiums, presumably related to some measure of ability to pay, from some or all, it would seem, of the 70 per cent not hitherto covered by *Jamkesmas*.

[For the 'Note on chapter 10: ambiguities, puzzles, and compromises', see Appendix 10.1.]

An apparent lesson from the Thai case is that there may be a diversity of ways of achieving protection, not all of them offering exactly the same range and quality of services, and it may be that no one of them will fulfil ideally all the requirements. Even if formal financial cover is universal, the degree of physical accessibility for some services at least will almost certainly vary across the population. A 'pluralistic' solution will make possible a range of compromises, without abandoning the most essential guarantees.

Conclusion

Formal financial coverage of health expenses – so that they avoid the possibility of impoverishing those who incur them, without unduly increasing dependence on outside finance – can be possible, at least with reasonably fast-growing middle-income countries. Thailand is striking evidence that it can happen. It is best sought initially through a variety of financial devices tailored to the country concerned and its institutional history.

A functional and equitable health service requires both physical and financial 'accessibility': a proper mix and geographical distribution of services as well as manageable ways by which people at all income levels can pay for their use. However, physical accessibility – the range of services effectively on offer – is a matter of degree; it will inevitably vary somewhat according to where people live and their level of mobility. There is also likely to be at least some difference in the perceived quality or range of services between delivery systems financed mainly by contributory insurance and those financed largely or entirely by the state.

Even when expenses are covered so as not themselves to impoverish the users, extreme poverty and destitution may still come about through the chronic disease, disability or death of able-bodied members of a household. That is another matter, calling for its own appropriate solutions.

Many low-income, as distinct from middle-income, countries will undoubtedly encounter particular difficulties in making health services that can be regarded as minimally adequate in prevailing conditions both physically and financially accessible. These countries are likely to have strong cases for international support.

Notes

1 Definitions used here are those that the present authors take to be expressed or implied in ILO 2008b, pp. 16–26.

2 This seems to fit what ILO publications mean by *access* (for example in the tables in ILO 2008b, pp. 77–90) when they do not specify that it is *effective access*, which would include financial, as well as physical and geographical, access.

3 Figures for Thailand in Appendix 10.1, Table 10A.2, would imply a somewhat smaller number 'uncovered'. Also the table in ILO 2008b, pp. 77–90, on which our Table 10A.2 draws, seems to overlook completely the 5 million holders of private health insurance.

Appendix 10.1: Health services in low- and lower-middle-income countries

Note on Chapter 10: Ambiguities, puzzles and compromises in the health-cover information

There are ambiguities and puzzles, beside the one already mentioned, connected with (a) the understanding of the completeness of formal financial cover and (b) the proportion which out-of-pocket payments for health services bear to total national health expenditure – as they are given in the form of percentages in columns (2) and (5) respectively of Tables 10A.1 and 10A.2. It would be expected that (a) and (b) would be reciprocally related, with the OOP ratio low where the percentage of cover is high and vice versa. Sure enough, in the source tables (ILO 2008b, pp. 77–90) from which the data in Tables 10A.1 and 10A.2 are extracted, South Africa is given a rate of formal coverage of 100.0 per cent and at the same time, as might be expected, the very low rate of 10.5 per cent for the proportion that OOP payments bear to total national health spending. But Namibia, with a formal coverage rate given as 22.5 per cent, extremely low by international standards, has a ratio of only 5.8 per cent of OOP payments to total health spending, even lower than South Africa's. One just possible explanation for this anomaly that Namibia seems to represent is that it has something to do with the attempt in Namibia to rely heavily on 'community', rather than state, activity for providing health care (Republic of Namibia 2007).

Further puzzles seem to arise over the difficulties of providing unambiguous definitions and classifications. An instance is where Xenia Scheil-Adlung and others, writing under the auspices of the ILO (2006), count South Africa at the time concerned as having only 12.3 per cent of the population covered by 'any form of health insurance', and appear to use 'health insurance' as synonymous with 'social health protection'. This would seem to imply that 87.7 per cent of South African people have no form of social health protection in a financial sense; and the analysis in the Scheil-Adlung paper is apparently conducted on that supposition. But, as we have mentioned, the tables in ILO (2008b) rate South Africa as having formal financial cover of 100.0 per cent (of which more than four-fifths was provided by the state). (A personal communication to one of the present authors would imply that, though 'formal' state cover in South Africa is universal, the state service, free of charge for primary care but requiring users of other services to pay or not according to their means, is heavily over-stretched and, for that reason if no other, offers an inferior service to that provided privately and largely financed through contributory insurance.) The apparent inconsistency between the Scheil-Adlung *et al.* 2006 paper and ILO (2008b) suggests that there is a need to distinguish 'insurance' in the narrow institutional sense from 'financial protection' as a much broader concept. We are interested in financial protection. However, our informant suggested that further reforms of the state system in South Africa are likely before long.

It is also no surprise that, as the WHO (2012a) renal-dialysis case mentioned in the text of the chapter appears to illustrate, not only physical cover but also financial cover can be a matter of degree. The wholly or largely state-financed system, even if it covers a great range of services, will probably be somewhat more selective, and possibly less attractive in other respects such as waiting times for operations, than one largely financed by users' contributions.

Selected indicators

Note: In the top row of each of these tables, figures in round brackets represent column numbers and their contents, so that, e.g. '(3)=(1)×(2)' means that the column (3) figure equals the product of the column (1) and column (2) figures. (see Tables 10A1 and 10A2)

Table 10A.1 Indicators of health-service coverage (*c.*2003–5) and projected patients' out-of-pocket expenses (*c.*2008): low-income countries

(1)	*(2)*	*(3)*	*(4)*	*(5)*	*(6)*	*(7)*	*(8)*	*(9)*
Country	*Formal cover (% population)*	*GNI (bil. PPP\$, 2005)*	*Health exp're (% of GDP)*	*OOP exp're (% health exp're)*	*OOP payments (bil. \$) = (3) × (4) × (5)*	*OOP (% of GDP) = (6) / (3)*	*Staff-related access deficit (SRA, %)*	*Birth-attended access deficit (BAA, %*
Bangladesh	0.4	55	7.5	58.9	2.4296	4.4	88	87
Benin	0.5	3	4.4	51.4	0.0678	2.3	72	34
Burkina Faso	0.2	4	5.6	52.2	0.1169	2.9	85	43
Burundi	13	1	3.1	76.7	0.0238	2.4	93	75
Cameroon		4	10.9	69.6	0.3035	7.6	76	68
Central African Republic	6.0	1	4.0	58.5	0.0234	2.3	88	56
Chad		2	6.5	57.9	0.0753	3.8	90	86
Congo Democratic Republic		5	4.0	81.7	0.1634	3.3	80	39
Eritrea		1	4.4	54.5	0.0022	0.2	80	72
Ethiopia		6	5.9	32.7	0.1158	1.9	93	94
Gambia	99.9	0.653	8.1	40.2	0.0213	3.3	59	45
Ghana	18.7	7	4.5	68.2	0.2148	3.1	66	53
Guinea	1.1	3	5.4	82.9	0.1343	4.5	79	65
Guinea-Bissau	1.6	0.386	5.6	43.5	0.0094	2.4	75	65

Haiti	60.0	3.5	7.5	43.0	0.2096	3.2	89	76
Kenya	25.0	29.5	4.3	50.6	0.6419	2.2	60	58
Lao P.D.R.	16.1	4.7	3.2	46.4	0.0698	1.5	49	81
Madagascar		7.8	2.7	33.6	0.0708	0.9	81	49
Malawi		4.1	9.3	27.7	0.1056	2.6	81	39
Mali	2.0	7.4	4.8	38.0	0.1350	1.8	82	59
Mauritania	0.3	2.6	3.7	23.2	0.0223	0.9	77	43
Mongolia	100	4.4	6.7	33.0	0.0975	2.2		
Mozambique		8.1	4.7	14.9	0.0567	0.7	93	
Nepal	0.1	11.5	5.3	66.6	0.4059	3.5	87	
Niger	0.7	2	4.7	41.9	0.0394	2.0	92	
Rwanda	36.6	2	3.7	23.6	0.0175	0.9	85	
Senegal	11.7	6	5.1	55.5	0.1698	2.8	88	
Sierra Leone		1	3.5	41.7	0,0146	1.5	88	
Tanzania	14.5	10	4.3	36.2	0.1557	1.6	88	
Togo	0.4	1	5.6	66.2	0.0371	3.7	85	
Uganda	0.1	6	7.3	36.7	0.1607	2.7	78	
Uzbekistan		11	5.5	54.4	0.3291	3.0		
Yemen	6.3	10	5.5	00.4	0.3102	3.1	69	
Zambia		4	5.4	33.1	0.0715	1.8	42	

Sources: Extracted from ILO (2007), pp. 59–71; ILO (2008b), pp. 77–90; and World Bank (2010), pp. 378–9.

Table 10A.2 Indicators of health-service coverage (*c.*2003–5) and projected patients' out-of-pocket expenses (*c.*2008): lower middle-income countries

(1)	*(2)*	*(3)*	*(4)*	*(5)*	*(6)*	*(7)*	*(8)*	*(9)*
Country	*Formal cover (% population)*	*GNI (bil. PPP$, 2005)*	*Health exp're (% of GDP)*	*OOP exp're (% health exp're)*	*OOP payments (bil. $) = (3) × (4) × (5)*	*OOP (% of GDP) = (6) / (3)*	*Staff-related access deficit (SRA, %)*	*Birth-attended access deficit (BAA, %*
Albania		6	6.5	58.2	0.2270	3.8		6
Angola		10	7.1	15.8	0.1122	1.1	62	53
Armenia	100.0	3	4.5	64.3	0.0868			3
Bolivia	66.9	8	6.7	28.5	0.1528	1.9		39
Bulgaria	100.0	17	7.5	44.8	0.5712	3.4		1
Cameroon	0.1	10	4.2	69.9	0.2936	2.9	44	38
China	23.9	1,417	5.6	55.9			34	17
Cape Verde	65.0	0.00156	4.6	26.7			57	11
Congo Democratic Republic		2	2.0	35.8	0.0143	0.7	64	64
Côte d'Ivoire	5.0	11	3.6	65.5	0.2594	2.4	77	37
Ecuador	73.0	23	5.1	54.1	0.6346	2.8	4	31
Egypt	47.6	94	5.8	53.5	2.9168	3.1	19	31
El Salvador	59.6	14	8.1	50.4	0.5715	4.1	36	31
Guatemala	72.6	23	5.4	55.4	0.6881	3.0		59
Honduras	65.2	7	7.1	37.3	0.1854	2.6	42	44
India	5.7	568	4.8	72.9	19.8755	3.5	56	57
Indonesia	54.6	173	3.1	47.6	2.5528	1.5	76	34

Iran		133	6.5	50.0	4.3325	3.3	45	10
Jordan	c.80.0	10	9.4	40.6	0.3816	3.8		
Kazakhstan	70–80	27	3.5	42.7	0.4035	1.5		
Lesotho		1	5.2	3.7	0.0019	0.2	79	45
Morocco	41.2	40	5.1	50.9	1.0384	2.6	59	37
Nicaragua	68.5	4	7.7	49.4	0.1522	3.8	55	33
Nigeria		43	5.0	67.9	1.4599	3.4	38	65
Pakistan		69	2.4	70.9	1.1741	1.7	62	77
Papua New Guinea		3	3.4	9.7	0.0099	0.3	82	82
Paraguay	63.7	6	7.3	51.1	0.2238	3.7	12	23
Philippines		88	3.2	44.0	1.2390	1.4	29	40
Serbia and Montenegro	96.2	16	9.6	20.9	0.3210	2.0		7
Sri Lanka	0.1	18	3.5	48.9	0.3081	1.7	33	3
Syria	29.2	20	5.1	51.8	0.5284	2.6		30
Thailand	97.7	136	3.3	28.7	1.2881	0.9		1
The FYR of Macedonia	100.0	4	7.1	15.5	0.0440	1.1		2
Tunisia	99.0	22	5.4	45.1	0.5358	2.4		10
Turkmenistan	82.3	5	3.9	32.6	0.0636	1.3		3
Ukraine	100.0	47	5.7	26.8	0.7180	1.5		1
Venezuela	100.0	89	4.5	53.2	2.1307	2.4	39	6
Vietnam	23.4	39	5.4	53.6	1.1288	2.9	66	15

Source: Same as Table 10A.1.

11 The 'other' Millennium Development Goals

Competition or synergy?

The objective advanced in this book, the achievement in each part of the world of a reliable floor to disposable income at least at a level deemed to be just above one of extreme poverty, has been exposed to two objections. One is that, if taken seriously, it would divert resources from the pursuit of economic growth, the only realistic path out of poverty. This is answered after a fashion in Chapter 3. The other objection is that the concentration on disposable income risks leaving out of account those contributors to material welfare – so-called public goods and merit goods – which can only be procured – or can most effectively be procured – through social action, that is by government or civil society. We consider that objection here.

The Millennium Development Goals (MDGs) are intended to express the highest-priority material needs of the world's people and therefore may go beyond goods such as food and shelter that can readily be obtained by individuals and households if they have the cash, and extend to environmental goods of either present or future utility, such as public-health measures and clean air and conserving fisheries and stabilizing the climate.

There were 8 MDGs adopted by the UN General Assembly in the year 2000, with 18 more specific 'Targets', all but the last three related directly to the Goals, and most expressed quantitatively, and with 48 'Indicators' for testing the extent to which the Targets have been fulfilled or been on track for fulfilment. The Indicators are mostly expressed as intended changes in the Target variables between 1990 and 2015. Wording and some details have been modified slightly in the repetition of the Targets and Indicators that has occurred since the millennial year.

Does the concentration on equipping every household with a modicum of disposable income (the first MDG) *risk the neglect of* needs that can only be satisfied, or most effectively be satisfied, by social action? Or may this attention to disposable income even *contribute to* procurement of the public and merit goods?

11.1 Goal 1: Eradicate extreme poverty and hunger

This book is directed to what is understood by the first MDG, essentially *maintaining a floor to disposable income* at or above the international extreme-poverty line, which, it would be hoped, would mean affording everyone, among some other essentials, *the capacity for acquiring* no less than the quantity and quality of food, especially in early childhood and in pregnancy and lactation, that provides adequate calorific content and prevents the development of clinical malnutrition. A highly important extra twist has been inserted in the present treatment as essential for fulfilling the intention of the Goal; this is that *medical expenses should be 'covered'*, directly or through contributory insurance, to the extent that they should not be 'impoverishing' to any household. (The compelling reason for this addendum, and what it means, is explained at the beginning of Chapter 10 above.) If the objective of preventing malnutrition is to be taken seriously, we should probably also include measures, often very low-cost, against harmful animal parasites such as intestinal worms.

What we aim to do in this short chapter is to consider the extent to which a commitment to this first Goal conflicts, or at least competes for resources, with the other Goals and their associated Targets. Does the concern on the part of governments for ensuring an essential minimum of disposable income and cover of medical expenses risk impairing for financial reasons access to clean water and sanitation, and expert care in childbirth, and schooling for girls, and environmental sustainability, and to vaccinations and other prophylactics against bacterial and viral and prionic and animal-parasite diseases? Or could the one help to validate the effects of the other? So we shall consider in turn each of the other Goals and attempt some judgement of whether they are likely to compete or to cooperate with this first Goal.

11.1.1 A digression on fulfilment of Goal 1 targets

Halving extreme poverty and hunger between 1990 and 2015 is taken to mean halving the *proportion* of the world's population below the extreme-poverty line. This appears in fact to have been achieved by 2010 (World Bank 2013). (The same test was applied to every region or other subgroup individually. The absolute numbers for the developing countries fell from 1.94 billion in 1981 to 1.29 billion in 2008. This represented a fall in the proportions of the people of those countries in extreme poverty from somewhere in the region of 58 per cent (if we take total numbers in 1981 as 3.34 billion) to 22 per cent, a fall of roughly two-thirds in the proportion. The fall was highly concentrated on the East Asia and Pacific region, which moved from 77 per cent to 14 per cent over the same period, and especially on China with its great weight in the total. But it was noted (ibid.) that between 2005 and 2008 every region's headcount fell both absolutely and proportionately, and (though on incomplete figures) absolute falls appeared to continue after 2008. Rapid growth, which has characterized much of the developing world, would seem very likely, if it continues, to produce more of the same fall in the poverty headcount. But Martin Ravallion (cited ibid.) cautions that there has been a build-up of numbers just above the extreme-poverty borderline and at the same time comparatively small absolute falls (from $2.59 billion to $2.47 billion) in two-dollar-a-day poverty, which might between the two lead to an unduly favourable impression of what is happening. He projects that on present trends there will still be a billion in extreme poverty in 2015.

11.2 Goal 2: Achieve universal primary education

Clearly public spending on supplementing the disposable incomes of the poor may compete for public resources with building, equipping and staffing primary schools. But extra public spending is not the only means by which elementary education can be advanced. This is not just because there are various ways in which, without further spending on salaries, buildings or equipment, the quality of teaching and rates of attendance (of both children and teachers) can be significantly improved, so greatly advancing the main objectives of schooling, namely the acquisition of knowledge and skills. (See Banerjee and Duflo 2011, ch. 4 *passim*, esp. pp. 97ff.)

Apart from the quality of what goes on in the classroom, there is also the question of what makes parents willing to put their children in school, forgoing the benefits of whatever else the children might be doing and, where there are fees, being prepared to pay them. The big increases in primary-school enrolment and attendance in several countries, such as Kenya, Uganda and Ghana, as soon as fees were abolished (Banerjee and Duflo 2011, p. 73) made it clear that there had been a large unmet demand for schooling. Reducing its cost to the households that were the potential users was apparently enough to release the demand. Many of the parents clearly set a value on education.

But it is a further question whether that release of demand was, at least in part, an 'income effect' (occurring because the abolition of fees increased the families' real incomes) or simply a 'substitution or price effect' (making the schooling relatively cheaper). This is a question of some importance: if it was an income effect, then an equivalent cash transfer to the parents (without abolition of the fees) might have had a similar effect. In fact, some evidence from Malawi and Morocco (Banerjee and Duflo 2011, p. 80), as mentioned in Chapter 9 above, on the effects of conditional cash transfers (CCTs) suggests that the behaviour aimed at (in the case of Malawi, putting girls into school in response to a cash sum for doing so) would be generated by the cash transfer alone, independently of the conditional element, that is of the cash as a *reward*. (The 'income effect', perhaps combined with the 'nudge' of calling attention to the desired behaviour, might, it seems, have been enough.)

Insofar as that is a valid interpretation and expectation, it suggests that there may often be no conflict, but rather synergy, between making cash transfers (even unconditional cash transfers) to the poorest households and increasing primary-school enrolment and attendance.

11.3 Goal 3: Promote gender equality

This, according to the Indicator attached to it, implies that there should be equal proportions of girls and boys entered for both primary and secondary schooling.

Much of what is said above over Goal 2 also applies here, except that the attitudes of parents, which are crucial, have in the past often treated women's education as less important than that of men. Casual perusal of the girl-to-boy ratios as percentages in primary and secondary schooling for the years 1991 and 2009 (World Bank, *WDI 2011*, pp. 14ff.) strongly suggest, however, that, where these attitudes have not already changed, they are now changing fairly fast. Where there have been significant changes in these ratios over the 18 years, these are almost all increases. (Changes of over 5 percentage points, where figures for both years were recorded in the source, numbered 31 increases and only five decreases.) Movement toward gender-parity in schooling appears to be happening spontaneously. Cash payments have been used on occasion to encourage girls' schooling specifically, but sums involved seem from examples to have been trivial in comparison with what would be required in approximating a safety-net of the sort discussed here. Any public-sector spending that is at all likely to be done specifically to provide a bait in order to encourage gender parity in schooling is likely to make little proportional difference one way or the other to what might be spent on maintaining a disposable-income floor. The two are not in any significant degree competitors.

11.4 Goal 4: Reduce child mortality

The stated Objective here is to reduce the under-five mortality rate by two-thirds between 1990 and 2015. An interim report for February 2011 indicated that, of 144 countries, only 11 had actually reached that target and 25 others were 'on track' to do so by 2015, with a further number of more than 100 off-track and unlikely to reach the target in time (World Bank, *WDI 2011*, pp. 5ff.). This sounds disheartening but, if we set the bar a little lower and ask which low-income and lower-middle-income countries have reduced their under-five mortality rates *by more than half* between 1991 and 2009, we find that they include Albania, Armenia, Bangladesh, Bolivia, China, Egypt, El Salvador, Eritrea, Ethiopia, Indonesia, Iran, Kazakhstan, Laos, Liberia, Madagascar, Malawi, Mongolia, Nepal, Nicaragua, Senegal, Syria, Thailand, Timor Leste, Tunisia, Turkey, Uzbekistan and Vietnam: in fact 27 countries including nine of the world's giants and covering quite a large part of global population, with India just narrowly failing to make it a tenth on that test. This is evidence, if evidence is needed that, for the great bulk of the diseases of childhood that in the past have often been fatal, the technology exists for greatly reducing death rates below pre-industrial levels. Then does directing resources into safety-net-type outlays threaten, or on the contrary further, the reduction of child mortality?

Part of the answer lies in the fact that a safety-net in our understanding itself includes important health-service requirements. Following UN/ILO interpretations, we have taken an income floor to imply that all essential medical expenses for procedures that are in practice physically and technically accessible should be financially 'covered' in such a way and to such an extent that no household should be 'impoverished' by them, and by implication that no household should be deterred from using medical services through fear of impoverishment.

We have distinguished in Chapter 10 between physical accessibility and financial accessibility of medical services. Physical accessibility refers to whether the medical infrastructure – of professionals, buildings, supplies and equipment – exists and is close enough transport-wise to the potential patients. Financial accessibility refers to whether the necessary services can and will be paid for without risk of any household's impoverishment. In our discussion of a safety-net we have emphasized financial accessibility. Both elements, advances on both fronts, are necessary. If health budgets are limited, the two may compete with one another for funding, and questions of priority have to be decided. Extending either may help to improve general health status and increase knowledge and awareness of hazards and of simple remedial measures, and hence to reduce child mortality.

On grounds of equity, we would argue on the whole for giving priority in cases of doubt to financial accessibility, that is, to the safety-net element: in other words that, where the medical infrastructure exists, it should be made available to all (through whatever method of financing) so that no one need be impoverished by out-of-pocket payments for services or deterred on that ground from using them.

11.5 Goal 5: Improve maternal health

A Target here is to reduce maternal deaths in childbirth by three-quarters between 1990 and 2015. (In 2011, 30 countries were judged to be on-track to achieve this.) Other objectives were to expand contraceptive use and to have each birth accompanied by a skilled attendant. As with child mortality, making medical services more accessible, financially as well as physically, can be expected to improve general health status, and with it knowledge and awareness of hazards, and hence to reduce the incidence of deaths of mothers in childbirth; so that again the safety-net agenda would be to a considerable extent working in cooperation with other health measures (provision and geographical spread of the medical infrastructure) toward realizing the (maternal-health) Goal.

11.6 Goal 6: Combat HIV/AIDS, malaria and other diseases

The first stated Target here is to have halted by 2015, and begun to reverse, the spread of HIV/AIDS. The judgement of the UNAIDS Report of 2010 (World Bank, *WDI 2011*, pp. 5,6) is that the number of new infections per year reported had fallen by 21 per cent from its peak in 1997, but that many developing countries lacked reliable estimates of incidence. Reducing the spread of HIV/AIDS is presumably in large part a matter of information and advocacy plus provision of condoms, with ARV drugs as therapy. These protective activities have their costs and to that extent may compete with transfers made to supplement the disposable income of the very poor.

The second Target is to have halted by 2015, and begun to reverse, the incidence of malaria 'and other major diseases'. There are a number of requirements specific to protection against particular diseases, such as impregnated bednets against malaria, and others such as adequate nutrition of wide importance but especially relevant to malaria. These requirements are likely to be encouraged by safety-net-motivated transfers.

11.7 Goal 7: Ensure environmental sustainability

Here the synergies with a safety-net programme may not be immediately obvious, and the range of needs is immense. Two Targets of prime importance to life and health are reducing by half both the numbers of people without access to an improved water source and those without access to improved sanitation. On the matter of possible competition for finance between improved water and sanitation on the one hand and disposable-income support on the other, Banerjee and Duflo (2011, pp. 46–7) point to possibilities of radically improving the trade-off if, as they argue is possible, annual cost of the water and sanitation can be reduced from a 'conventionally cited' $20 to $4 per household. This suggests that accessible clean water and sanitation, if they can be acquired at cost, may be at least on the borderline of eligibility to be fitted into the household budgets of many of the very poor, and their uptake therefore is likely to be increased by small rises in the households' disposable incomes.

11.8 Goal 8: Develop a global partnership for development

This is a goal of a different order, and the question of rivalry or synergy does not arise in the same way.

Conclusion

If, as it appears, very poor people in general care no less deeply than others about their own and their families' health, educational level and general (future as well as present) material well-being, their spending of any additional disposable income is likely to reflect these concerns, so that, provided they have access to the relevant information and suitable local institutions, there is a strong potential synergy between the safety-net objective on the one hand and the other objectives in the areas of education, water and sanitation, and general health on the other, and hence between the first Millennium Development Goal (food and poverty) and key elements of six of the others.

12 Politics of safety-nets

Turning aspiration into reality

> The rapid introduction of social protection programmes based on income transfers has resulted in a sharp rise in coverage. New forms of assistance introduced in the last decade now reach in excess of 150 million poor households in developing countries, with perhaps half a billion people benefiting. Notable recent initiatives include: South Africa's Child Support Grant, implemented in 2003 and now reaching 7.2 million children; the Minimum Living Standards Scheme in China initiated in the late 1990s and reaching 22.4 million by 2006; Mexico's Oportunidades started in 1997 and now reaching more than 5 million households; Bolsa Familia in Brazil with coverage of 12 million households; Indonesia's Safety Net Scheme introduced in 2005 and planned to reach 15 million households; and India's National Rural Employment Guarantee Scheme expected to reach 26 million households during 2008.
>
> (Barrientos and Hulme 2008, p. 3)

The central purpose of this chapter is to give plausible reasons how and why, in a number of countries, including some of the poorest, an effective social safety-net, not just a proliferation of anti-poverty measures but a genuine, largely consistent, floor to disposable income maintained at no lower than the extreme-poverty margin, not only may be possible but indeed can be seen as on the way to being realized. The plausible reasons lie in what is already happening, and in how – through what devices and procedures and what changes in the political climate – it has done so.

On the optimistic side, we could cite not only the cases mentioned in the 2008 quotation above from Barrientos and Hulme, but also other major advances, brought in or promised, some of which we shall mention in Section 12.12 below.

There is a strong sense that bit by bit fundamental change is under way – as if the tectonic plates were moving.

This book has considered the possibility of safety-nets at a fairly high level of generality. At the same time we have taken it for granted that a safety-net will need to be applied country by country, with the relevant country's government in the driving seat. So realizing the aspiration will entail bringing each government on board. Individuals and institutions that wish to generate a commitment to having disposable-income floors over as much of the world as possible will need to consider how that commitment in each particular country can be brought about. This will mean inevitably attending to the politics.

The idea of maintaining no less than a certain minimum value of purchasable goods and services for all is of course not new. But thinking of it as a controlling and urgently needed principle of practical policies capable of implementation, with real numbers attached, that should apply to everyone, not only in the rich countries but also among the huge part of the world's people in the low-income and low-middle-income categories – that was a step that probably seemed to most concerned people as too far from the realms of practical possibility until shortly before the start of the present century. How actually to bring it about was hardly a subject of serious debate.

Yet since then there have been three striking applications of distinctive options available for practical use by national societies against severe poverty: the conditional cash transfers that have spread widely through Latin America; the employment guarantee of so many days of paid work for any household in a year that has been instituted to run across rural India; and the combination of contributory and non-contributory health insurance devices that seems to have enabled Thailand to provide an almost complete range of recognized medical services virtually without risk of impoverishing the service users. These are among the potential building-blocks for universal safety-nets, even if verdicts about the effectiveness of their practical manifestations, especially that of the second, are not yet final. But until recently we could probably say that few if any low-income or low-middle-income countries (certainly few of those with predominantly market-based economies) had yet adopted, with signs of serious intent or as an explicit policy, the goal of a clear income floor for all.

12.1 A manifesto of social protection for everyone

However, there are convincing signs that this is in process of changing. The 'Text of the recommendation concerning national floors of social protection' issued by the 101st International Labour Conference in Geneva on 14 June 2012 (ILO 2012a) would appear to imply wide international agreement to the principle of a safety-net. Admittedly, international declarations of laudable principles are not necessarily pledges of what is likely to happen, and the recent 'recommendation' may seem superficially a noble document with no real force. As is the custom in such declarations there is exhaustive definition of terms and listing of qualifications to the main theme, ostensibly to ensure first that no form, aspect or mechanism should appear to be excluded or overlooked when it ought to be allowed as a possible, or enjoined as a necessary, feature of the activity advocated; and second that none should appear to be included when it ought to be forbidden.

But the essence of the 'recommendation' is in its Clause 4:

> Members [that is, governments and other representatives of nations that are members of the ILO] should, in accordance with national circumstances,

> establish as quickly as possible and maintain their social protection floors comprising basic social security guarantees. The guarantees should ensure that, over the life cycle, all in need have access to essential health care and to basic income security which together ensure effective access to goods and services defined as necessary at the national level.

Elsewhere (Clause 1 b) there is an aspiration that over time the floors established *should be progressively raised.*

Maybe some of the definitions and clarifications in the recommendation seem to overdo the degree of specification expressed. But no doubt the ILO, in practice taking the lead in the movement to establish social safety-nets, would want to have as clear an agreement as possible of what was and what was not being advocated.

12.2 A process with a concrete target

However, a feature of this statement, in contrast to some UN declarations, is that, rather than being a voice crying in the wilderness – preaching in part to the converted who do not need its message and in part to those who will simply ignore it – the recommendation has provided authority *for a process that has already begun to take place* well beyond the relatively rich countries that embraced similar ideals in the twentieth century, not just a variety of moves of one sort or another 'to help the poor' but a procedure for building in each cooperating country a consistent floor that no one can fall through. The hope is to extend the building of safety-nets beyond the giants – China, India, Indonesia, Brazil, Mexico, Thailand – that have already taken important steps in that direction – to the many other countries whose participation is needed.

What follows aims to see this process – a process of mutual consultation and clarification of possibilities – through three pilot-studies of countries from among those whose governments have opted to undergo it. The countries are Vietnam, El Salvador and Mozambique. At the time of drafting of this chapter Vietnam had proceeded further than the other two.

12.3 Alliances and fairness

On the face of it the politics of establishing safety-nets might appear to be a matter of *forming alliances* of those whose aspirations and interests in favour happen to coincide or can be made to coincide. With talk of alliances we might imagine an opposing force that would have to be resisted and overcome. But this does not quite fit the present case. Even if a country's safety-net would have to be provided in essentials by its own institutions, with any help from abroad only a minor element, the main political obstacle would seem likely to be *inertia* rather than active opposition. Few would openly reject the general aim of supporting the very poor, the weak, the vulnerable – even though they might not be positively enthusiastic for making personal sacrifices in the cause. The political skill in deflecting potential opposition to a safety-net would lie partly in arranging that any unavoidable financial cost should be widely spread with some colour of fairness so that its adverse impact on any class of individuals would be barely noticeable, or at least be tolerable, and not clearly out of line with sacrifices elsewhere. Furthermore, if the prospective safety-net appeared to be reliably consistent, its *insurance* character might extend its appeal beyond those who might expect to be its immediate beneficiaries, to those who recognize that they might need to rely on it *in case they themselves should fall on hard times for their productive activities or into disability or treatable but costly illness.*

12.4 Costs of filling the gaps

Moreover filling the extreme-poverty gap, except in the very poorest countries, seems unlikely to require a huge financial effort. It has been mentioned above that the apparent size of the gap in 2005 for the low-income and low-middle-income countries together[1] amounted to about 0.2 per cent, that is 1/500, one five-hundredth, of world gross income (GNI). Among the three countries serving as pilots for present purposes, figures for Vietnam put its extreme-poverty gap then at 1.0 per cent, 1/100, of its GNI. El Salvador gave a figure even lower at 0.6 per cent. So covering the gap in these two cases need not, it would seem, demand any massive redistribution of income, even if there is to be no simultaneous dividend from economic growth and no additional drawing of resources from the rest of the world. However, the figure for the third pilot country, Mozambique, was a daunting 19.6 per cent, and here some external support is likely to prove essential unless realization of the objective is to be pushed far into the future. (The corresponding figure for Bangladesh in the same year appears to be 2.9 per cent.)

12.5 Channelling attainable moves

All this leaves open the possibility that, for a number of the developing countries above the ranks of the very poorest, an operational policy for establishing a safety-net may require something in the nature of a 'nudge' rather than a campaign or massive external aid. In these cases – probably including those (comparatively few) of the then-low-income countries asterisked in Table 4A.7 in Appendix 4.2 above, but almost all of the lower-middle-income countries – the general desire to help the very poor may need only to be channelled into the tactful selection – through a consensual process – of specific measures that are attainable.

The encouraging development in the century's second decade, as we shall explain below, is that a definite procedure for administering the necessary nudge has been outlined and has already begun tentatively to be put into effect. An aspiration is being turned into a programme.

And, as figures given above suggest, two of the first three countries in which the procedure is being piloted – El Salvador and Vietnam – are not on the face of it especially difficult targets: respectively one small low-middle-income country in Central America, and one South East Asian giant on the cusp between lower-middle and low. But there is also one medium-sized African state, Mozambique, that has gone through a recent period of very fast growth but is now still far down in the low-income category.

12.6 Clarifying paths to safety-nets: the UN's Social Protection Floor (SPF) Initiative

The ILO describes the UN's Social Protection Floor (SPF) Initiative as 'the most tangible outcome of the renewed international interest in social protection' (ILO 2012b, p. 3). The Initiative requires the formation as a first step in each interested country of a task force or working group comprising UN agencies and 'development partners' (foreign donors) present in the country, together with representatives of interests from within the society, 'to build or further develop' its national social-protection floor. Nine (mainly low-income) countries are listed (as of May 2012) as examples of those that have formed such task forces. The task forces' role is clearly to deploy both domestic and international knowledge and expertise, in order to identify gaps in protection-floor coverage, and possible routes to filling those gaps, with the options fully costed.

The costing of each option would allow a form of cost-effectiveness judgement to take place, with the cost of each measure and each plausible combination of measures set against the reduction in the poverty headcount and in the poverty gap that it would bring about. This would provide information needed for guiding the setting of priorities among the actions that are possible.

In some cases the IMF is brought in to undertake or validate the costing and to estimate how far, if at all, revenue sources or economies ('fiscal space') may be expected *to expand* through background growth in the revenue base or *to be capable of expansion*, presumably through, for example, redirecting of existing outlays (such as general subsidies on consumer goods), or additional taxes, or increased tax rates, or spending economies, or reduction of evasion and avoidance.

A UN agency – or more than one – is to take the lead in each instance of the process's application. The identity of this lead agency varies from case to case, including, individually or in combination, UNICEF, the World Bank, ILO and WHO. Having the IMF and one of the other institutions together in the lead is presumably some defence against two forms of wishful thinking: underestimation of the costs, and overestimation of the benefits and the extent of cover (as some assurance perhaps that awkward groups, such as parentless children or beggars, are not overlooked).

Most countries have some programmes ostensibly designed to help the poor and vulnerable, often no doubt instituted with good intentions and of value to their beneficiaries. But *these* schemes are often fragmentary and uncoordinated. There are contributory social-insurance schemes that are confined to particular groups such as government servants and their families, or to all formal-sector workers. These may cover medical expenses or retirement pensions but typically have no provision for those who are or have been working in the informal sector or have never been consistently in the paid labour force. The challenge faced is to transform these manifold programmes in each country into something consistent and available at need to all.

To this end one step in the SPF is to set out for the country considered its existing social provisions. This is done for Vietnam in ILO 2012c (pp. 48–9), which gives the 'baseline social budget, actual' for the years 2003–10, and corresponding baseline forecasts for the following ten years. Much of this budgeted expenditure could presumably be incorporated into the safety-net, either through actual redirection or on paper through redesignation. The expenses for completing the safety-net would thus not by any means represent a full net addition to the baseline spending, the status quo.

12.7 Analytical tools in the SPF Initiative

The purpose of the analytical tools devised for fulfilling the SPF Initiative is represented by the ILO (2012b, p. 3) as providing 'the factual bases for national dialogues on alternative policy options, implementation priorities and the phasing in of SPF policies'. In abridged form the tools listed are as follows:

- A procedure to assess the state of national Social Protection Floor Policies and identify coverage gaps…
- An ILO-UNICEF costing tool that allows users to estimate the cost of different social protection measures…
- A rapid assessment protocol (RAP) … that enables users to evaluate the cost of steps that could be taken to close social protection coverage gaps … The tool further provides a basis to discuss and simulate alternative financing options and fiscal space.
- A … methodology that [makes it possible] to assess the … impact of alternative benefits on poverty headcounts and the poverty gap on the basis of household survey data.

(Ibid.)

Briefly what this appears to mean is:

1. Identifying gaps in safety-net coverage that are present under current practice and future plans;
2. Estimating the costs of various possible benefit measures for filling the gaps;
3. Compiling the costs of various (possibly acceptable) combinations of those benefit measures and simulating various (possible and possibly acceptable) means of paying for them;
4. Judging the impact of various packages of benefits on the numbers of people in extreme poverty and the aggregate depth of the poverty.

The pilot studies show how applying this set of tools can lead to a rough form of cost-effectiveness comparison of alternative courses of action, which can help in informing the decision-makers in the country concerned.

An example from Vietnam is given below of how a choice between two variants of a policy package for social protection of children can be illuminated by comparing the respective costs of the two variants and the respective reductions in the child-poverty headcount that they are estimated to bring about.

But there is a further element of assessment that inevitably comes into the process of selection of social-protection measures. This is how the chosen actions are to be financed, the question we have explored in Chapter 7.

As the ILO paper classifies them, there are five broad possibilities (ILO 2012b, p. 6): economic growth with the consequent revenue bonus; revenue mobilization; increasing expenditure efficiency; reallocation of spending; and external finance.

Summarizing features of the Social Protection Floor Initiative reflected in the pilot studies, the authors of ILO 2012b make four important points (p. 6).

First, the studies are '*demand-driven*': each undertaken at the request of the authorities in the country concerned and pursued in close collaboration with them.

Second, the findings are '*non-prescriptive* and tailored to particular country circumstances'.

Third, the studies are directed to *coordination* of policies covering various sectors and to 'the coherence of these approaches with national social protection policy and overall development priorities'.

Fourth, '*implementation is flexible*': it is taken that timing must depend on circumstances.

Once the first of these four points is made – that there is to be no attempt to impose anything from outside – maybe the others necessarily follow. And that first point is critical. It implies that, unless the authorities in a country have *some inclination* toward eliminating extreme poverty in disposable income, the procedure envisaged here can simply not take place. There are various ways in which that inclination may be generated. Influential strands in the population may of course have a variety of motives that might push their governments in this direction: purely humanitarian concern; fear of social disturbance in case severe and unaccustomed poverty is excessively concentrated; or considerations of national prestige if a country's poverty is notorious. All three motives can co-exist even in a single person. Declared international standards such as the Millennium Goals may fortify the third type of motive. The current movement of opinion and awareness in support of the idea of a social safety-net is likely to draw on the prestige-shame concern and so add its force to the others in favour.

However the inclination of national authorities toward a social-protection floor has been generated, the important point for our purposes is that it does seem to exist. Otherwise it is hard to see why, as we have mentioned, a number of developing-country governments have taken steps toward participating in the SPF Initiative, why India has sought to introduce its rural-employment-guarantee scheme and its public-distribution scheme and health cover for the poorest and why so much of Latin America has adopted as policy conditional cash transfers to families with children. Given the inclination, the consultative procedure with which we are concerned here can chart for each country various ways for getting there that seem potentially acceptable. Making them concrete and costed, with clearly unacceptable options removed from consideration and with their benefits in poverty-reduction also estimated, clears the path for the next steps toward a social-protection floor and makes informed choice possible.

To give some idea of how and to what outcomes the 'tools' listed above may be applied, we present briefly the outline of a 'national social-protection strategy' for Vietnam (ILO 2012c) and more preliminary analyses and proposals of a similar character for El Salvador and Mozambique (ILO 2012b). Explicitly in the case of Vietnam, implicitly in the other two, the consideration of gaps in coverage and how to fill them is given under four heads corresponding to the four guarantees sought by the UN's Social Protection Floor Initiative: for medical expenses, to children, to working-age adults and to the elderly, with the invalid and handicapped treated in one or other of the last two categories.

In comparing the pilot studies it is well to remember the huge differences in average income across the three countries. El Salvador in 2009 had a gross income per head of PPP$ 6,420, more than twice that of Vietnam (PPP$ 2,790), which was about three times that of Mozambique (PPP$ 880).

12.8 Vietnam pilot study

On Vietnam (ILO 2012c, pp. 9ff.) we are told that there had been, in the decade since 2002, 'the development of a fairly extensive set of social protection policies … including a social insurance system for both formal workers and the poor and vulnerable … and several social assistance benefits targeting vulnerable groups excluded from the labour market'. And there was more: 'programmes targeted to specific groups, areas and sectors to provide access to basic social services'. A draft Social Protection Strategy, to run from 2011 to 2020 but with its approval as of mid-2012 delayed, was promulgated to extend the system of social protection in ways that went well beyond social transfers (cash grants).

The ILO, on behalf of the UN SPF Initiative, 'assessed the existing social protection system of Vietnam using the four "guarantees" of the SPF as benchmarks: health for all, and income security for children, for working-age population and for the elderly' (ILO 2012c, p. ix).

The 'Rapid Assessment Matrix' mentioned above was used for Vietnam. The matrix involved the areas of these four guarantees as what might be called its 'rows', and, as its six 'columns', 'existing provisions', 'measures foreseen in the social protection strategy', 'policy-design gaps', 'implementation gaps', 'agencies involved' and 'priorities'. In practice the use of the matrix in rapid assessment involved mainly setting out the first, third and fourth of these (existing provisions, design gaps and implementation gaps), leaving the priorities to be determined by dialogue with the government). The existing provisions and the gaps identified are set out at length in ILO (2012c, pp. 8–16). What follows is drawn from the very brief executive summary there.

First, on *health*, the government had adopted as a target the achievement of universal health-insurance coverage by 2014. More than 60 per cent of the population were covered by some form of health insurance in 2010 (ILO 2012c, p. 9), some of it subsidized in varying degree, and some not. *For those included*, the 60 per cent, social health insurance covers between 80 and 100 per cent of costs for most of the health services. But it still seemed to be the case that patients' out-of-pocket expenses accounted for nearly half of the total costs. Presumably the projected *universal* insurance coverage would significantly reduce the out-of-pocket outlays overall. However, there was uncertainty in 2012 over how, and therefore whether, the cover would be applied by the target date to all of that large proportion of households that were in the informal sector (ibid.).

For Vietnam's *children*, there were already benefits for orphans and for 'children living in vulnerable regions or children of ethnic minorities', but the judgement made was that tight criteria and low benefits meant that adequate living standards were generally not being attained for poor children in these groups.

To meet the needs of *working-age adults*, there was an unemployment-insurance scheme introduced in 2009 for formal-sector workers, but nothing comparable for the much larger numbers in the informal sector: 'only a scattered series of individual programmes [providing] some *ad-hoc* support to specific groups of people'.

Of the *retired* population in Vietnam,

> only 9 per cent ... received retirement pensions from the compulsory insurance system. Apart from this formal pension scheme, people over 80 or poor or vulnerable elderly are supposed to benefit from a universal non-contributory social pension ... [but] around 30 per cent of the eligible elderly [which appears to mean here mainly those aged 80 or over] are not covered by social pensions. Furthermore, by design, income security of elderly people aged between 65 and 79 is not guaranteed.
>
> (ILO 2012c, p. 9)

As an outcome of dialogue with the Government of Vietnam and the 'social partners', *the ILO formulated the following suggestions* (ILO 2012c, pp. xff.), which we paraphrase in the four paragraphs that follow. (We suppose that the health-finance commitment for 2014 mentioned above has been costed and counted in existing plans as part of the status quo.)

- For the *elderly* a choice is outlined between two possible combinations of increases in the level of benefits and extension of the age-range eligible for receiving them, either combination to be introduced gradually. Added cost would be 0.6 per cent of GDP in one case and 0.8 per cent in the other. One of the options would be expected to reduce the extreme-poverty headcount for old people from 14.5 per cent in the status quo to 12.2 per cent. The longer-term aim would be movement towards a universal non-contributory retirement pension.

- For poor *children* under 16 there were again two options mentioned, either to be gradually implemented over five years. One would provide targeted benefits (a cash allowance according to need, 'educational services' and one meal a day) for no more than two children per household; the other would give the same package per child for as many children as there happened to be. Costs by 2016 would be 0.47 per cent of GDP for the first option and up to nearly 0.87 per cent for the other, but there would be a big difference between the two in the reductions they would be expected to make in the poverty headcount: from 20.8 per cent in the status quo to 12.2 per cent in one case and to an extremely low 2.2 per cent in the other.
- For *people of working age* the recommendations included guaranteed employment of 100 days a year per household along Indian lines, stipends for the disabled, training for the unemployed and encouragement of micro-enterprises. The maximum cost estimated would be 1.14 per cent of GDP by 2020. The reduction in the extreme-poverty headcount, apparently for the whole age-group, would be from 12.1 per cent in the status quo down to 5.3 per cent, and for the disabled from 25.8 per cent down to 9.4 per cent.
- Various compromises mooted in a package *covering the three age categories* (including eventually the targeted benefits to *all* children qualified by their degree of poverty, and retirement benefits from the age of 72 to all old people otherwise uncovered) would cost around 2.3 per cent of GDP by 2020.

This brief summary for Vietnam serves to show the possibility of careful assessment of fiscal costs against poverty-reduction benefits that the procedure can involve. It is an example of poverty-budgeting that is not exactly made easy but is both comprehensible and apparently well informed.

The passage reporting these proposals adds, however, that it seems unlikely, because of the revenue prospects in 2012, that all the gaps in SPF protection cover could be closed over the following four years; that is, by 2016. This appears to mean that not all the measures mooted above are likely to come into force at the times proposed. However, 'fiscal space' might open up around the middle of the decade, and, if revenue were to be restored to its level of a few years earlier, 'a sequence of policy actions could be designed that would envisage a successive closing of gaps in child, active-age and old-age income security', without raising the annual deficit above the target level accepted of 3 per cent of GDP.

The report seems to give, on the most probable revenue outcomes, an informed choice between alternative courses of action. On the revenue side, it is projected that, if the personal income tax is increased by 1 per cent of GDP and value-added tax by 1 percentage point, the SPF gap, presumably as opened by the extra expenditures proposed, might be closed by 2017–18. Without any such major increase in revenues over pre-crisis levels, the SPF gap might be gradually closed over the next 10 to 15 years (ILO 2012c, p. xi).

These proposals and projections for Vietnam come out as hopeful. But there are clearly a number of conditions to be fulfilled for achieving the near-term targets. The findings recorded in the assessment matrix make it clear that, beside the policy-design changes, there are plenty of implementation gaps that would need to be closed for the planned outcomes to be achieved.

In what follows we aim to give some idea of the general drift of the preliminary reports of pilot studies on El Salvador and Mozambique.

12.9 El Salvador pre-pilot study

The El Salvador study (ILO 2012b, pp. 13–15) compares the costs of four 'scenarios', of which number 4 comprises the current official proposals, derived from the government's five-year development plan, the Plan Quinquenal, designed for the years 2009–14. All scenarios are to involve 'basic cash transfers and basic health care protection programmes'. Scenarios 1, 2 and 3 include targeted (that is, means-tested) transfers to families with children and to pregnant women, non-contributory pensions for the elderly and disabled, temporary transfers to the unemployed and expanded health benefits. The three scenarios differ in the ambition of their proposed provisions: scenario 1 directed at the 'extremely poor'; scenario 2 – more inclusive and hence more costly – at the 'poor'; and scenario 3 – the most costly – proposing unemployment relief, elderly and disabled pensions and health-care expenses, for all those not covered by existing insurance for these contingencies. Confusingly scenario 4, the official plan, is the least costly and least ambitious and thus most similar to scenario 1.

Figures 5 and 7 in ILO 2012b (pp. 14, 15) show graphically, in per cent of GDP and dollars respectively, the projected costs of the four scenarios over the ten-year period 2011–20, with different assumptions on how the first three might be phased in. Figures 6 and 7 project possible funding for the two quantitatively similar scenarios 1 and 4 (the least ambitious), and Figure 6 projects seven components by which the extra funding supposed in Figure 7 might be made up (including reduced subsidies, reduction in cost of the minimum pension, improved tax collection, a new excise tax and increased income-tax and VAT rates). We are told that the completed study will comment on existing tax arrangements and give ideas on improving the coverage of the existing contributory social-security schemes.

So the study at its present stage (as in mid-2012) does not propose any particular package but enlarges the scope for informed choice on the part of the government while steering attention toward a possible combination of scenario 1 and the official plan, that is, toward the less costly end of the range.

12.10 Mozambique pre-pilot study

Here (ILO 2012b, pp. 7–9) there are five simulations designated A, B, C1, C2 and C3.

A is essentially the existing plan for the period to 2014, but extended to 2022 in several versions, all apparently keeping within the 'programme' agreed with the IMF as necessary for stability and debt-sustainability. It allows budgetary costs of social protection to rise faster than income rises, from 0.25 per cent of GDP to 0.8 per cent by 2016, with the possibility of further rises thereafter, as finances are enhanced by the phasing-out of the fuel subsidy, and possibly by introduction of further taxes on the extractive industries and/or extra aid from external donors.

B is an expanded version of A that allows costs to rise to as high as 1.6 per cent of GDP by 2021, with increases in the rates and scopes of some transfers.

Scenarios C1, C2 and C3 are versions of what might be done from 2015 on, after the end of the current Basic Social Security Strategy in 2014. The Social Protection Floor is to be based around what are called 'two main pillars: a social pension and a child benefit focused on the poor'. Targeted maximum costs for these three scenarios by 2022 are respectively 1.4 per cent, 2.5 per cent and 2.75 per cent, of GDP.

Financially there might be scope for 'a significant expansion of basic social security programmes', possibly beyond those recently proposed officially.

'Nevertheless', as the brief pilot report admits (ILO 2012b, p. 9), 'the implementation challenges are enormous'. It details a number of moves, past and prospective, for improving administrative capacity and obtaining further donor resources. 'Should these challenges be overcome', it concludes, 'progressively building a Social Protection Floor in Mozambique, adapted to the context and country pace, could be affordable and implemented in a way that does not threaten fiscal sustainability.'

12.11 Broad conclusions from the three pilot studies

We may paraphrase briefly the 'Conclusions and lessons learned' from the pilot studies (ILO 2012b, p. 17) as follows:

1. Social protection floors (SPFs) are possible, 'even in resource-constrained low-income countries', if they are progressively introduced – though we believe we need to add the further proviso that for some countries significant help from abroad will be needed.
2. Discussions and exchanges on financing, bringing in the IMF among others, can be fruitful in expanding the range of recognized possibilities.
3. Having several UN agencies involved in an assessment enhances both the technical quality and the political force of the recommendations.
4. Both the feasibility of an SPF and its potentially beneficial effect on the wider economy may be revealed by studies of the present kind.

12.12 Movement of the tectonic plates: radical changes introduced or promised in the world's giant economies

The 2008 quotation from Barrientos and Hulme at the start of this chapter mentions most of the striking developments up to that time. We had also had the Public Distribution System in India with parliamentary moves on improving its implementation through changing to all-cash transfers and electronic means of making them. India, as mentioned in Chapter 6, under Section 6.1.3, is also actively developing a system of individual biometric identification, with the possibility of readily identifiable ownership of individual bank accounts and of electronic transfer of funds to identified individuals that might greatly reduce the leakage of cash and goods in the transfers involved in creating a comprehensive safety-net. There is the promise in Indonesia of extending by 2014 a single-payer health service from the present *Jamkesmas* (which has covered free of charge about 30 per cent at the poorest end) to the whole population (though very probably, it seems, with the help of some form of mandatory means-related insurance contributions from those newly included). And, as expounded in Chapter 10, there is the actual free health service that has been in effect since 2003 for roughly one-third of the Thai population, together with the nearly free service for another third, these two components designed to pick up between them all the people within physical range not otherwise financially covered. Nandi (2013) has mentioned India's scheme for financial cover of medical treatment for the poorest, introduced in 2008 and known by its initials as RSBY, with currently (early 2013) 33 million families enrolled, each covered up to the exchange-equivalent of about $500 in any year, which each can pay through an electronically readable card, though there are doubts about adequate financing. More spectacularly but without further detail, Nandi records that China has introduced three health-insurance programmes since 1998, with 1.1 billion people covered by early 2013. Christine Wong (2012) gives recent detail on one of these, the rural 'new cooperative medical scheme', with 835 million participants, which was able to raise its cover per participant from 20 million yuan in 2003 to 240 million in 2012. Nandi (2013) also lists health-cover schemes (beside Indonesia's, China's and India's) introduced in five developing countries since 1992. There will also in Chapter 13 be brief mention of a great variety of transfer schemes in Bangladesh, mostly so far very small, including a cash-for-work system that might come to be developed on the lines of India's. Indonesia also has had a cash-for-work scheme (Sudarto 2005), though, unlike India's, directed primarily at the urban rather than the rural unemployed, but subject apparently to similar imperfections of targeting.

There may be a temptation to think that the world is coming round fast to the safety-net principle, and hence that there is no need for the case to be pushed or argued. Where the giants – India, Indonesia, China, Thailand, Brazil, Mexico, South Africa – are going, the rest will follow. But complacency should go only so far.

First, those that have made big moves all appear to be *middle-income* countries, though a number of them are admittedly among the world's largest.

Low-income representatives seriously aspiring after a safety-net seem at least until very recently to have been rare. We have seen that Bangladesh's last-resort transfer programmes are fragmentary and so far lack a sense of coherent direction. Vietnam, as has been shown in this chapter so far, seems to be taking the objective of a safety-net seriously and has given some signs of achievement, but, though its income now brings it at least to the borderline of the lower-middle-income category, it appears to be having difficulty in fitting in reforms that it regards as necessary. And there is also a mass of really low *low-income* countries (Mozambique has been mentioned as an extreme example) that are so poor that without external help they would inevitably find it very difficult to provide a consistent safety-net even marginally above the extreme-poverty level. Only careful and reasonably impartial investigation can reveal what is and what is not possible as things are, and thus tell whether a powerful case can be made for external help. Hence the ostensible value of the procedures outlined in this chapter.

Second, some of the promising devices that are mentioned are at an early stage of application, and in some cases implementation appears to be patchy (see, for example, Chapter 9 on India's employment guarantee). Funding of programmes may be inadequate, and there may be leakage of public resources through various forms of plunder. This underlines the importance of the devices under preparation in India for making watertight properly authorized transfers from the state to social institutions and even to particular individuals.

Third, there are also circumstances in particular places – such as frequent crop failures, especially if they are combined with inadequate management of staple-food stocks – that may make an effective and sustainable safety-net impossible without external aid. Even with prudent stockpile management, some countries may need to draw on external help in times of difficulty.

A fourth corrective to complacency is to recognize that politicians and their constituencies have a natural tendency to be attracted to big projects, often with less inclination to fill in the cracks or to make adequate fiscal provision for their initiatives.

The routine described and exemplified above in sections 12.5–12.10 of this chapter is designed to find those cracks, as well as the chasms, and to attend to the people who may remain in them, the people who are in danger of being forgotten. This is the essence of the idea of a safety-net: to catch and support those who, for whatever reason, find themselves below a very meagrely defined subsistence level. Governments prepared to go through the process for detecting weaknesses in their own arrangements with a view to subsequently filling the gaps would appear to be showing a commendable humility as well as good will.

Conclusion

The world is experiencing two remarkable movements that can be seen as directed, systematically or otherwise, at the creation of social safety-nets in each jurisdiction.

One of these movements, starting around the turn of the century, is the gradual introduction, one piece at a time and on no single pattern, of a set of major initiatives that will substantially affect huge numbers of people in gigantic middle-income countries, initiatives with an excellent case (not always fully exploited) for international attention, sympathetic criticism, and respect.

The other is a less spectacular process in which the governments of what are mostly smaller and often much poorer countries are prepared to work out carefully in discussion with representatives of international organizations what their options in the safety-net direction are, which they choose to adopt and what as a result are their firmly grounded claims if any on international help.

Note

1 This is the gap as we have estimated it in Chapter 4 and Appendix 4.2, with the extreme-poverty *headcount* of around 1.3–1.4 billion that we have used for 2005 close to the 1.29 billion in the World Bank's latest complete estimate for 2008 (see http://econ.worrldbank.org/povcalnet, accessed 19 February 2013), suggesting that the absolute number of extremely poor people had not fallen much in the intervening three years.

Part III

Another window

13 The NGOs and microcredit in Bangladesh

> Eventually, when the roof of their tiny hut was about to collapse, having no jewellery or other assets to pledge for a loan, Saraswati sold her seven-year old daughter into bonded labor to a local merchant for 2000 Indian rupees (about US$40).... Five years later, Saraswati joined Working Women's Forum, a women's self-help and microcredit program based in Madras, India. With her first loan she paid off her debt to the merchant, freeing her daughter, who now attends school, and began a small vegetable-selling business.
>
> Daley-Harris (2002, p. xi)

13.1 Introduction

This chapter aims to provide information relevant to the question how far microcredit, in forms and on terms available in Bangladesh, could create, or contribute to, or substitute for, a social safety-net against extreme poverty. It leads to the extraordinary story of the Bangladesh non-government organizations (NGOs), a triumph of civil society and a notable example of what we have elsewhere called *active humanity*.

Based on 2,122 calories intake per person, in Bangladesh the poverty figures were 44.3 per cent of the total population in 2000 and 40.4 per cent in 2005, as given in the *Household Income and Expenditure Surveys*. However, assessment of the proportion in 'poverty' on another criterion (cost of basic needs), has the proportion falling from 48.9 per cent in 2000 to 40.0 per cent in 2005, and further to 31.5 per cent in 2010 (GOB 2011b, Part 3, p. 48). A recent assessment, carried out by the World Bank, attributes much of the advance to general economic growth – itself of course the outcome of a number of recognized developments – with reduced human fertility and increased remittances from workers abroad also contributing (Inchauste *et al.* 2012).[1]

But in this book we are concerned with the occurrence and possibilities of *social interventions* to shift the *distribution* of income in favour of the poorest.

One potential source of such interventions is obviously the state. Since independence in 1971, Bangladesh has accumulated a number of programmes involving credits or transfers, in cash or in kind, conditional or unconditional, to groups of the public. The targeted beneficiaries of these programmes are generally extremely disadvantaged or vulnerable people, such as poor widows or the physically handicapped. No less than 89 of these schemes have been listed (GOB 2011b, Part 2 pp. 438–42), some of them extremely small or highly localized or both. The criticisms made of them collectively as a response to extreme poverty are that their value in recent years represents in aggregate a small proportion of national income by the standards of comparable countries;[2] that they are uncoordinated with each other and therefore fail to approach the provision of any consistent safety-net; and that their multiplicity wastes administrative resources.

The other potential source of social intervention for poverty reduction is 'the NGO sector' – consisting of organizations that are neither necessarily run by the state nor motivated by the prospect of personal gain for their owners or promoters – which has come to play what is probably a far more important role in Bangladesh than in any other country.

In Bangladesh, non-government organizations have been actively involved in providing a variety of services to poor people. Among these services microcredit has been dominant, though far from being the only one. But the term 'NGO' covers a wide range of organizations, with varying functions and styles of work. Also, as observed by Zohir (n.d., p. 1), there are two important ways in which

> the NGOs in Bangladesh stand out from the traditional private voluntary organisations (PVOs). First, NGOs engage in activities, which had traditionally been the domain of government agencies, and it is the failure of the latter, which prompted donors to route funds through these organisations. Second, NGOs are largely participatory in their approach – at least, during the early phase of their development, which enables them to deliver services to targeted groups of [the] population better than the hierarchically structured government agencies.

The regulatory structure of the NGO sector in Bangladesh is, however, somewhat less formal, especially at the lower end. In the words of Zohir (n.d., p. 1):

> Normally, NGOs are required to register with the department of social welfare, for the purpose of claiming to be a non-profit organisation. [However], some NGOs have sought registration with the directorate of women's affairs, and yet others have registered as a cooperative society. In some exceptional cases, an NGO may register itself with the registrar of joint stock companies as a not-for-profit organisation. Since the formation of the NGO Affairs Bureau (NAB) in 1990, the NGOs have to register with the bureau in order to avail [themselves] of foreign funds. For the purpose of our exercise, we consider as NGOs all such organisations which are outside the direct control of government or semi-government agencies…

However, because there is no one authority with which any particular NGO is required to register, and

> because more than one kind of organisation may register with the same authority, there is no exact estimate of the number of NGOs. If non-registered societies (such as, clubs and informal savings and credit associations, many of which may operate within the periphery of a single village), are included, then some guesstimates put the figure in the range of 22,000 to 24,000. However, it is only a small subset of these, whose work style and activities appear to be similar, that are commonly considered as NGOs.
>
> (Zohir n.d., p. 2)

A list published by the NOAB (Newspaper Owners' Association of Bangladesh) gives some 2,170 registered NGOs, of which 1,981 are of Bangladesh origin (Table 13.1).

Thus, over 90 per cent of the NGOs registered with the NGO Bureau are of local origin. However, the list does not include the Grameen Bank which, strictly speaking, though an NGO, is considered a specialized bank in Bangladesh. A historical comparison shows that the number of registered NGOs has been significantly higher in 2012 than the number, for example, in 1996–7.

13.2 NGO activities in Bangladesh: an overview

The NGO sector of Bangladesh appears to be well covered in the literature (see, e.g. Gauri and Galef (2005), World Bank (2006b), Osmani and Khalily (2011) and Zohir (n.d.).

Table 13.1 Registered NGOs operating in Bangladesh, by country of origin, 2012

Country of origin	*Number of NGOs*	*% distribution*	*Country of origin*	*Number of NGOs*	*% distribution*
Australia	5	Neg.	New Zealand	2	Neg.
Austria	2	Neg.	Norway	4	Neg.
Bangladesh	1,981	91.3	Qatar	1	Neg.
Belgium	4	Neg.	Saudi Arabia	4	Neg.
Canada	7	Neg.	South Korea	6	Neg.
Denmark	3	Neg.	Spain	4	Neg.
Finland	3	Neg.	Sudan	1	Neg.
France	6	Neg.	Sweden	7	Neg.
Germany	3	Neg.	Switzerland	2	Neg.
India	3	Neg.	Thailand	1	Neg.
Ireland	1	Neg.	UAE	2	Neg.
Italy	3	Neg.	UK	33	1.5
Japan	16	0.07	USA	60	2.8
Kuwait	2	Neg.	Total	2,170	100
Netherlands	4	Neg.			

Source: Calculated by the authors from NOAB (2012).

Note
Neg. = Negligible.

In the words of Gauri and Galef (2005, p. 2045):

> The NGO sector in Bangladesh is highly organized and relatively homogeneous. Most NGOs utilize a branch and headquarters structure in which branches have limited autonomy from headquarters. At the branch level, most NGOs in the country, whether big or small, focus on credit services, derive more of their income from fees for services than from grants, rely on salaried rather than voluntary staff, keep detailed financial accounts that are externally audited, and hire middle-class college educated men as managers. The convergence to a modal institutional form probably is the result of the persuasive power of ideas, sociological pressures toward acculturation and conformity, as well as material incentives.

However, viewed in a historical context, as observed by Zohir (n.d., p. 2):

> During most of the 1970s, the NGOs were providing services in social sectors, e. g., education, health and sanitation, family planning, etc. There were also some local movements for self-reliance, culminating in the formation of Swanirvar Bangladesh. Pilot experiments into the provision of micro credit to small groups were made only towards the end of the 1970s. With the success of the Grameen Bank, the 1980s experienced a gradual acceptance of micro credit activities [conducted] by NGOs. New institutions, often with indigenous effort, emerged during the late 1980s and early 1990s, though many of the first generation NGOs continued to engage in the delivery of [a range of] social services.... [However], many of the newly emerging micro-finance institutions (MFIs), which are also included in the domain of NGOs, have exclusive focus on microcredit.

As may be seen from Figure 13.1 which is based on a survey carried out by the World Bank in 2003,

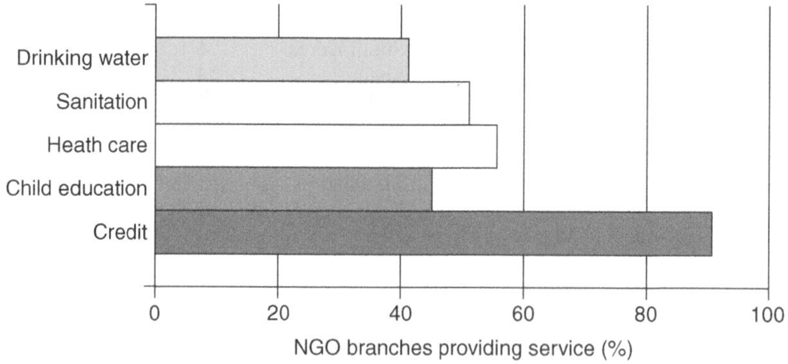

Figure 13.1 Main services provided by NGOs, 2003 (source: as taken from World Bank (2006b, p. 15), reproduced with kind permission from the World Bank).

> most NGOs offer four or five different services. Credit is by far the most common activity, with about 92 percent of all NGO branches providing it. The second most common area of service activity is health and sanitation, involving slightly more than half of NGO branches, followed by the provision of child schooling and provision of clean drinking water. However, NGOs do differ in their 'product range' within these sectors.
>
> (World Bank 2006b, p. 15)

However, according to Zohir (n.d., p. 2):

> In the specific context of Bangladesh, the distinction between NGOs and MFIs ... often gets blurred. While the act of financial intermediation may require special focus, the micro credit organisations (MCOS) quite often engage as agents [for other activities] in the NGO sector as well.... Most NGOs engage in group-formation and provide financial services to group members. Some also engage in providing social services – health, education, water and sanitation, training and skill development, and awareness building. There are others who may also engage as economic agents, such as, through providing marketing support to the beneficiaries, or, as provider[s] of wage employment. The currently observed mix of activities has a long history; and the NGO sector in Bangladesh has been an ever-changing sector. Broadly speaking, while the NGOs may differ in their early engagements, their commonality is derived from the network of groups, of primarily women members, which underlie most NGO activities.... While primary research into the paths of institutional savings and asset accumulation is yet absent, there is enough anecdotal evidence to suggest that this is underway in a significant way.

As further observed by Zohir (ibid., p. 2):

> Two other areas of engagements, often undertaken in conjunction with one or more of the ... interventions listed above, are advocacy and research. Advocacy is a tool used to promote improved performance, shift priorities and highlight areas of concern. It is also an essential ingredient to social mobilisation. Thus, advocacy may overlap with all the [classes of activity identified in Figure 13.1].... The same holds for research. However, both these activities may turn out to be saleable services, which a commercially motivated NGO may decide to deliver.

There is, however, some concern regarding the regional distribution of the NGOs as is apparent from the following observation:

> The regional imbalance of NGOs has led to concerns about overlapping NGO programs and underserved pockets. Microcredit coverage remains uneven, varying from 100 per cent of households below the poverty line in

> Meherpur district to only 31 per cent of poor households in Sunamganj. The 2003 World Bank NGO survey also shows considerable variation: while 17 *thanas* have only one NGO, Mohammadpur in central Dhaka boasts 192. The average number of NGOs per *thana* across the country is 15.
>
> (World Bank 2006b, p. 16)

Within this wide range of services, however, it is microcredit (also known as microfinance) which is considered as the main contributory factor to the growth of the NGO sector in Bangladesh. As expressed by Mahmud (2012): 'One of the main reasons for the growing presence of NGO programmes is the expansion of microfinance.' The overwhelming importance of microcredit is also apparent from the following table which shows the rankings by focus groups of the various categories of community services as reported by the NGOs surveyed by the World Bank in 2003.

13.3 The Bangladesh microcredit sector

A systematic overview of the evolution of microcredit programmes is provided by Khandker (1998, ch. 2). Given the focus of our study in this chapter and also the dominance of microcredit among the NGO activities in Bangladesh, we now concentrate on microcredit. Indeed, as already mentioned, an important factor in the spectacular growth of the NGO sector in Bangladesh is the rapid expansion in microfinance during the 1980s and especially the 1990s, as may be seen from Figure 13.2.

Table 13.2 Rankings of community services as viewed by the focus groups, May 2003

Name of the service	*Groups indicating the service as a priority*		*Name of the service*	*Groups indicating the service as a priority*	
	No.	*%*		*No.*	*%*
Access to credit	252	81	Road construction/ repair	87	28
Health care	224	72	Non-formal adult education	79	25
Safe drinking water	213	68	Electricity system	69	22
Employment generation	182	59	Other	49	16
Non-formal child education	181	58	Transportation services	46	15
Sanitation (waste disposal)	156	50	Land rights/tenure	35	11
Agricultural training for adults	96	31	Telephones/other communications	13	4

Source: World Bank (2006b), p. 16.

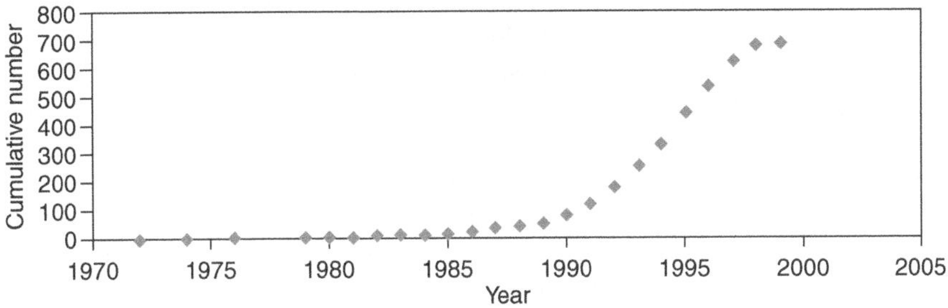

Note: This captures only those MFIs which responded to CDF query during their bi-annual surveys.
Source: compiled from CDF data.

Figure 13.2 Growth of MFIs in Bangladesh, 1970–2000 (source: Ahmed (2004), p. 29, reproduced with kind permission from the author).

A similar picture of a significant jump around 1990 in the number of the NGOs is also shown by Datta (2004).

Table 13.3 helps us to see some recent data of the NGO-microcredit providers registered under the Microcredit Regulatory Authority (MRA) of Bangladesh and, as may be seen, on various accounts including the number of registered NGOs under MRA and the total number of borrowers, there has taken place a gradual increase from 2008 to 2011. As of June 2011, 20.6 million borrowers were provided with microcredit by some 576 NGOs registered under MRA. However, it should be noted that this figure does not include the microcredit borrowers of Grameen Bank (8.35 million in October 2011, www.grameen-info.org) as it is not considered as an NGO, as already mentioned, because of its

Table 13.3 Basic statistics of NGO-microcredit providers registered under Microcredit Regulatory Authority of Bangladesh, 2008–11

Particulars	*June 2008*	*June 2009*	*June 2010*	*June 2011*
No. of licensed NGO-MFIs	293	419	516	576
No. of branches	15,007	16,851	17,252	18,066
No. of employees	98,896	107,175	109,597	111,828
No. of clients (million)	23.45	24.85	25.28	26.08
Total borrowers (million)	17.79	18.89	19.21	20.65
Amount of loan* outstanding (Tk. million)	134,680.96	143,134.03	145,022.66	1,73,797.60
Amount of savings* (Tk. million)	47,386.19	50,610.04	51,362.93	63,304.44

Source: MRA (2012), reproduced with kind permission from the Executive Vice Chairman of MRA.

Notes
* The figures are in current prices, so a time-period comparison needs to be treated with caution.

status of a specialized development bank. Moreover, this total of 20.6 million does not include the borrowers of PROSHIKA as it is not covered in the current statistics provided by MRA, but in June 2011 this NGO had a total number of 1.36 million primary group members, most of whom are presumably active borrowers (PROSHIKA 2013). Thus, one can perhaps safely say that in 2011 the number of microcredit borrowers in Bangladesh was over 30 million. (The corresponding figure was 29.28 million in 2008 (GOB 2011b, Part 2, p. 417).)

However, the microcredit sector, though it has grown significantly over the last three decades, is very small relative to the total credit market in Bangladesh, providing only 5 per cent of the total private-sector credit (World Bank 2006b, p. 18). Moreover, the sector is dominated by a handful of the microcredit providers, called the Big Four (Grameen Bank, BRAC, ASA and PROSHIKA) with a share of over 82 per cent of the total microcredit provided, as found in a survey conducted in 2003 (ibid.). Current figures as provided by the Microcredit Regulatory Authority (MRA) show that the sector is still dominated, though slightly less so now, by a small number of large microcredit providers. As of June 2011, BRAC and ASA which are two of the largest microcredit providers in Bangladesh were each providing microcredit to over five million borrowers, while

> the smallest 428 NGO-MFIs (out of a total of 524 on the list) have contributed only 4 per cent of total loan outstanding and 5 percent of total savings. [Thus, the] institutional concentration ratio is highly skewed in favour of large MFIs: just 22 institutions are in control of 76 percent of the market share while three largest organisations have control of over 50 percent in terms of both clients and total financial portfolios.
>
> (MRA 2011, p. 7)

According to the above mentioned World Bank study (2006b, p. iii), based on its 2003 survey covering some 300 NGO branches in Bangladesh, microcredit 'reaches as many as 43 per cent of all Bangladeshi households and about 70 per cent of poor households'. The spectacular growth of the sector has, indeed, attracted a lot of interest from a number of contributors and, in the five paragraphs below of which the first is a direct quotation, we present a brief picture based on a highly informative paper by Zaman (2004).

'The growth in the poor's access to credit took place', as observed by Zaman (2004, p. 4):

> in several distinct phases over the last three decades [from the mid-1970s]. The origins of the current microcredit model can be traced back to action research in the late 1970s, carried out by academics as well as practitioners in organizations that were created to deal with the relief and rehabilitation needs of post-independence Bangladesh. The 1980s witnessed a growing number of non-governmental organizations (NGOs) which experimented with different modalities of delivering credit to the poor. The various models converged in the beginning of the 1990s toward a fairly uniform

'Grameen-model' of delivering microcredit. It sparked a sharp growth of access to microcredit during this decade. In recent years, the standard Grameen-model has undergone more refinements in order to cater to different niche markets as well as to different life-cycle circumstances.

The 1970s: Bangladesh in the early to mid-1970s was preoccupied with relief and rehabilitation after the independence war and the 1974 famine. Experiments began in providing credit to households considered unbankable by the existing financial institutions. What became the microcredit movement had to resist on one side ideological pressure to concentrate on agitation and mobilization against injustice and on the other side 'elite capture'. BRAC and PROSHIKA, which were to grow into giant NGOs, responded with a target-group approach, bringing in the poor as partners. Simultaneously researchers at Chittagong University, led by Mohammad Yunus, experimented with lending to small peer-groups of borrowers, with each group of four or five people accepting joint responsibility for servicing of the loans. With research and experience continuing into the early 1980s, occupational groups and men-women groups of borrowers were dropped in favour of village-based groups each of one gender. Group loans were also dropped in favour of loans to individuals, but with peer-group monitoring and strong follow-up by staff of the microcredit institution. This became the predominating Grameen model, and the Grameen Bank was instituted in 1983.

The 1980s: In the 1980s ASA, which was to become one of the big three NGOs, went from being a people's organization agitating against oppression to working with target-groups of the poor and then providing financial services. It has been notable for offering uniquely low-cost delivery, partly through devolving decisions to the field. The management capacity of microfinance institutions was enhanced by their undertaking of large projects in other areas of activity, such as, to take one of the first notable cases, the training by BRAC of 13 million women for administering oral-rehydration therapy.

Early to mid-1990s: The early to mid-1990s saw rapid expansion of NGOs in which new branches, following the practices set by their parent institutions, proliferated. The country's coverage of NGO branches came to be widespread though not uniform. PKSF was set up in 1990 as a wholesale financing institution, presumably to spread risks and otherwise to reap economies of scale. It has not only lent to microfinance institutions but also acted to strengthen their capacity, and helped to develop a regulatory framework for them.

Mid-1990s onward: Now research and experience were leading to increasingly diversified financial services in order to meet the needs of different groups of potential borrowers. The uniformity of the Grameen model, with rigid repayment schedules, narrow limitations on terms on which clients could withdraw their capital, and maximum and minimum sizes of loans, had great advantages in cost reduction but did not suit everyone, including especially those who were not in extreme poverty and also the very remote and near-destitute. So there was attention to various niche markets, such as larger loans for some of those who had already borrowed and repaid successfully; loans to the small end of the small-enterprise sector (BRAC); and attention to beggars and those so poor that they might have difficulty in finding co-guarantors for their loans.

The same study by Zaman (2004, pp. 9–12) details important explanatory factors behind the phenomenal growth of the NGO sector, and specifically the microcredit sector, under four main heads cited below, most of the factors relating to decisions, choices and endeavours of various of the actors involved.

1 **'Institution building – leadership, staff incentives, and learning by doing':** A host of more or less detailed characteristics are mentioned by Zaman under this head: the vision, persistence and persuasiveness of the leaders of the movement; their humility in learning from mistakes; intelligent measures for staff 'recruitment, motivation, and retention'; decentralization of responsibility; systems of internal control; and use of staff and client feedback for consistent improvement. Briefly we could say that a high degree of professionalism seems to have been combined with systematized openness to possibilities.
2 **'A constructive donor-client relationship':** 'External resources played an important part in the experimentation, subsequent growth in outreach, and institutional strengthening of the microfinance industry. At the same time, the large microfinance institutions have been successful in "managing donors".' (ibid.)

From relying heavily in the early stages on grants from international NGOs, the main MFIs moved to a point around the start of this century at which expansion of their lending and of their other development programmes has been very largely (albeit controversially, partly because of 'cross-subsidization') financed from their own earnings.

The big NGOs, with a variety of activities, had to deal with numerous potential donors, all usually inclined to finance particular projects and not to cooperate among themselves. BRAC most notably, with its excellent track record, manifest professionalism and wide range of activities, was able to persuade donors instead to form a consortium geared to pooling funds. The consortium committed its members, for example, to supporting BRAC's five-year Rural Development Programme.

3 **'A progressive government stance':** The point here is that the regulatory framework for microcredit and the NGO sector generally has been fairly benign, and there have been important sources of encouragement and support from within government circles.
4 **'A professional apex body for microfinance':**

> The Palli Karma Sahayak Foundation (PKSF) was created in 1990, and is governed by a board composed of both public and private sector representatives. It is a public-private apex body that channels funds for microfinance to MFIs, and has been critical to the expansion and

> improved professionalism of the microcredit industry in Bangladesh. PKSF's core functions include (1) lending money to MFIs which meet certain eligibility criteria, to expand their microfinance operations; (2) building capacity and giving hands-on assistance to strengthen MFIs and move them towards financial sustainability; (3) [advocacy on] microfinance issues and helping develop an appropriate regulatory framework for the industry.
>
> PKSF played an instrumental role in contributing to the sharp increase of access to microcredit that took place in the 1990s by expanding the capital base for MFIs to lend to the poor. For instance, as of December 2003, PKSF loans [constituted] around 30 percent of ASA's current revolving loan fund. PKSF is also widely credited with sharpening the focus of many MFIs on financial sustainability and setting appropriate standards to pave the way to a strengthened regulatory structure for microfinance.
>
> (Ibid., pp. 10–11)

13.4 Socio-economic impact of microcredit: results of studies

The alleviation of extreme poverty is taken here as a matter of course to be the major criterion for judging the success of microcredit. The main indicators of poverty alleviation are taken to be:

- Increase in income, leading to increase in consumption;
- Asset creation, to reduce household vulnerability to various risks;
- Improvement in various social conditions, such as women's empowerment and children's education.

There is now a large body of literature, most of it empirically based, that has set out to assess the impact of microcredit in the country. Most of the evidence that emerges from these studies is positive, but criticisms, some of them harsh, have also been made against the operation of microcredit in Bangladesh. Because of the profusion of studies that have come out with favourable verdicts, we have collected summaries of the results in an appendix (Appendix 13.1, at the end of this chapter).

Then below, in Section 13.5 within the main text of the chapter, we give summaries of the more or less adverse judgements on microcredit, several of which strictly refer to Bangladesh.

This is followed by discussion of the debate and an attempt to judge the relevance of the Bangladesh microcredit experience to the quest for social safety-nets that can offer consistent protection against extreme poverty in disposable income.

13.5 Criticisms of microcredit in Bangladesh

The apparently positive findings shown in Appendix 13.1 need to be viewed against the various criticisms that have been made of microcredit as it has been practised in Bangladesh. Such criticisms as advanced are found to come from three major groups: aid practitioners, politicians and academics.

13.5.1 Practitioner critics

The practitioners of microcredit (i.e. the NGO owners/managers), though actively working in the field, usually have to struggle to find the funds required. They often do not have the luxury of a liquidity surplus enjoyed by many commercial banks. This difficulty leads many of them to criticize the dependency mode of the sector, in particular the heavy dependence suffered by many of the microfinance providers on aid and charities. In fact, Professor Yunus himself has emerged as a critic of the conventional NGO-supported charity work for helping the poor. Such microcredit delivery relying on charitable donations, in the opinion of Yunus (2010, p. 6):

> is not a sustainable way of running an organization. It forces NGO leaders to spend a lot of time, energy, and money on fund-raising efforts. Even when these are successful, most NGOs are perennially strapped for cash and unable to sustain, let alone expand, their most effective programs.

This view of Yunus's has understandably emerged from his long years of searching for funds to carry out the microcredit programmes of Grameen Bank for which he was constantly on the lookout for obtaining grants and donations: from the Government of Bangladesh, and also from international organizations and developed-country governments. His recent emphasis on social enterprise for alleviating poverty is directed at escaping from dependence on grants.

Yunus is not alone in this aspiration.

13.5.2 Politician critics

Some senior government officials in Bangladesh are highly critical of microcredit in general and the Grameen Bank and its founder Professor Yunus in particular. They appear to be angered by the suffering, as at times reported in the press and other media, experienced by some microcredit borrowers in repaying their loans. Also, they appear to be moved by the high level of poverty still persisting in spite of the active roles played by the various NGOs in providing support with microcredit for a number of years. There is even a suggestion that the suffering of the borrowers is so acute that many of them will commit suicide.

The following two are perhaps the main criticisms as advanced by a number of senior politicians of Bangladesh: (i) Grameen Bank (and by implication the other microcredit providers as well) is charging a very high interest rate, and consequently the borrowers are being ruined; and (ii) microcredit, so widespread and claimed to be so effective, has nonetheless failed to eradicate poverty in Bangladesh.

Although no suicides are reported to have taken place over microcredit loan repayments in Bangladesh, one needs to assess these criticisms carefully. The first of them has also been advanced by a number of academic critics (see, e.g. Chang 2010). However, in Bangladesh microcredit providers are no longer free to charge any interest they wish. The interest rate ceiling, which is currently at 27 per cent, is set by the Microcredit Regulatory Authority (MRA) of Bangladesh, which is a government agency.[3] As may be seen from Table 13.4, although some of the microcredit providers including BRAC and TMSS charge the maximum rate as set by the MRA, there are some that charge a lower rate, including the Grameen Bank which charges an effective annual rate of interest of 20 per cent.[4] Given that the microcredit providers generally make weekly collections of repayments from their borrowers, and hence have high administrative costs, the fact that the interest-rate ceiling is currently as high as 27 per cent can perhaps be better understood. So it will be wrong to make comparisons with the lower interest rates (often around 12–15 per cent) charged by the commercial banks. Also, it needs to be kept in mind that in providing microcredit an NGO, if it is committed to being self-reliant, will need to be cautious about the prospect of repayment and hence (even though it is a non-profit organization) will naturally charge a risk-premium.

Also, it may be mentioned that although the interest rates charged by the MFIs might appear high, in Bangladesh the borrowers do not have to pay bribes for obtaining microcredit. Thus, a knowledgeable Bangladeshi commentator, Dr Akbar Ali Khan, has recently observed that, compared to the state-run commercial banks, the interest-rate cost effectively borne by the Grameen Bank's borrowers is much lower, if one calculates the money and the time one has to spend for getting loans from the commercial banks (Khan 2012).

Table 13.4 Interest rates charged by various major microcredit providers in Bangladesh, 2012

Microcredit providers	*Effective annual interest rate (%)*	*Rate differing from the maximum allowed by the MCRA (27%)*
Grameen Bank	20	–7%
BRAC	27	Same
ASA	20	–7%
TMSS	27	Same
POPI	25	–2%
CLP	27	Same

Sources and notes: Field surveys by the authors. Also consulted was the published information available from the respective NGOs. Often the microcredit providers charge different rates depending on the size, the duration and even the purpose of the loans, so that the rates quoted need to be treated with caution.

Moreover, the criticism of high interest rates charged by the microcredit providers fails to consider the fact that to many of the borrowers the alternative would be usurious loans from village money sharks (known as '*mahajans*'), commonly at 10 per cent per month (Hossain 1985).

The second criticism is even more serious, and it also appears to have a strong appeal. However, as in the case of the first criticism, it arises out of failure on the part of the critics to recognize that there are serious limitations on the role that the private sector including charities can play in determining income distribution (see, e.g. Brown and Jackson 1990, ch. 2). In fact, as is evident in West European countries, the state in a democratic society is required to play a major role toward ensuring a just income distribution and alleviating poverty. Poverty alleviation also takes place through income growth and employment generation as the economy expands. Thus various agents, including not only microcredit providers but also private investors and the state, are relied on to contribute to poverty alleviation. So, if microcredit providers are attacked for their failure to eradicate poverty, other agents including the state and the private sector also need to be criticized. In making this attack on MFIs the critics appear to be treating microcredit as if it can be expected to act as a substitute for official cash transfers in the provision of a social safety-net. In this respect, Professor Yunus should perhaps share some of the criticism as he gives the impression that microcredit programmes and other social enterprises have the potential on their own for eradicating poverty, and in the process he downplays the role of the benefits provided by the state. Indeed, he appears to be convinced that introducing 'social businesses' into the global framework can enhance the globalization process 'making sure that it works for the poor people and [the] poor countries' (Yunus 2010, p. 200).

Yunus also appears to be critical of welfare institutions especially as he believes that all 'welfare laws all over the world are so generous as to make sure people feel very comfortable to live in welfare' (Yunus 2011, p. 22). While there may be some truth in this, one also needs to recognize the vital contribution to poverty alleviation made by social-safety-net-type provisions such as monthly benefits provided to destitute widows, the elderly poor and disabled people. Unfortunately, the state of Bangladesh is still failing to provide help to many of these very poor people, mainly because of the very low level of government expenditure for this purpose and the inefficiency in the administration of the limited benefits provided.

13.5.3 Academic critics

Surprisingly perhaps, microcredit has also attracted a number of academic critics. While several of these could be described as *selective critics* (e.g. Hulme and Mosley 1996; Sinha 1998; Wright 2000; Navajas *et al.* 2000; Chowdhury *et al.* 2004; and Banerjee and Duflo 2011) who, while generally praising the poverty-alleviation role played by microcredit, point out what they regard as some of the weaknesses of the system, there is a small group including Morduch

(1998), Ahmad (2007), Bateman and Chang (2012) and Roodman (2012), who could be considered as harsh in their criticisms.

While acknowledging the role microfinance has been playing to reduce poverty in Bangladesh, Hulme and Mosley (1996, p. 134) concluded that most 'contemporary schemes are less effective than they might be' and further that 'the poorest people have little access to these schemes'. Sinha (1998, pp. 2–3) argues that it is notoriously difficult to measure the impact of microfinance programmes on poverty; also, it is difficult to isolate the impact of any particular loan, partly because of the definition of 'poverty', how it is measured and who constitute the 'poor' – some 'fiercely contested issues'. Wright (2000, p. 262) states that the 'traditional Microfinance programmes are not reaching the "poorest of the poor" – indeed they are rarely reaching the bottom 10–15% of the population'. Furthermore, as he observes (ibid., p. 260): 'There has been inadequate analysis of the effects of Microfinance on health and education indicators.' This latter argument is in line with the views of Navajas *et al.* (2000, p. 345) who question whether 'microcredit is the best way to spend public funds earmarked for development'.

Also, as observed by Chowdhury *et al.* (2004, p. 292), 'considerable debate remains about the effectiveness of microfinance as a device for directly reducing poverty', and about the characteristics of the people it benefits.

Banerjee and Duflo (2011, pp. 173–4) also list some limitations of microcredit. They see drawbacks in the highly risk-averse approach adopted by the MFIs. As they argue, the insistence of the microfinance providers on 'zero default' generates 'a clear tension between the spirit of microcredit and true entrepreneurship, which is totally associated with taking risks and, no doubt, occasionally failing'. Also, according to these authors (ibid., p. 173):

> The rigidity and specificity of the standard microcredit model mean, for one thing, that since group members are responsible for each other, women who don't enjoy poking into other people's business don't want to join. Group members may be reluctant to include those they don't know well in their groups, which must discriminate against newcomers.

In response, however, it is worth mentioning the readiness of some of the major NGOs (expounded in the article by Zaman (2004), extensively quoted/paraphrased above) to modify their MFI conditions and to issue new variants, in order to take account of new or inadequately met needs.

The defects in microcredit asserted by these 'selective critics' mostly have the potential, insofar as they are genuine failings, of being corrected while the essentials of microcredit are preserved. Below we present now the more fundamental criticisms advanced by Morduch (1998), Ahmad (2007), Roodman (2012) and Bateman and Chang (2012), who have emerged as harsh critics. (Recently, Duvendack and Palmer-Jones (2012) have also emerged as two harsh critics, with an equally harsh response from Pitt (2012). However, we have checked our temptation to include this new debate here as we believe that our coverage adequately encompasses the controversies.)

Morduch (1998): Morduch's criticisms were first voiced in a paper which he brought out in 1998, analysing the household-level data set originally collected by BIDS in collaboration with the World Bank, 'the survey [covered] 87 villages and was completed in 1991–92' (ibid., p. 6).

Though Morduch is using the same data set as used by Pitt and Khandker (1998), the findings are different. One of Morduch's important findings is that 'no evidence was found to support claims that the programme increases consumption levels or increases educational enrolments for children relative to levels in control villages'. As observed by Morduch (p. 30),

> few microfinance programmes have received rigorous statistical evaluation. Attempts at such evaluation are complicated by biases due to non-random programme placement and participation by others. Simple measures of impacts are thus likely to be driven partly by correlations of unobserved client quality and patterns of lending, with respect to both participation and the size of borrowings.

However, in his analysis Morduch appears to challenge the findings of Pitt and Khandker, in particular the findings that there are positive impacts on household consumption and negative impacts on male labour supply 'compared to lending to women'. Indeed, Morduch finds that microcredit does not have a significant impact on consumption *levels* and therefore on income poverty.

Morduch, however, also finds that consumption *variability* is 47 per cent lower for eligible Grameen households, 54 per cent lower for eligible BRAC households and 51 per cent lower for eligible BRDB households, than for a control group. This consumption smoothing is driven by income smoothing as evidenced by the significantly lower labour-supply variability experienced by microcredit members than by the control group. The importance of this result cannot be over-emphasized, given the fact that seasonal deficits play a key part in the poverty process in Bangladesh. Essentially, Morduch's results seem to indicate that programme participants do not benefit by enjoying higher consumption levels, but probably participate because they benefit from risk reduction.

The criticisms voiced by Morduch have, however, been attacked, among others, by Pitt (1999) who himself was closely involved in the original investigation analysing the impact of microcredit on poverty alleviation in Bangladesh, using the extensive data collected in the early 1990s. However, the same data were also used by Morduch, although the analysis he carried out led him to reach a set of conclusions which were different from the original findings of Pitt, derived from the study which he carried out jointly with Khandker (Pitt and Khandker 1998). The reply given by Pitt (1999) perhaps deserves mention. Pitt addresses the concerns which have been raised by Morduch and 'finds them lacking because Morduch has misunderstood and mischaracterized the methods of [Pitt and Khandker], and has applied incorrect methods to obtain his new evidence' (Pitt 1999, p. 1).

Ahmad (2007). Q.K. Ahmad, who is currently the Chairman of the PKSF (the major provider of the microcredit funds given to the NGOs by the Government of Bangladesh) is one of the vocal critics.

The findings of a survey covering a representative sample of 2,501 rural micro-borrowers, carried out in January–February 2006 by his team of researchers, appear to form the main foundation of Ahmad's criticisms. The following points as summarized in this report (Ahmad 2007, pp. 45–9) can be considered as the main criticisms.

- While 'some of the micro-borrowers have benefited in terms of reasonable increases in income',... 'in a majority of the cases there has not been a significant increase in income and about a quarter earn from micro-credit-related activities and other sources taken together only about or below the average income of the rural poor.'
- '[A]ccess to adequate food even in quantitative terms remains insecure for about one-fifth of the respondents interviewed, while this is so for about another third in qualitative terms if not in quantitative terms. About 39% are unsure of any change in their access to food since enrolment and only about 7% have access to sufficient food in both qualitative and quantitative terms. Also, there has not been any improvement worth noting in ... ownership of land ... [or of] large livestock since enrolment.'
- 'In terms of overall living conditions, only about one-third of the respondents have indicated some improvement, while the rest have experienced no change or deterioration since enrolment. Clearly, therefore, the majority of the respondents have remained marginal in ... their living conditions now as [they were] before enrolment.'
- 'On the satisfaction scale, just over a quarter of the respondents are satisfied, while about 50% are dissatisfied, and just under a quarter are neither satisfied nor dissatisfied, with their present living conditions. As to the future prospects [from] relying primarily on micro-credit, just over a third believe that the prospects are good but a third are apprehensive of bad prospects. In ... social position, well over half of the respondents have reported no change and another 13% have reported deterioration, while about 28% have experienced an improvement. For this majority, therefore, there has been no improvement in social standing since enrolment.'
- 'Overall, therefore, [the] socio-economic impact of micro-credit, as indicated by this study, is marginal. Obviously, some micro-borrowers have benefited to an extent but many have experienced no improvement. There are also those who have experienced even deterioration in certain respects.' '[R]egarding debt burden, the micro-borrowing process seems to continue endlessly for most of the clients of the MCIs. It has been found that while they pay base interest rates between 10% and 15% (in some cases up to 18%), the effective rate of interest and the effective cost of borrowing are as high as 27.5 and 31% respectively for Grameen Bank and even higher at 39% and 41% for PROSHIKA and 42% and 45% for both BRAC and ASA.'

Roodman (2012). Of those who can be considered as the most vociferous critics of microcredit, Roodman probably tops the list. In his latest book (Roodman 2012), *Due Diligence: An Impertinent Inquiry into Microfinance*, which is a follow-up of several of his papers and postings, the central message, as summarized in the Preface of the volume, is that 'microfinance does not live up to its popular image'. There are several strands of his attack including the following three. First, he is dubious of the benefits derived from microcredit and hence categorically states that the 'microfinance industry will probably never play a critical role in the transformative economic processes that increase productivity, create jobs, and lift people from poverty' (ibid., p. 251), and further that good studies on 'microcredit so far have found no impact on poverty' (ibid., p. 290). Second, he is critical of what he calls the huge amount provided for microcredit through foreign aid as he believes that such 'money came easily because of microfinance's exaggerated reputation for fighting poverty and empowering women' (ibid., p. 267). Third, a follow-up of the second point, the availability of ample and cheap finance undermined the 'initiative to take savings as an alternative source of funds' (ibid., p. 275).

As Roodman is not raising these points with specific reference to Bangladesh, it is difficult for us to make any serious judgement on this part of his argument given our specific country-focus here. However, for Bangladesh, there are now findings from various rigorous studies that provide strong evidence that microcredit is not only helping to reduce poverty but also helping to raise savings on the part of the poor. Indeed, thanks almost certainly to the initiative taken by the MFIs in Bangladesh, there has been a huge growth of savings from the recipients of microcredit. Indeed currently the net savings of the microcredit borrowers amount to more than one-third of the amount distributed as loans by the NGO-MFIs of Bangladesh (MRA 2012). Also, as Roodman is perhaps unaware, a number of the major microcredit providers in Bangladesh, including Grameen Bank, ASA and BRAC, are no longer taking foreign aid. In fact, dependence on foreign aid has come down to only 3 per cent of the total microcredit distributed in Bangladesh, although in the past such dependence was very high (Rahman 2012).

While Roodman's assertions in his 2012 book are directed at microcredit in general, he had earlier drawn attention more specifically to what he claimed were substantive weaknesses in the impacts of microcredit in Bangladesh. For example, in an article which he has jointly produced with Morduch (Roodman and Morduch 2011), there is a strong critique of the positive findings of Pitt and Khandker (1998) that 'microcredit for women had significant poverty-reducing impacts'. However, in their response Pitt and Khandker (2012) strongly rejected the claims of Roodman and Morduch, asserting that they had failed to investigate properly the properties of the econometric methods used, so that their criticisms were not valid.

So, though what is said here is far from comprising a comprehensive rejection of Roodman's whole case, at least it can be said that some of his generalizations are inconsistent with known and important public facts in Bangladesh and some of his interpretations of the results of econometric studies appear to be open to debate.

Bateman and Chang (2012): Like Roodman, Bateman and Chang are highly sceptical of the true benefits of microcredit; they challenge 'the view that the microfinance model has a positive association with sustainable poverty reduction and local economic and social development'. They concede that 'the microfinance model may generate narrow positive short-run outcomes for a few lucky individuals', but claim that 'these outcomes are limited in number and anyway swamped by much wider longer run downsides and opportunity costs at the community and national level' (p. 13).

Their main attack is that the case made for microcredit is a neoliberal view, a part of the globalization project, supported strongly and uncritically by the international development community as it suits their 'preferred economic and societal model based on self-help and individual entrepreneurship' (Bateman and Chang 2012, p. 30). Two of the key arguments advanced by them against the microfinance model are that, first, it 'ignores the crucial role of scale economies' (ibid., p. 17) and second, it 'greatly reduces the ability of developing countries to promote their industrial upgrading' by misdirecting scarce resources into wrong types of investment (ibid., p. 25).

Bateman and Chang firmly assert that microfinance is an institutional and political barrier to sustainable economic and social development, and to poverty reduction. They claim indeed that the microfinance model:

- Is likely to lock people and communities in a poverty trap;
- Has had catastrophic outcomes in a growing number of microfinance-saturated countries, regions and localities;
- Still retains its popularity within the international development community, despite growing evidence that it has failed to reduce poverty; and
- Remains attractive because of its political serviceability to the neoliberal worldview that locates individual entrepreneurship as the main driver of economic development.

Separately, Chang (2010) has strongly attacked the model of development and poverty alleviation championed through self-enterprise growth via microcredit, especially as he is convinced that this is contrary to the actual mode of development in the developed countries where self-employment is only a fraction of total employment (for example, only 7.5 per cent in the USA and 8.6 per cent in France), compared to a high figure such as 75.4 per cent in Bangladesh and a staggering 88.7 per cent in Benin.

Similarly, Bateman (2012) suggests that microfinance is actually a major 'poverty trap' and that almost all of the main claims made on behalf of microfinance are myths:

> Let's not kid ourselves that this recent interest in financial inclusion is anything other than the start of a sophisticated, carefully managed – but supremely cynical – PR campaign that attempts to cover up for local neoliberal policies and programmes that have actually failed the poor.

He and Chang (2012, p. 30) advocate what they claim are better local and national financial-institution alternatives such as financial cooperatives, credit unions, building societies and local and national development banks.

13.6 Response to the debate

There has continued to be huge interest from various quarters in the impact of microcredit, and a number of studies directed at assessing its value in poverty reduction. Of the studies those cited here (in the main text of this chapter and in Appendix 13.1) are only a selection, though they probably suffice to give the main features of the case made on both sides of the argument. Table 13.5 attempts to summarize the findings and the assessments made.

Although microcredit is often – correctly in our view – credited with poverty alleviation, it was not deliberately designed as a formal tool of income redistribution. Nor was it set up to answer the (policy) question: how may society set a floor to disposable income? That is the question we are trying to answer in this book when we consider governmental transfers in cash or kind, conditional or unconditional, cash- (or food-) for-work programmes, and financial arrangements for preventing anyone from being impoverished by medical expenses.

Rather microcredit is set up to answer either one of two questions. One is what poor people are to do when they have a desperate need for cash and all the known ways of getting it are inaccessible or intolerable (the situation faced by Saraswati in the true incident, typical of many, recorded at the start of this chapter). The other is how very poor people can improve their condition, their standard of living, through their own actions. Ideally government might be able to answer these questions or make the answering of them unnecessary. Where it does not, the possibility exists that, as in Bangladesh, 'civil society' – non-government organizations – can provide answers.

Before the days of microcredit, the poor, faced with an urgent need for cash, often had no alternative to obtaining usurious loans – or to something even worse such as selling children into servitude. Since microcredit is provided without requiring any collateral, which very poor people would be simply unable to provide, it is no surprise that its loans have had a great appeal to many from the lower-income groups, in whom the high-street banks have generally not shown serious interest.

Some of the conflict between supporters and opponents of microcredit arises over empirical studies from *different methods or interpretations of quantitative findings*. On these we do not here propose to attempt precise judgements. Yet, given the mass of evidence outlined in our Appendix 13.1, especially that based on the apparently extensive studies that have been conducted in recent years (see, e.g. GOB 2011a and 2012a), it seems difficult to deny the huge positive impacts of microcredit on income growth and poverty alleviation in Bangladesh. So it does not at all appear that the microcredit providers are 'blood suckers' as has been claimed (BBC 2012) on the ground that they charge too much for the cost of their operations and for surpluses that can pay for expansion of the circle

Table 13.5 Summary of impact assessments: selected studies of microcredit programmes

	Year considered for the analysis	*Overall assessment*	*Key findings*
Pitt & Khandker (1998)	1991–2	Strongly positive	Large positive impacts on the income of poor households especially as microcredit programmes favour women.
Khandker (1998)	1991–2	Strongly positive	Significant positive effects on household per capita expenditures.
Morduch (1998, 1999b)	1991–2	Negative	No significant increase in consumption levels of microcredit borrowers.
BIDS (2001)	1997–2000	Positive	Positive and significant effect on poverty status of the programme households.
Mahjabeen (2008)	1999–2000	Strongly positive	Microcredit institutions raise income and consumption levels of households.
Ahmad (2007)	2006	Generally negative	Socio-economic impact is marginal. No significant increase in income of microcredit borrowers.
Asian Development Band (2007)	2006–7	Generally positive	Increase in income of the participating households and increased role of women in accessing finance.
Govt of Bangladesh (2011a)	2010–11	Strongly positive	Microcredit contributed to poverty reduction.
Govt of Bangladesh (2012a)	2011–12	Strongly positive	Poverty alleviation following increase in employment and income.
Bateman & Chang (2012)	The study is not survey-based	Strongly negative	Positive outcomes are very limited; the microfinance model is likely to lock people and communities in a poverty trap.
Huq & Salimullah (2012)	2012	Strongly positive	Most microcredit borrowers experienced income growth and this is particularly marked in urban poor households.
Roodman (2012)	This is not survey-based	Strongly negative	Doubts whether microcredit helps to remove poverty and questions the wisdom of the huge US aid given for providing microcredit in developing countries.

Source: Summarized by the authors.

of those that benefit; nor are the benefits confined to 'a few lucky individuals' (Bateman and Chang 2012, p. 13); nor are they 'marginal' as asserted by Morduch (1998) and Ahmad (2007).

A number of the adverse critiques depend on assertions about *opportunity cost*: that the same resources could be better used, for example, in big, formal-sector organizations, state-run or private. Maybe, if the big, formal-sector organizations that could satisfy the urgent needs of some 30 million poor households existed and needed for their operation to take over the resources that have been put into microcredit in Bangladesh, this argument would have weight. But, in the absence of a realistic alternative programme that meets the expectations and hopes of the people who would otherwise be microcredit borrowers, it can easily amount to a recipe for doing nothing.

And some of the criticisms seem to depend on *ideological labelling*, as if calling some strategy 'neoliberal' or 'individualist' was enough to condemn it.

But, on the question whether microcredit *has been generally beneficial for the poor*, it will seem to many that the figures speak for themselves. No one is compelled to borrow from microcredit institutions. Yet nearly half of the households in Bangladesh, and more than two-thirds of the poor households, have done so. No one, having borrowed and repaid, is compelled to come back for more. Yet millions have done, and are doing, just that. And the figures seem to be holding up as the personnel gradually changes, with deaths and births and the formation of new families. Unless there is an immense delusion – unless the millions who have come back for more are simply mistaken about their own interests – microcredit appears to be a real boon for tens of millions of people.

However, it would be wrong to consider microcredit as an activity that is, or is likely to be, or should be, centrally coordinated. Its dispensers consist of a number of NGOs that are operating in a competitive marketplace, providing 'freedom of choice' as is emphasized by Yunus in his schema of social business (Yunus 2010, p. 22), giving the borrowing household the capacity to obtain what it uniquely wants or needs. In fact, the existence of a market, with competition among the lenders, the sellers, is what gives the buyers, the borrowers, a choice, and also confidence that the price charged, the interest-rate, will genuinely reflect costs and *not* be excessive.

But equally microcredit-dispensing NGOs cannot be expected to perform a 'universal' role, by setting a consistent floor to disposable income. That is a task for government. By reducing poverty among their clients, the MFIs may make that task easier for government, but they cannot substitute for it. This is because of some in-built limitations of the charitable activities of private agents (Brown and Jackson 1990, ch. 2). Also it is asserted in a study conducted by the Asian Development Bank (2007, p. iii), that 'targeting microfinance on the poorest households may not be the most appropriate way to help them escape poverty'. Indeed, to have a universal and coordinated approach for attacking disposable-income poverty, the state needs a major role.

Conclusion

Microcredit administered by NGOs, as experienced in Bangladesh, must be judged, with only minor reservations, as improving the lives of tens of millions of poor people, through modest and completely non-coercive interventions, and in ways largely determined by each household for itself. It is probably essential for this task – certainly for its efficient performance – that the intermediaries, the MFIs, remain non-governmental. There is at the same time a governmental role involved in creating a safety-net, a consistent floor to disposable income. These are two distinct roles, both directed to the fight against poverty, and they need to be considered and pursued separately.

Notes

1 This is a major recent study and the assessment includes Peru and Thailand as well, extensively analysing the contributory factors towards the decline in these three countries (for the period 2000–10 for Bangladesh and Peru and 2000–9 for Thailand).

2 Bangladesh is found to be spending a very low amount on social safety-net programmes. Data as available from 1996–7 to 2004–5 show that the figure never reached 1 per cent of GDP. As observed by the World Bank (2006a, p. 19),

> Even if expenditure on social protection programs (pensions, labor market) is included, Bangladesh still seems to spend somewhat below the norm (less than two percent of GDP) – as compared to two percent for Africa and close to five percent for South Asia.'

However, in recent years, expenditures on social safety-net programmes have been on the increase. As estimated by Ahmed (2007, p. 4), the proportion was 1.21 per cent in 2006–7 and 1.6 per cent in 2007–8. The rate appears to have been maintained in 2011. As observed by Rahman and Choudhury (2012, p. 3): 'Annual outlay on social safety net programmes amounts to Taka 11,470 Crores (US$1.64 billion) which is approximately 1.6% of GDP (2011).'

3 The Microcredit Regulatory Authority, which for the first time started fixing the interest rate in July 2011, is now reported to be working on reducing the current maximum rate of 27 per cent to 26 per cent, in line with the maximum interest rate the microcredit providers are allowed to charge in India. For further details, see Jibon (2013).

4 Grameen Bank has various types of interest rates for its loan programmes:

> 20% for income generating loans, 8% for housing loans, 5% for student loans, and 0% (interest-free) loans for Struggling Members (beggars). All interests are simple interest, calculated on the declining balance method. This means, if a borrower takes an income-generating loan of say, Tk.1,000, and pays back the entire amount within a year in weekly instalments, she'll pay a total amount of Tk.1,100, i.e. Tk.1,000 as principal, plus Tk.100 as interest for the year, equivalent to 10% flat rate.
>
> (www.grameen-info.org/index.php?option=com_content&task=view&id=26&Itemid=175)

Appendix 13.1: Microcredit: selected studies showing positive impacts

Here we have included a selection of studies which are generally favourable to microcredit. The discussion is organised as follows. Section 13A.1 will list a number of early studies analysing the socio-economic impact of microcredit, while Section 13A.2 will include some recent studies. Finally, in Section 13A.3, a brief idea of women's empowerment following microcredit, based on some early studies, is provided. As will be found, the coverage is selective, however we believe that it is highly representative of this type of studies which have been conducted over the years.

13A.1 Early studies: Pitt and Khandker (1998); Khandker (1998); BIDS (2001); and Mahjabeen (2008)

i Pitt and Khandker (1998)

This is the first major study available which attempted to assess the impact of microcredit, using data collected in the course of a special multipurpose household survey covering 87 Bangladeshi villages during July 1991 to June 1992, undertaken jointly by the BIDS and the World Bank.

> The survey's main focus was to provide data for an analysis of three major credit programs (Grameen Bank, BRAC, and RD-12). The survey covered both program villages of each of these programs and villages in which neither of these programs nor any other program providing credit or other activities operated.
>
> (Khandker 1998, p. 38)

It was an extensive survey, covering 72 villages that had one programme and 15 villages that had no programmes.

All these early microcredit-programme surveys are devoted exclusively to the rural poor, with women featuring prominently. A sophisticated econometric test is used to assess the programme effects in a limited-information maximum-likelihood framework.

Pitt and Khandker examine the 'impact of participation, by gender, in each of the three group-based credit programs on women's and men's labour supply, boys' and girls' schooling, expenditure, and assets' (ibid., p. 960). Microcredit is found to be a significant determinant of many of these outcomes. In particular, it is found that:

- 'credit has a larger effect on the behaviour of poor households in Bangladesh when women are the program participants. For example, annual consumption expenditure increases [by] 18 taka for every 100 additional taka borrowed by women from three credit programs, compared with 11 taka for men' (ibid., p. 958).

- 'participation in credit programs by women increases the value of their nonland asset holdings, whereas male participation does not. For women at the mean, every increase of taka 100 of credit from BRAC, BRDB and Grameen Bank increases the value of their nonland assets [in the three groups] by 15, 29 and 27 taka, respectively' (ibid., p. 982).

ii Khandker (1998)

Separately, in a book published in 1998 (*Fighting Poverty with Microcredit: Experience from Bangladesh*), Khandker analyses the impact of the microcredit programme in Bangladesh in a bigger dimension, using the same set of data which formed the basis of the above-mentioned study that he jointly conducted with Pitt (Pitt and Khandker 1998).

All the three microcredit programmes were found to have 'significant positive effects on household per-capita expenditures'. Khandker (1998) meticulously estimated the rates of poverty and net-worth accumulation before and after programme-participation.

> The estimated impact coefficient of credit from Grameen Bank was 0.043 for women and 0.018 for men. That is, a 10 percent increase in borrowing increases expenditure by participating households by 0.4 percent when women borrow and by 0.2 per cent when men borrow. Mean per-capita expenditure in the survey households was Tk.4,004 a year. Average cumulative borrowing for all three programmes was Tk.5,499 for women and Tk.3,692 for men. Assuming an average family size of six, the average annual household expenditure was Tk.24,024. [There was implied by the results of the previously reported study] an estimated marginal increase in household consumption of 18 per cent for women's borrowing and 11 per cent for men's borrowing.
>
> (Ibid., p. 55)

Similar estimates were also made to analyse the impact of poverty at the village and the national level and the results were robust. All the three microcredit programmes reduced both moderate and extreme poverty. 'Aggregate village-level moderate poverty was 14 percent lower in RD-12 villages, 12 percent lower in Grameen Bank villages, and 10 percent lower in BRAC villages' (ibid., p. 57).

Similarly, at the national level,

> [B]orrowing from a program was estimated to reduce poverty among participants by as much as 20 percent and extreme poverty by as much as 22 percent. This means that as many as 5 percent of program participating households should be able to lift their families out of poverty every year by borrowing from a microcredit program.
>
> (Ibid., pp. 59–60)

The conclusion reached was that 20 per cent of the population of Bangladesh effectively benefited from microcredit programmes. Moreover, microcredit programmes also helped to attack poverty on the social front.

> They empower women and thereby increase their role in household resource allocation. This effect directly increases the welfare of children.... Women's credit has the largest impact on per-capita consumption and nutritional status of children. Microcredit programs have substantial impacts on children's schooling, which in turn enhances the human capital status of a country. Microcredit programs also seem to attack poverty from a population growth perspective.
>
> (Ibid., p. 60)

iii Study by BIDS (2001)

The Bangladesh Institute of Development Studies (BIDS) carried out an extensive study covering a three-year period. It was commissioned by the Palli Karma-Sahayak Foundation (PKSF) and was aimed at assessing the impact of the microcredit programmes conducted by the Partner Organizations (POs) of PKSF. Three repeat surveys were carried out during 1998, 1999 and 2000. The study covered 3,026 sample households from 91 villages (from a census of 19,151 households conducted in 1997) under 13 POs of PKSF. In an attempt to have a comprehensive study, other microfinance institutions operating in the area (i.e. non-PKSF POs) were also included.

In this robust study, the impact of microcredit on various economic and social aspects was extensively analysed, in particular taking into account the participants and the non-participants of microcredit, and the former was divided into regular and occasional participants.

> On the whole, the study finds positive impacts of program participation, if it is regular (i.e. continuous). More importantly, such positive impact is more visible in case of land-poor households, who are alleged to be the target population. Multivariate analyses show that there is significant positive effect of regular program participation on income and on average consumption of poor households. There is some indication that average consumption tends to rise with increase in the length of membership. Analysis on the determinants of income changes, however, suggests that the impact is less visible in case of the non-target population.
>
> (Zohir *et al.* 2001, p. 258)

Furthermore, 'both head-count and poverty-gap measures show that regular participants registered a faster rate of poverty reduction than occasional participants and non-participants and [the] estimated rate of poverty reduction was higher for occasional participants than non-participants' (ibid., p. 259).

Positive impacts were also observed in terms of social well-being and women empowerment:

> Participation in MFI programs in general, and regular participation in particular, had positive effect on household resource allocation on house repair, schooling and health care. All these had improved the social wellbeing of the participant households more than the non-participants. More importantly, participation had led to reduced gender gap in access to modern health care.
>
> (Ibid., p. 259)

There was also a positive impact on social attitude as, for example, 'the rise in contraceptive prevalence has been particularly high in households that are regular participants or past participants [of microcredit], compared to the non-participants or new participants' (ibid., pp. v–vi).

The study also attempted to make an assessment of the capacity of micro-credit borrowers to cope with vulnerability, especially as the study period coincided with the 1998 flood which was particularly disastrous for the poorest of the poor.

> The group-specific squared poverty gap (SPG) index show[s] noticeable impact of program participation in protecting from such shocks – value of SPG increased by only two percentage points between the first and the second round, for the regular participants. During the same period, SPG had increased by 11 percentage points for the non-participants. Both head-count and poverty gap measures show that regular participants registered a faster rate of poverty reduction than occasional participants, and [the] reduction in poverty among the latter was faster compared to the non-participants.
>
> (Ibid., p. v)

iv Findings by Mahjabeen (2008)

Mahjabeen examined the welfare and distributional implications of microfinance institutions in Bangladesh in the context of a general equilibrium framework, constructing a financial Social Accounting Matrix (SAM) of Bangladesh for 1999–2000 and taking Grameen Bank as a representative of the MFIs, comparing

> the welfare, income, consumption and utility of households under the basic model (without the MFIs) and the extended model (with the MFIs). The social welfare function is defined as the weighted sum of household utility. [It is assumed] that all households have a Cobb–Douglas utility function.
>
> (Ibid., pp. 1088–9)
>
> The major findings are that MFIs raise income and consumption levels of households, reduce income inequality and enhance welfare. This implies

> that microfinance is an effective development strategy and has important policy implications regarding poverty reduction, income distribution, and achievement of millennium development goals (MDGs).
>
> (Ibid., p. 1083)

Some key findings of this study are shown in Tables 13A.1 and 13A.2. The first table shows the change in household income, consumption and utility that has taken place in the extended model compared to the basic model. Thus viewed, the researcher finds that the

> provision of financial services to the rural poor in Bangladesh enhances income of all types of households, specially the rural poor the most, by 73%. [Her] results show that consumption of all households including the rural poor increased by more than 50% for all commodities after [she] extended the CGE model of Bangladesh by including MFIs as another type of financial intermediary. ... Consumption of agricultural commodities does include consumption of food. [It is also found] that there is a 258% increase in the value of social welfare from the basic to the extended version.
>
> (Ibid., p. 1089)

Table 13A.1 Change in consumption, income and utility in poor and rich households: as observed in the extended model compared to the basic model (% change)

	Consumption		*Income*	*Utility*
	Agriculture	*Industry and service*		
Poor households				
Rural	*65*	*56*	*73*	*228*
Urban	*65*	*70*	*60*	*288*
Rich households				
Rural	65	59	*42*	*270*
Urban	65	75	*72*	*266*

Source: Based on Mahjabeen (2008), p. 1089.

Table 13A.2 Distribution of income between the poor and the rich households: under the basic and the extended models (% of total income)

Poor households	*Basic model*	*Extended model*	*Rich households*	*Basic model*	*Extended model*
Poor rural	2	13	Rich rural	53	36
Poor urban	2	16	Rich urban	43	35
Total	4	29	Total	96	71

Source: Based on Mahjabeen (2008), p. 1089.

Table 13A.2 shows the distribution of income under the two models. Computational findings show that the

> provision of financial services to the rural poor enables the Bangladesh economy to reduce the income inequality. Under the basic model, poor households (rural and urban) earned 4% of total income. However, under the extended model their share in total income increases to 29%. Changes in the household share in national income imply that there is a change in the magnitude of the national poverty.
>
> (Ibid., p. 1089)

The study also examines

> the effect of MFIs on the labor market and profits of the commercial banks. The percentage change in labour demand from the basic to the extended model is 14% increase in the agriculture sector and 41% increase in the industry and service[s] sectors. These results strongly suggest that MFIs generate employment opportunities. Also, results show that the profits of commercial banks increased by 50% and the MFIs earned positive profits (i.e., did not go bankrupt) in the extended model.
>
> (Ibid., p. 1089)

13A.2 Selected Recent Impact Assessment Studies (ADB 2007; GOB 2011a and 2012a; and Huq and Salimullah 2012)

i Study by the Asian Development Bank (ADB 2007)

This study, conducted by the ADB for assessing two of their projects in three developing countries (Bangladesh, Philippines and Uzbekistan), helps us, in the investigators' words, 'to assess the extent to which microfinance projects have reduced the poverty of rural poor households and improved the socioeconomic status of women' in these countries. However, for conducting the Bangladesh case study, sample surveys were undertaken during October 2006 to January 2007 covering a sample of 200 microfinance clients, 'intended to generate the socioeconomic profile of target groups reached by ADB microfinance projects rather than measure impact quantitatively'. Below we list, in the words of the study's authors, a number of the major positive outcomes that were reported referring to the Bangladesh part of the project (ibid., pp. 24–30).

- 'Almost all of the survey respondents in Bangladesh reported that their incomes rose after participation in the programme.'
- 'Most of the respondents did not experience hunger in their households. Only 3 of the 200 respondents reported they had taken less food for the last three months. In terms of food quality, three quarters reported that they had had more food after participation in the programme. The purchase of clothing and health services also increased.'

- There was a marked enabling effect as 'participation in the microfinance programme enabled them to expand their microenterprises and start new businesses'.
- 'Ownership of assets changed positively after participation in the programme for about 90 per cent of the beneficiaries.'
- There was a significant positive impact in the acquisition of productive assets. Also positive changes 'were observed in the purchase of household furniture, TVs, electric fans, and clothing'.
- Participation in the microfinance programme enabled the women 'to save ... in group savings schemes, pension schemes, or in their homes. With the improved technical knowledge and skills, they were able to contribute to family income.' The finding is particularly marked in the Participatory Livestock Project, where the participating women who had no savings at the pre-project stage were having 'savings ... in the group savings scheme, in banks, or in their houses' and every one experienced this.
- 'Increased knowledge and self-confidence in doing business, and increased experience in dealing with people, were among the benefits reported by these women.'
- '70 per cent of the women felt that they were more empowered because of participation in the project and this was reflected in greater self-confidence in managing microenterprises (about 60 per cent of the respondents).'
- 'The women felt that they had greater control over money matters after participating in the microcredit programme (78 per cent for the Rural Livelihood Project and 66 per cent for the Participatory Livestock Development Project).'

ii Findings of a study by the Government of Bangladesh (GOB 2011a)

Published in June 2011, this study extensively evaluated the Microcredit Programme for the Handloom Weavers. The Microcredit Programme for the Handloom Weavers (Revised) under the Ministry of Textile and Jute was implemented by the Bangladesh Handloom Board from July 1998 to June 2006 with an investment cost of Tk.500 million.

The survey was conducted during 2010–11, with a sample of 696 households who were borrowers from the Bangladesh Handloom Board (BHB) and 296 from control areas, i.e. non-borrowers, thus a total sample of 992, covering all the eight administrative Divisions of Bangladesh. A multi-stage random-sampling method was used to select the ultimate sample for this study from a population of. handloom weavers/marginal weavers each owning no more than five handlooms.

For assessing this microcredit programme a project-and-control-area approach has been used. Thus assessed, the findings show some marked improvement in the employment and socio-economic status of the handloom weavers under the BHB when they are compared with the control households (i.e. non-project handloom weavers). The handloom weavers under the BHB were found to be satisfied with the loan-repayment period and the interest rate on the loan but complained of the inadequacy of loan amount, of delays in getting the loan on time and of the lack of competitiveness of their products in the market. The key findings include the following:

- Microcredit has helped the handloom weavers generate high-wage employment and other income-earning activities at a level equivalent to full-time employment.
- Though the average incomes per capita of both the borrower group (i.e. Tk.36,877) and the control group (i.e. Tk.32,660) are reasonably high, the former is a much higher figure than the latter.
- 72 per cent of weavers in the project area and 68 per cent of weavers in the control area are above the poverty line.
- 43.3 per cent of the handloom weavers in the project area are self-employed, compared to only 18.4 per cent in the control area.
- Only about 15 per cent of households use *katcha* (i.e. non-sanitary) latrines against the national average of 37 per cent.
- 84.3 per cent of the weavers in the project area have been brought into the electrification network against 74.5 per cent in the control areas.
- The literacy rate of the male population (aged 7 years and above) has been estimated at 86 and 81 per cent respectively in the project and the control areas; for females, the corresponding rates are 82 and 76 per cent, respectively.

iii Findings of a second study by the Government of Bangladesh (GOB 2012a)

The **second study** by the GOB evaluated in great detail the impact on rural women's development (under the Rural Women's Development Project under the Ministry of Women's and Children's Welfare, which was implemented by the National Women's Society (*Jatiya Mohila Sanghstha*), with a sample size of 353 as project households and 249 as control households (a total of 602), covering ten randomly selected sub-districts (Upajilas) from the seven Divisions of Bangladesh.

Overall, the 'Study findings show that the project has achieved its targets in respects of poverty alleviation' including structural changes in employment, employment generation, raising of income and creation of new assets (ibid., p. iii). Table 13A.3 gives an idea of the impact of the Rural Women's Development Project (RWDP) on those who participated in it.

The project has revealed a 'very positive impact at various stages' of the investigation, in the fields listed below:

a Demographic and land-ownership status;
b Education, dwelling houses, water, sanitation and electricity;

Table 13A.3 Assessment of benefits derived by women microcredit borrowers

Indicators	*Impact as % the total response*			*Total*
	Increased	*Remained the same*	*Decreased*	
Improvement in business decision-making	92	7	1	100
Improvement in confidence and leadership	88	11	1	100
Find easy to visit banks and other places	63	34	2	100
Contribution made to family expenses	73	27	0	100
Change in violence and torture	1	12	87	100
Improvement in status as a family member	78	23	0	100

Source and note: GOB 2012a, Table 3.29. The total may not exactly add to 100% because of the rounding off.

c Employment, economic participation and income growth;
d Credit, asset-accumulation and food security; and
e Women's empowerment.

The following can give an idea of the benefits as reported (GOB 2012a, ch. 4):

- The average number of children pursuing education is 1.88 in project households against 1.70 in the control households.
- The proportion of household members with no education is 1.30 per cent for the project area against 10.2 per cent in the control area.
- About 93 per cent of beneficiaries owned dwelling units against about 84 per cent in the control area.
- 99.4 per cent of beneficiaries use drinking water from tube wells against 96 per cent of those in control groups.
- Users of sanitary latrines and of ring-slab latrines jointly represent 91.8 per cent of households in the project area against 59.8 per cent in the control area, and the use of open fields or bushes is nil in the project area.
- About 78 per cent of RWDP beneficiaries are connected with electricity against 45.28 per cent in the control area
- The economic participation rate of women in beneficiary households is 44.31 per cent against 18.87 per cent in non-beneficiary households.
- The economic participation rate of beneficiary households is about 66.19 per cent against 57.23 per cent in the control area.
- The employment intensity is 124 per cent in the project area compared to 113 per cent in the control area.
- The status of women in households has progressed outstandingly from their position prior to joining the RWDP. Various selected indicators have shown progress (sufficient and moderate progress).

iv Findings of a study by Huq and Salimullah (2012)

This study is based on two series of field surveys carried out during 2010 and 2012. The 2010 survey, though focused mainly on social-safety-net transfers, attempted to get a feeling for the satisfaction resulting from microcredit in a rural location. However, the 2012 survey has been entirely focused on microcredit with a sample of 224 households in a rural location of northern Bangladesh (in Lalmonirhat district) and 217 households in an urban location (selected '*basti*' areas of Dhaka city).

One particular finding of the 2010 survey is shown in Table 13A.4 and, as may be seen, 96 per cent of those receiving microcredit expressed some level of satisfaction (high, medium or low), with about half of them reporting high (significant) benefits in terms of increase in income and, in the process, the alleviation of poverty.

In an attempt to pursue the impact of microcredit on poverty alleviation further, in 2012 two surveys, one covering a rural and one an urban location, were conducted during March to May, investigating in particular income growth and consequent rises in the consumption of households. In the rural survey, a total of 224 households were interviewed, consisting of 186 borrowers (i.e. recipients of microcredit) and a control group of 38 (i.e. non-borrowers). In the urban survey, the total sample was 214 (borrowers 151 and control group 63). (As the households were selected without initially enquiring whether they received loans or not, the difference in the control-group proportions between the rural and the urban survey appears to be purely fortuitous.)

Table 13A.5 shows the distributions in the rural and urban surveys as conducted in 2012.

The average loan size was relatively small – urban: Tk.13,694 (£110 approx.); and rural: Tk.20,662 (£165 approx.). So the average loan size of microcredit provided to rural borrowers in the sample was much lower than that to urban borrowers. Also, as shown in Table 13A.6, relatively small loans up to Tk.10,000.00 feature prominently in the rural survey, going to 58.6 per cent of the total number of borrowers, while in the urban survey loans of over Tk.10,000 feature prominently, three-quarters of the borrowers having loans in that range. The difference is perhaps understandable: in the urban survey a large percentage of the

Table 13A.4 Level of satisfaction as perceived by microcredit borrowers, 2010

Level of satisfaction perceived	*No of respondents*	*% of respondents*
High	24	47.1
Medium	10	19.6
Low	15	29.4
Negative	2	4.0
Total respondents	51	100

Source: Field surveys, September–October 2010.

Table 13A.5 Distribution of the borrower and the control groups in the rural and the urban surveys, 2012

	Borrower group	*Control group*	*Total*
Rural survey	186 (83.04%)	38 16.96%)	224 (100%)
Urban survey	151 (70.56%)	63 (29.44%)	214 (100%)
Total	337 (76.94%)	101 (23.06%)	438 (100%)

Source and Note: Field surveys carried out in April–May, 2012. Figures in brackets show percentage distribution.

borrowers took loans for business purposes, while the main purpose of the loans received by the rural borrowers was for agriculture.

It is found that a large number of microcredit providers including Grameen Bank, BRAC and ASA have remained highly active. Indeed, when they are judged against their score in helping to generate income and employment, there is a strong similarity across the NGOs (including Grameen Bank): all are perceived by the borrowers as helping highly effectively, and there is a strong liking on the part of the borrowers for doing business with them.

As may be inferred from Table 13A.7 (also plotted in Figure 13A.1), the impact of microcredit on income growth appears very positive (helping in leading to higher consumption and poverty alleviation) on the evidence of both rural and urban surveys: over 90 per cent of the rural borrowers reported positive income growth (with just over 8 per cent experiencing 'no-income growth' and 1.1 per cent with 'negative-income growth'), while in the urban survey 98.7 per cent reported positive income growth (with less than 1 per cent each reporting 'no-income growth' and 'negative-income growth'). In the case of the control group (i.e. those who did not take loans), in the rural survey about 8 per cent reported 'negative-income growth' and of the remaining over 80 per cent experienced 'no income growth', while only about 11 per cent had some income growth; the corresponding figures in the urban survey were 4.8, 6.5 and 31.7 per cent respectively, i.e. only about 32 per cent of the urban-survey respondents in the control group witnessed income growth. So, given that there are over 30 million microcredit borrowers in Bangladesh, the positive impact of microcredit on poverty alleviation can perhaps be easily appreciated.

13A.3 Women's empowerment: some early findings

As reported in Zaman (2004, pp. 13–14), several early studies also attempted to assess various socio-economic factors, one of which is women's empowerment.

> Empowerment of women in Bangladesh can be viewed against the backdrop of patriarchy, defined by Cain *et al.* [1979] as a 'set of social relations with

Table 13A.6 Distribution of microcredit by size of loans in Taka (no. of borrowers)

	Up to Tk.10,000	*>Tk.10,000 to 20,000*	*>Tk.20,000 to 30,000*	*>Tk.30,000 to 40,000*	*>Tk.40,000 to 50,000*	*Over Tk.50,000*	*Total no. of borrowers*
Rural borrowers	109 (58.60%)	45 (24.19%)	15 (8.06%)	10 (5.38%)	4 (2.15%)	3 (1.61%)	186 (100%)
Urban borrowers	38 (25.17%)	56 (37.09%)	37 (24.50%)	6 (3.97)	10 (6.62%)	4 (2.65%)	151 (100%)
Total	147	101	52	16	14	7	337

Source: Sample surveys, 2012.

Notes
Figures in brackets show percentage distribution.
Average size of the loan: Rural: Tk.13,694.35 and Urban: Tk.20,660.00.

Table 13A.7 Distribution of income growth: borrower and control groups

		Negative growth	*No growth*	*Growth of 25%*	*Growth of 50%*	*Growth of 100%*	*Total*
Rural	Borrower group	2 (1.07%)	15 (8.06%)	70 (37.63%)	81 (43.55%)	18 (9.68%)	186 (100%)
	Control group	3 (7.89%)	31 (81.57%)	4 (10.52%)	–	–	38 (100%)
Urban	Borrower group	1 (0.66%)	1 (0.66%)	18 (11.92%)	64 (42.38%)	67 (44.38%)	151 (100%)
	Control group	3 (4.76%)	40 (63.49%)	20 (31.74%)	–	–	63 (100%)
Total	Borrower group	3 (0.89%)	16 (4.75%)	88 (26.11%)	145 (43.03%)	85 (25.22%)	337 (100%)
	Control group	6 (5.94%)	71 (70.29%)	24 (23.76%)	–	–	101 (100%)

Source and Note: Sample surveys, 2012. Figures in brackets show percentage distribution (respondents).

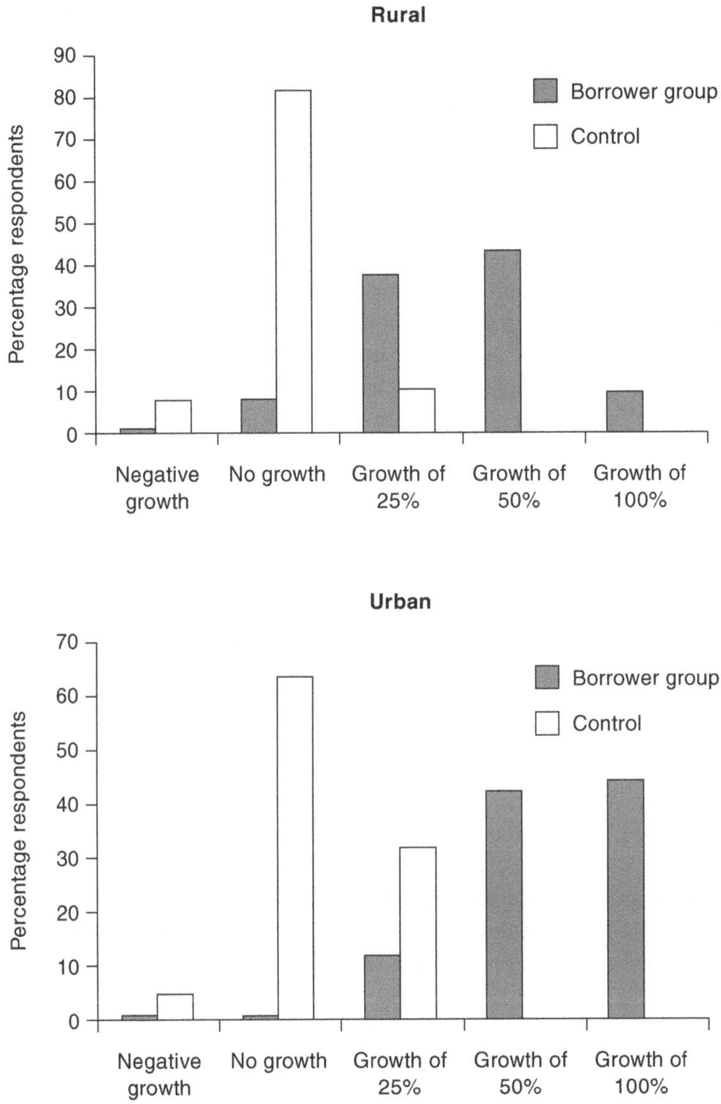

Figure 13A.1 Bar graphs showing income growth of microcredit borrowers (compared to control-group respondents) in rural and urban surveys (source: Sample surveys, April–May, 2012).

> a material base that enables men to dominate women.' Hence, [empowerment of women] can be thought of as an improvement in intra-household gender relations. Moreover, given the institution of *purdah* (loosely translated as 'veil'), a pervasive social construct which restricts the female sphere within a typical Bangladeshi household, empowerment can also be viewed in terms of a woman's interactions outside the homestead and the acquisition of skills, knowledge, and confidence that such interactions can bring.
>
> (Zaman 2004, p. 13)

> The work by Amin *et al.* [1994] in 36 villages in Bangladesh showed that membership in microcredit programs positively affected a woman's decision-making role, her marital stability, her control over resources, and her mobility, but had less impact on her attitude regarding marriage and education of daughters. Naved [1994] finds that the women participants in credit programs, in her sample felt their status had improved due to the fact that they were seen as income earners for the family because of their access to credit.
>
> (Zaman 2004, p. 14)

> Hashemi *et al.* (1996) developed an 'empowerment index' based on eight empowerment indicators. Their analysis establishes that contributing to her household's income is a significant factor contributing to a woman's own empowerment. However, Hashemi *et al.* also show that credit programs can empower women independently of whether they contribute to family income or not, after controlling for other factors.
>
> (Zaman 2004, p. 14)

As Zaman (2004, p. 14) concludes:

> On the whole, the evidence presented by those who argue that microcredit improves the status of females within a household appears more convincing than that argued by the sceptics' camp. There are two main reasons for this contention. First, the underlying thread of the argument, that access to an important household resource (credit) enhances a female's status within the household, is both intuitively appealing and resonates with the theoretical literature on bargaining models of the household. Second, the focus on female control over loans, as a key component of the sceptics' argument, fails to recognize that credit enters the overall household income pool and that household members jointly participate in the loan investment.

Part IV

Summary

14 Imperative and hope

14.1 A half-open door

In writing this book we hope and believe we are pushing on a half-open door. What was scarcely considered a serious project as little as 20 years ago is now – quietly and almost unnoticed among the affluent segment of the earth's people – becoming a matter of practical policy and politics. Four of the world's five largest nations, with 40 per cent of the global population, have all, within the last 15 years, taken deliberate measures more or less in the direction of a floor, a safety-net, to their people's disposable incomes. And they are not alone.

14.2 Three possible routes to getting things done

The three potential routes for social reform and improvement are the market, the state and civil society: the market working its magic through competition, the state through regulation; and civil society through mutual trust and responsibility. Each of the three depends to a degree for success on the other two. All flourish through the exercise of ingenuity and creativity. In our Chapter 13 we display the great apparent gains in material welfare made within Bangladesh by millions of very poor people, gains that result from the work of *non-government organizations (NGOs)*, principally in dispensing *microcredit*. The motivation and ethos of these organizations is that of civil society, but at the same time they work in competition with one another under the disciplines of a market. These conditions have been made into strengths. The NGOs, voluntary bodies with voluntary clients, can afford to be open-ended, spotting and pursuing opportunities of service to society that they can take without resort to coercion.

But a safety-net must involve some redistribution of income, which will need to be largely in the interest of those least favoured by the market and by the endowments, natural and social, with which they have started their lives. In order to make their material position better, less precarious, government must be able to transfer income or assets to them from others, and this entails an element of coercion. By its nature a safety-net must be all-inclusive, supporting all who might otherwise slip through. In the techniques used it may be ingenious and creative, but it must also be consistent and impartial, relying on principles of fairness, not simply goodwill.

So, in the last resort, the responsibility for creating a safety-net must fall to a *government.* It should certainly not seek to suppress or obstruct (but should rather encourage) the very real contributions that can be made to the reduction of disposable-income poverty (and poverty in all its strands) by market-oriented and civil-society institutions. But it should not expect, nor should its public expect, these institutions, lacking coercive powers, to replace it in its role of safety-net creation.

14.3 Conquering weakness in implementation

It is easy to see holes and gaps in the nets that the big middle-income countries have begun to weave. But the bugbear is so often implementation, falling far short of enactment, let alone of aspiration. Sometimes too the quality of implementation within a nation varies sharply from one state or province or district to another, even between nearby villages.[1] The nations of the modern world, and their institutions of government, especially in low-income and lower-middle-income countries, are vast sprawling organisms with diverse loyalties and cultures that resist rationalization.

Yet it is impressive that the implementation weaknesses are often widely recognized and discussed, and, as the case of India strikingly exemplifies (with its universal system of biometrically recognizable identity cards now in course of introduction), amazingly ambitious measures may be taken in the hope of countering them.

14.4 Both ... and ..., rather than either ... or ...

The objective, as we see it, following the institutions of the UN family, is to draw *everyone* above the level of extreme poverty in disposable income. We stress again that tedious word *disposable*, and emphasize that this is only one strand of the fight against extreme poverty. It is not the be-all and end-all of the struggle. But it is an essential part.

Beside the disposable-income objectives, it also goes without saying that clean accessible water is necessary. So are vaccinations, and latrines, and impregnated mosquito nets, and de-worming treatment of various kinds. So – before *financial* accessibility of medical treatment can become an issue – are suitably placed and professionally staffed clinics for primary medical treatment, and, for those who have serious but treatable illnesses, hospitals with specialist staff and equipment. But people also need food, for which, if they do not grow it themselves, they need a flow of cash; and in many places they also need cash to buy schooling and even water itself. For this they must have *disposable income.*

There are of course agonizing questions of priorities among these good and even necessary claims on resources. But, as we argue in Chapter 11, it does not always need to be a matter of *either* ... *or*.... More personal disposable income – more cash in hand – for those at the bottom of the heap may, often will, mean more educated people, more vaccinations, safer water, more de-worming, more and better food, more professionally attended births, less child labour and debt-slavery. Free or nearly free medical treatment, at least for the poorest, which we follow the UN and ILO in treating as a necessary part of the safety-net package, can – apart from its direct impact on health, comfort, physical capacity, self-respect, sometimes life itself – be a marvellous defence against indebtedness and consequent financial disaster for any family facing a major surgical procedure.

In the elaboration of this book's title we have claimed, for the safety-nets whose case we are advocating, a combination of four powerful reasons for acting: *pressing need, manageable cost, practical possibilities* and *favourable spillovers.*

14.5 Pressing need

It is to our shame, all of us in the rich world and the rich segments of middle-income countries, that we have hitherto been leaving so many people, more than one and a quarter billion on the estimates made around 2005 and again in 2008,[2] without any secure source of income to feed themselves and their families, abandoning them in many cases to genuine hunger, at least in certain seasons of even normal years or when crops and demand for casual work are weak. *If* the scarcity for so many millions were *unavoidable*, requiring an intolerable amount of spending-power from the rest of the world in order to escape it, we might be obliged to ignore it, but what this exercise has revealed (see chapters 3 and 4) is that the cost of filling the gap with cash, on the supposition that that would be administratively possible, is very small change when set against global income.

People whose spending power is *less than what $1.25 per person per day would buy in New York or Peoria*: such people at least may surely regard themselves as hard-pressed, and, even if they are not completely destitute now, will be aware of living under the ever-present shadow of destitution. As we have stressed, it is *the known risk of even more extreme deprivation*, for people's families as well as for themselves, that adds extra bitterness to whatever degree of want they are currently undergoing. The pressing need is *to know there is a floor*, a limit to how bad it can get. If their governments, whether with little help or much from the rich world, can give them that assurance – at a level that can at least allow them to eat, and to spend on some other functions that are socially necessary in the communities where they live – this surely, for many millions, even hundreds of millions, would be a step forward of incalculable worth. And this is still true, even today, when the big battalions of Latin America and Monsoon Asia have already begun to lumber into position.

14.6 Manageable cost

Here we recall the paradox mentioned in Chapter 1 that, though a fifth of the world's population are, or were around 2005 and 2008, in extreme disposable-income poverty, the size of the total poverty gap – representing the amount in actual US dollars that, if it went in precisely the right distribution *to all and only* the people below the extreme-poverty line, would suffice to bring them up to it – would be about 80 billion dollars a year, around one five-hundredth of world income. Admittedly, this maybe makes filling the gap seem easier and less costly than it would be in practice. For one thing, the willingness of the high-income countries to pay the bills, even for transfers of cash to the poorest people in the poorest countries, will at best be limited. And, in any case, making sure that the gap in any country is filled by cash transfers will almost certainly entail a certain amount of over-filling and will therefore cost more than the sheer size of the gap would suggest. And in this simple calculation we have left out of account (though with some crude indicators inserted in Chapter 4) the cost of health-care finance, which we have emphasized is a necessary addition if a safety-net is to be effective.

Probably a more sober comparison will be the one involving the three pilot-study countries featured in Chapter 12: Vietnam, El Salvador and Mozambique. For Vietnam, at the bottom of the lower-middle-income range, the extreme-poverty gap in 2005 was about 1 per cent of its national income. This seemed in 2012, from the reported discussion of what could be done, to postpone the expected completion of the safety-net for some years but not to put it out of sight. El Salvador's proportional gap was less: about 0.6 per cent of its income. The discussion reported in Chapter 12 of what might be possible had not gone as far there as in Vietnam. But the gap in Mozambique, with an extremely low income per head, amounted to 19.6 per cent of income. It was fairly obvious that Mozambique was a long way from being able to fill the gap without significant outside help.

This leads to a possible path ahead. 'The world', if it set its mind and will to the task, could fill the gap – universal medical cover on the Thai pattern and all – without great difficulty. But the rich OECD countries are very unlikely to be prepared to carry the whole burden or even a very large part of it themselves. And it is to be hoped that (directly or through the international agencies) they will still be joining in other anti-poverty measures, taking a large share in providing the public goods and merit goods that are necessary or highly desirable complements to what can be bought with disposable income. Lower-middle-income countries such as India, China and Indonesia seem to be gradually working their way through to filling their own gaps without international help, and will do so all the more readily if, through some of the measures now or recently taken, they can get the implementation largely watertight. That might be a reasonable thing to expect of the *upper-middle-income* countries such as Mexico and South Africa, and of all, or all but the lowest, of the *lower-middle-income* countries. But the *low-income* countries (numbering about one-eighth, 12.5 per cent, of the world's people in 2009) should be agreed to have a right to ask for substantial help if they commit themselves seriously to extreme-poverty-gap filling. On those terms the costs should be manageable.

14.7 Practical possibilities

As interest has begun to develop over the need for a safety-net or income floor, plenty of ideas have surfaced on how it might be done; and there is already a mass of evidence of how the methods have worked in practice. The 2008 book *For Protection and Promotion* (by Grosh *et al.*), published by the World Bank, gives a wealth of reasoning and experience. In our Chapter 5 we have outlined seven conceptually different methods for 'targeting' the very poor,[3] that is to say concentrating benefits on them.

Filling the gap neatly, no more and no less, for each one of those 1.3 billion or so people, might naturally have seemed an impossible task. And strictly, literally, no doubt it was, at least if emphasis was to be put on the 'no more' as well as the 'no less'. Most of the methods of 'targeting', either by their nature leave out a segment of the population who might from their poverty be eligible (for example, households without children in the case of the standard form of CCTs, or people with certain physical disabilities in the case of rural public works) or have to make a compromise between errors of exclusion (leaving out some of those that ought to be in) and errors of inclusion (including more than strictly necessary). But often it will be evident or likely that combining *two or more* of the approaches together will give better results than the use of any one alone, especially if economy and speed are among the criteria on which the methods are judged.

If the administering authority is serious about leaving no one *out* who ought to be *in*, then there will inevitably be some over-filling: some of the not-quite-so-poor will be included. That will have a fiscal cost, but that cost may often be trivial against the cost entailed by attempts at greater accuracy; and in any case helping some of the not-quite-so-poor will surely in itself be good as long as it comes in the course of helping the extremely poor rather than at their expense.

The two approaches that have received particular attention recently are conditional cash transfers (CCTs) – popular on all sides with their dual purposes – which have taken off widely in Latin America; and rural public works that allow self-targeting and in principle employment guarantees, in which the great Indian experiment, despite its apparent problems and deficiencies, has shown flickering signs of being replicated elsewhere, as in Indonesia and Bangladesh.

Another development in the present century, which will surely begin to seem inevitable in its broad outlines, is Thailand's 'pluralistic' approach to enabling everyone, without risk of impoverishment, to pay for the health care that is available. This entails having a section of the population – roughly those in the formal sector – on state-run conventional contributory health insurance; a small number who so choose on private health insurance; and a large part of the people, all those otherwise unsupported, who are catered for by a separate system of primary-care centres and hospitals, to which about half have access completely free of charge, and the rest pay a small nominal fee per unit of service.

We have also in Chapter 7 outlined no less than five ways of financing the cash transfers that will be needed (dispensed either gratis or as wages) to constitute a safety-net. Not all of the five will be appropriate in all circumstances, but we stressed that the first place to look is for opportunities of reallocation of existing outlays. This will often reveal rich possibilities, especially if at the starting-point there are extensive subsidies on consumer-goods, which typically go indiscriminately to both rich and poor. This very often means in practice that the rich get absolutely more per head of the subsidy. The case against using subsidized goods in the belief or pretence that it is a way of helping the poor is that awkward fact about the distribution of the benefit, together commonly with a lack of transparency (the realities are conveniently obscured), and the fact that state distribution of subsidized goods is plunder-prone. Happy is the country whose leaders have the courage to reallocate what is spent on these false chimeras of social justice so as to create a genuine income floor.

14.8 Favourable spillovers

Creating a safety-net can be expected to have two valuable classes of spillover effects. One of these results from the sheer shift of a certain amount of spending-power from the relatively rich (from those at home and to some extent also perhaps from abroad) to the very poor. No elaborate proof is needed for most of us to establish that the part removed from the rich will mean less, will be valued at a lower rate, than the part of equal monetary value received by the poor. It goes without saying that a gift of £20 that can be a big bonus if given to someone living on £10 a week will be of virtually no account to someone living on £200 a week. £20 *taken away* in the form of tax from the richer person may be rated a bit more highly than that: most of us set a higher value on what we have, or have had, than on what we do not yet have. But the principle remains: a given sum means more, sometimes much more, to the poorer than to the richer person.

And the very poor household will tend to spend the extra on something it considers important. If it considers schooling important (they mostly do) and is also concerned about nutrition and general health care (for which some information or nudging may be needed to generate the best response, but which is still likely to be the case), then making that household a little less poor is likely to lead to some investment in education and nutrition and general health, while the same sum taken from the much richer party is *unlikely* to lead to *any comparable disinvestment* in education and health. So, establishing a safety-net above the previous living standard of a large segment of the population, at the expense only of a much smaller, much richer segment, will contribute to a better educated, better nourished and physically stronger, population. Surely that would be a public good, a bonus *for the society* over and above the *individual* gains of those who as a result are better informed, more competent in highly important ways and healthier. In general, we can expect an equalizing redistribution with its benefits concentrated on those who are otherwise most firmly trapped in poverty – giving them a few extra degrees of freedom – to make the society more productive in the ways that matter.

The second class of spillover, one that we have referred to already, is related but conceptually and practically different. As well as entailing equalizing income redistribution, establishing a safety-net, if it is fully effective and trusted to continue, will give the individual household a firm base, reducing the downside risk of any venture. For operators in the informal economy, who are a large proportion of the workforce in many developing countries, productive life is highly precarious. A false business move may lead to the loss of everything. It makes sense to stick to known ways: to be unenterprising. But a credible safety-net is favourable to *enterprise*, to *investment*. Each of the investments so encouraged may well be very modest in scale, but that is very far from meaning that, separately or together, they are of little worth.

Conclusion

Need, finance, practicalities, positive spin-offs: all this creates a powerful *imperative* for each of us – as states, as civil associations and individually – to press toward the creation of safety-nets in the spheres in which we have opportunity or responsibility. It is necessary and it is possible.

Add to the generalizations the fact that we have been witnessing an advancing range of working exemplars of how it can be done; that there has been increasing public awareness of need and opportunity in the giant nations where a large proportion of the world's extremely poor still live; and that unthreatening and non-coercive routines have been laid out by which hesitantly willing states may be coaxed, or coax themselves, into the fashioning of their own safety-nets.

As poor nations become richer, communication also continues to improve exponentially, and poor and near-poor people become better informed and increasingly aware of their latent power. These developments give ground for hope that a world of safety-nets – floors to disposable income that can gradually be raised over time – may increasingly prevail and form one immensely important strand in the attack on world poverty.

Notes

1 See, for example, *The Economist* (2012d).
2 See above in Chapter 4 and also World Bank at http://econ.worldbank.org/povcalnet.
3 Without including conditional cash transfers (CCTs) as a separate method.

Postscript

We are adding this Postscript, after the text of the book has gone to press, in order to update readers with some relevant recent developments and, in particular, with some information which has just been published in *The Economist* (2013).

Summarizing some of the latest estimates of the numbers of people in the world whose disposable income is below the extreme-poverty borderline, the *Economist* report cites the rather remarkable fall in their numbers over 20 years: from 43 per cent of the populations of developing countries (1.9 billion people) in 1990 to 21 per cent (1.2 billion on an only slightly altered criterion) in 2010 (ibid., p. 23).

It also summarizes some evidence relating to the prospects for actually ending 'extreme hunger and poverty' in the sense understood under the first Millennium Development Goal. This is taken to mean reducing the headcount of extreme (disposable-income) poverty effectively to zero (say to 1 per cent of world population) by 2030, the date mooted as a target by the new President of the World Bank, Jim Yong Kim, a goal quite likely to form one of the post-2015 successors to the MDGs. Simply on the arithmetic, meeting the target 'would mean maintaining the annual one-percentage-point cut in the [extreme-] poverty rate achieved in 1990–2010 for another 20 years' (ibid., p. 24).

Yet some of the reductions in developing countries since around 1980 have been spectacular. In China the fall between 1981 and 2010 amounted to 680 million people. Not only that but for the rest of the developing world, the world outside China, Martin Ravallion's calculation[1] is cited to the effect that, in the single decade after 2000, the number fell by 280 million. These two figures alone add to almost a billion. Could a fall of a further billion be brought within view?

Falls in the poverty headcount may come about either 'spontaneously' – through economic growth largely as a matter of the impersonal working of the economic system – or else as a result of deliberate distribution policies, with combinations of the two possible and to be sought and expected.

The three main reservoirs of extreme poverty in the closing years of the last century were in China, India and Sub-Saharan Africa. *The Economist* supposes the possibility of three main movements to the goal: three main acts in the drama. China, entirely through its rapid economic growth and in the absence of deliberate redistribution policy ('targeting'), has already cut its extreme-poverty rate 'from 84 per cent in 1980 to about 10 per cent now' (ibid., p. 24). This is the first act and on its own might give abundant ground for hope that the virtual-zero target may be achievable within a very few years.

But India over roughly the same period, despite almost comparably fast GDP growth for much of the latter part of the time, had its extreme-poverty rate fall only from 59.8 per cent in 1981 to 41.6 per cent in 2005 (World Bank, *WDI 2011*, p. 66). This suggests that, if India is to follow China in making huge reductions of the extreme-poverty-headcount proportion, that will probably have in large measure to be through deliberate government action directed at equalizing distribution, such as transfers in cash or kind and 'self-targeting' public-works employment. Despite the heavy dependence of poverty reduction on general economic growth, the crucial role in addition of measures of equalizing redistribution is apparent from an estimate made by Martin Ravallion to the effect that a 1 per cent increase in incomes would cut extreme poverty 'by 0.6 per cent in the most unequal countries but by 4.3 per cent in the most equal ones' (*The Economist* 2013, p. 24). The *Economist* writer by implication expresses the hope that the ambitious Indian moves of the last few years, including the unique biometric identification of individuals to fortify against misappropriation of cash remunerations and transfers, will come to fruition. India's example in these respects might then be followed more or less by other big Asian countries such as Indonesia and Bangladesh, so forming the second act of the drama and making further big inroads into extreme-poverty reduction.

The third large reservoir of extreme poverty is in Sub-Saharan Africa; and here there is much less ground for optimism. Though on Ravallion's estimates (*The Economist* 2013, p. 24) overall 'consumption in the developing world has grown by just under 2 per cent a year since 1980 … [with] … a sharp increase since 2000' from a rate of 0.9 per cent before to 4.3 per cent after that date, and there is no general recent sign of diminishing returns; yet in much of Africa poverty rates are still very high, with average consumption in the six poorest countries as low as 50 cents a day (ibid., p. 26). *The Economist* expresses grounds for hope, but also fears that the last remnants of extreme poverty will prove hardest to remove; and also that concentrations will remain in failed or fragile states such as Congo and Somalia.

Doubtless with the (divergent) experiences and policies of both China and India in view, *The Economist* posits that moving to really low levels will require *both* growth *and* deliberate distribution measures, and (implying increased reliance on the latter) that further extreme-poverty reduction will be increasingly a matter of 'identification, targeting, and distribution' (ibid.) and to that extent may be capable of being achieved by public policy.

With the mixed record so far of successes and failures of realizing the MDGs, it is apparent that there is now a firm desire on the part of the world community to move towards new targets including the ambition of ending extreme disposable-income poverty within a specified time, possibly by 2030, a date that is now being flagged up from various quarters. Economic growth may do much toward making this achievable, but without deliberate safety-net policies – such as targeted transfers, self-targeting employment and, to enforce the rest, the devices that modern technology makes possible for ensuring that payments reach those for whom they are intended – gaps will remain.

In conclusion, the guiding principle of a universal social safety-net for ensuring that the gaps are filled becomes if anything ever more relevant.

Note

1 The sources cited in *The Economist* (2013) article are: Martin Ravallion, 'How long will it take to lift one billion people out of poverty?' World Bank Policy Research Working Paper 6325; and Laurence Chandy, Natasha Ledlie and Veronika Penciakova, 'The Final Countdown: prospects for ending extreme poverty by 2030', Brookings Institution Policy Paper 2013-04.

Bibliography

ADB (Asian Development Bank) (2007) *Effect of Microcredit on Poor Rural Households and the Status of Women*, Special Evaluation Study, Operations Evaluation Department, Metro Manila: ADB. Online. Available at: www.adb.org/documents/effect-microfinance-poor-rural-households-and-status-women (accessed 11 November 2012).

Ahmad, Q.K. (2007) *Socio-economic and Indebtedness-Related Impact of Micro-Credit in Bangladesh*, Dhaka: University Press Ltd.

Ahmed, S. (2004) 'Microcredit and poverty: new realities and strategic issues', in S. Ahmed and M.A. Hakim (eds) *Attacking Poverty with Micro-Credit*, Dhaka: University Press Ltd, pp. 23–40. See also, Ahmed, S. (2004) 'Microcredit in Bangladesh: achievements and challenges'. Online. Available at: www.microfinancegateway.org/gm/document-1.9.24645/22944_Microcredit_in_Banglades.pdf (accessed 1 November 2012).

Ahmed, S.S. (2007) *Social Safety Nets in Bangladesh*. Online. Available at: http://siteresources.worldbank.org/BANGLADESHEXTN/Resources/295759–1240185591585/BangladeshSocialSafetyNets.pdf (accessed 27 December 2012).

Amin, R., Kabir, M., Chowdhury, J., Ahmed, A.U. and Hill, R.B. (1994) 'Poor women's participation in income-generating projects and their fertility regulation in Bangladesh: evidence from a recent survey', *World Development*, 22 (4): 555–65.

ASA (2013) *ASA Profile*. Online. Available at: http://asa.org.bd/?page_id=12 (accessed 18 February 2013).

Banerjee, A.V. and Duflo, E. (2011) *Poor Economics: A Radical Rethinking of the Way to Fight Global Poverty*, New York: Public Affairs.

Barrientos, A. and Hulme, D. (2008) 'Social protection for the poor and poorest in developing countries: reflections on a quiet revolution', BWPI Working Paper 30, Manchester: Brooks World Poverty Institute.

Bateman, M. (2010) *Why Doesn't Microfinance Work?*, London: Zed Books.

Bateman, M. (2012) 'Let's not kid ourselves that financial inclusion will help the poor', *Guardian Poverty Matters Blog*, 8 May 2012. Online. Available at: www.guardian.co.uk/global-development/poverty-matters/2012/may/08/financial-inclusion-poor-microfinance (accessed 20 November 2012).

Bateman, M. and Chang, H.-J. (2009) *The Microfinance Illusion*. Online. Available at: www.microfinancetransparency.com/evidence/PDF/App.3%20Chang%20Bateman%20article.pdf (accessed 20 November 2012).

Bateman, M. and Chang, H.-J. (2012) 'Microfinance and the illusion of development: from hubris to nemesis in thirty years', *World Economic Review*, 1 (1): 13–36.

BBC (2012) *Hard Talk: Interview with Sheikh Hasina*, BBC World Service, 30 July 2012. See also 'PM Blasts Dr Yunus', *Daily Star*, Dhaka (30 July 2012). Online.

Available at: www.thedailystar.net/newDesign/latest_news.php?nid=39530 (accessed 20 February 2012).

BBS (Bangladesh Bureau of Statistics) (1998) *Report on the Household Expenditure Survey 1995–96*, Dhaka: Government of Bangladesh (Statistics Division, Ministry of Planning).

BBS (Bangladesh Bureau of Statistics) (2003) *Report of the Household Income & Expenditure Survey 2000*, Dhaka: Government of Bangladesh (Statistics Division, Ministry of Planning).

BBS (Bangladesh Bureau of Statistics) (2007) *Report of the Household Income and Expenditure Survey 2005*, Ministry of Planning, Dhaka: Government of Bangladesh (Statistics Division, Ministry of Planning).

BBS (Bangladesh Bureau of Statistics) (2011) *Report of the Household Income and Expenditure Survey 2010*, Dhaka: Government of Bangladesh (Statistics Division, Ministry of Planning).

BBS (Bangladesh Bureau of Statistics) (various years) *Statistical Yearbook of Bangladesh*, Dhaka: Government of Bangladesh (Planning Division, Ministry of Planning).

BIDS (Bangladesh Institute of Development Studies) (1990) *Evaluation of Poverty Alleviation Programmes* (Manuscript), Dhaka: BIDS.

BIDS (Bangladesh Institute of Development Studies) (2001) *Monitoring and Evaluation of Microfinance Institutions*, Dhaka: BIDS.

BIDS (Bangladesh Institute of Development Studies) (2010) BIDS-PRP Working Paper Series No. 5, 'Safety-net programs in Bangladesh: assessing the performance of selected programs', Dhaka: BIDS.

Bland, A.E., Brown, P.A. and Tawney, R.H. (eds) (1914) *English Economic History: Select Documents*, London: Bell.

BRAC (2013) *Microfinance*. Online. Available at: www.mixmarket.org/mfi/brac/report and www.brac.net/content/microfinance# (accessed 18 February 2013).

Brown, C.V. and Jackson, P.M. (1990) *Public Finance Economics*, Oxford: Basil Blackwell.

Cain, M., Khanum, S.R. and Nahar, S. (1979) 'Class, patriarchy and women's work in Bangladesh', *Population and Development Review*, 5 (3): 405–38.

Chang, H.-J. (2010) *Poverty, Entrepreneurship and Development*, Helsinki: UN-WIDER. Online. Available at: www.wider.unu.edu/publications/newsletter/articles-2010/en_GB/10–2010-Chang/ (accessed 12 January 2013).

Chowdhury, M., Mosley, P. and Simanowitz, A. (2004) 'Introduction: the social impact of microfinance', *Journal of International Development*, 16 (3): 291–300.

CLP (2012) *Chars Livelihood Programme (CLP)*. Online. Available at: www.rdcd.gov.bd/dmdocuments/Success%20Story%20of%20CLP.pdf (accessed 12 February 2013). Also see *Char Livelihoods Programme (CLP): Microfinance on the Chars: A Review of the Microfinance Situation and the Need for Innovative Products and Extended Services*. Online. Available at: www.clp-bangladesh.org/pdf/mf%20needs%20and%20coverage%20report%20%20final%2025.03.12.pdf (accessed 18 February 2013).

Clunies-Ross, A., Forsyth, D. and Huq, M. (2009) *Development Economics*, London: McGraw-Hill.

Coady, D., Grosh, M. and Hoddinott, J. (2003) 'The targeting of transfers in developing countries: review of experience and lessons' (no publisher given; comments to d.coady@cgiar.org, m.grosh@worldbank.org or john.hoddinott@dal.ca).

Collier, P. (2007) *The Bottom Billion: Why the Poorest Countries Are Failing and What Can Be Done About it*, Oxford: Oxford University Press.

Daley-Harris, S. (ed.) (2002) *Pathways out of Poverty: Innovations in Microfinance for the Poorest Families*, Bloomfield, CT: Kumarian Press.

Datta, D. (2004) 'Microcredit in rural Bangladesh: Is it reaching the poorest?', *Journal of Microfinance*, 6 (1): 55–81. Reprinted in S.R. Osmani and B.A. Baqui Khalily (eds) (2011) *Readings in Microfinance: Reach and Impact*, Dhaka: University Press Ltd, pp. 81–99.

Drèze. J. (1995) 'Famine prevention in Africa: some experiences and lessons', in J. Drèze, A. Sen and A. Hussein, *The Political Economy of Hunger: Selected Essays*, Oxford: Clarendon Press, pp. 554–604.

Dutta, P., Murgai, R., Ravallion, M. and van de Walle, D. (2012) 'Does India's employment-guarantee scheme guarantee employment?' World Bank, Development Policy Research Group Working Paper 6003, March.

Duvendack, M. and Palmer-Jones, R. (2012) 'High noon for microfinance impact evaluations: re-investigating the evidence from Bangladesh', *Journal of Development Studies*, 44 (4): 463–84.

Easterly, W. (2006) *The White Man's Burden: Why the West's Efforts to Aid the Rest Have Done so Much Harm and so Little Good*, New York: Penguin Press.

Economist, The (2005) 'Corruption in Kenya: feat of clay' 12 February 2005, p. 56.

Economist, The (2006) 'Kenya: caught in the act', 28 January 2006, p. 61.

Economist, The (2008) 'Nigeria: the good, the bad and the President', 5 January 2008, p. 46.

Economist, The (2012a) 'Asia's next revolution', 8 September, pp. 11–12; and 'Asian welfare states: new cradles to graves', 8 September 2012, pp. 22–4.

Economist, The (2012b) 'Bangladesh and development: the path through the fields', 3 November 2012, pp. 23–5.

Economist, The (2012c) 'Welfare in India: money where your mouth is', 10 November, pp. 58–9; and 'Warding off danger – money with strings attached', 10 November 2012, p. 59.

Economist, The (2012d) 'A tale of two villages – in rural India there is hope that the worst policies can be improved', 17 November 2012, pp. 63–4.

Economist, The (2012e) 'India's UID scheme: reform by numbers', 14 January 2012, pp. 51–2.

Economist, The (2012f) 'On the prowl', 1 December 2012, p. 68.

Economist, The (2012g) 'Can't get the help', 22 December 2012, p. 81.

Economist, The (2013) 'Briefing poverty', 1 June 2013, pp. 23–6.

Fiszbein, A. and Schady, N. *et al.* (2009) *Conditional Cash Transfers: Reducing Present and Future Poverty*, Washington DC: World Bank.

Gaiha, R., Kulkarni, V.S., Pandey, M.K. and Imai, K.S. (2009) 'National Rural Employment Guarantee Scheme, poverty and prices in rural India', Manchester: Economics, School of Social Sciences, University of Manchester, May.

Gauri, V. and Galef, J. (2005) 'NGOs in Bangladesh: activities, resources and governance', *World Development*, 33 (12): 2045–65.

GOB (Government of Bangladesh) (2003) *Bangladesh: A National Strategy for Economic Growth, Poverty Reduction and Social Development*, Dhaka: Ministry of Finance (Economic Affairs Division), March 2003.

GOB (Government of Bangladesh) (2004) *Bangladesh: Preparation of Poverty Reduction Strategy Paper: A Status Report*, 14 July 2004.

GOB (Government of Bangladesh) (2005) *Unlocking the Potential: National Strategy for Accelerated Poverty Reduction*, Dhaka: Planning Commission, Government of Bangladesh (October 2005).

GOB (Government of Bangladesh) (2011a) *Impact Evaluation of the Project 'Microcredit Programme for the Handloom Weavers' (Revised)*, Dhaka: Implementation Monitoring & Evaluation Division, Ministry of Planning (June 2011).

GOB (Government of Bangladesh) (2011b) *6th Five Year Plan 2011–2015: Accelerating Growth and Reducing Poverty* (Parts 1–3), Dhaka: Planning Commission, Ministry of Planning.

GOB (Government of Bangladesh) (2012a) *Impact Evaluation of Rural Women Development Project (Revised)*, Dhaka: Implementation Monitoring & Evaluation Division, Ministry of Planning (June 2012).

GOB (Government of Bangladesh) (2012b) *Perspective Plan of Bangladesh 2010–2021: Making Vision 2021 a Reality*, Dhaka: General Economics Division, Planning Commission.

GOB (Government of Bangladesh) (2012c) *Bangladesh Economic Review 2012*, Dhaka: Economic Advisor's Wing, Finance Division, Ministry of Finance.

Goetz, A. and Sen Gupta, R. (1996) 'Who takes the credit? Gender, power, and control over loan use in rural credit programmes in Bangladesh', *World Development*, 24 (1): 45–63.

Grameen Bank (2012) 'Grameen Bank at a glance', in *Bank for the Poor*. Online. Available at: www.grameen-info.org/index.php?option=com_content&task=view&id=26&Itemid=175 (accessed 18 February 2012).

Grieve, R.H. and Huq, M.M. (eds) (1995) *Bangladesh: Strategies for Development*, Dhaka: University Press Ltd.

Grosh, M., del Ninno, C., Tesliuc, E. and Ouerghi, A. (2008) *For Protection and Promotion*, Washington DC: World Bank.

Hanlon, J., Barrientos, A. and Hulme, D. (2010) *Just Give Money to the Poor: the Development Revolution from the Global South*, Herndon, VA: Kumarian Press.

Hashemi, S., Schuler, S. and Riley, I. (1996) 'Rural credit programs and women's empowerment in Bangladesh', *World Development*, 24 (4): 635–53.

Hossain, M. (1985) *Credit for the Rural Poor: The Experience of Grameen Bank in Bangladesh*, Dhaka: BIDS.

Hulme, D. and Mosley, P. (1996) *Finance Against Poverty* (Vol. 1), London: Routledge.

Hulme, D. and Shepherd, A. (2003) 'Conceptualizing chronic poverty', *World Development*, 31 (3): 403–423.

Huq, M. and Salimullah, M. (2012) 'Microcredit and poverty alleviation: a case study of Bangladesh', presented at the DSA Scotland Conference held at the University of Edinburgh on 14 September 2012.

ILO (International Labour Organization/International Labour Office) (2006) 'What is the impact of social health protection on access to health care, health expenditure and impoverishment? A comparative analysis of three African countries', by X. Scheil-Adlung, J. Juetting, K. Xu, G. Carrin and associates, ESS Paper no. 24.

ILO (International Labour Organization/International Labour Office) (2007) 'Social health protection: an ILO strategy towards universal access to health care, a consultation', Issues in Social Protection, Discussion Paper 19.

ILO (International Labour Organization/International Labour Office) (2008a) 'Can low-income countries afford basic social security?', Social Security Policy Briefings Paper 3.

ILO (International Labour Organization/International Labour Office) (2008b) 'Social health protection: ILO strategy towards universal access to health cover', Social Security Policy Briefings Paper 1. Online. Available at: www.ilo.org/public/english/protection/secsoc/fdownloads/policy/policy1e.pdf.

ILO (International Labour Organization/International Labour Office) (2008c) 'Universal health-care coverage through pluralistic approaches: experience from Thailand', by Thaworn Sakuphanit, Global Extension of Social Security. Online. Available at: www.socialsecurityextension.org/gimi/gess/RessShowRessource.do?ressourceId=6612.

ILO (International Labour Organization/International Labour Office) (2012a) International Labour Conference Provisional Record, 101st session, 'Text of the recommendation concerning national floors of social protection', Geneva, 14 June 2012. Online. Available at: www.ilo.org/wcmsp5/groups/public___ed_norm/___relconf/documents/meetingdocuments/wcms_183326.pdf (accessed 14 June 2012).

ILO (International Labour Organization/International Labour Office) (2012b) 'Towards effective and fiscally sustainable social protection floors', Preliminary report for the meeting of the G20 Labour and Employment Ministers, Guadalajara, 17–18 May 2012. Online. Available at: www.ilo.org/gimi/gess/RessShowRessource.do?ressourceId=30810 (accessed 18 May 2012).

ILO (International Labour Organization/International Labour Office) (2012c) 'Analysis of the Vietnam National Social Protection Strategy (2012–2020) in the context of social protection floor objectives: a rapid assessment', by M. Cichon, F. Bonnet, V. Schmitt, C. Galian and G. Mazeikaite. ESS Paper No. 32. Online. Available at: www.ilo.org/gimi/gess/RessShowRessource.do?ressourceId=30497.

IMF (International Monetary Fund) (2005) 'Vietnam's health-care system: a macroeconomic perspective', author Adams, S.J., Paper prepared for the International Symposium on Health-care Systems in Asia, Tokyo, 21–22 January 2005, IMF.

Inchauste, G., Olivieri, S., Saavedra, J. and Winkler, H. (2012) *What is behind the decline in poverty since 2000? Evidence from Bangladesh, Peru and Thailand*, World Bank Policy Research Working Paper No.WPS6199. Background Paper for the *World Development Report 2013*, Washington DC: World Bank (18 December 2012). Online Available at: http://siteresources.worldbank.org/EXTNWDR2013/Resources/8258024–1320950747192/8260293–1320956712276/8261091–1348683883703/WDR2013_bp_What_Is_Behind_The_Decline_In_Poverty.pdf (accessed 6 December 2012).

Institute of Microfinance (2012) *Bangladesh Microfinance Statistics 2010*, Institute of Microfinance, Dhaka. Online. Available at: www.inm.org.bd/statistics/2010/content_pre.pdf (accessed 28 October 2012).

Jibon, S.I. (2013) 'MRA moves to cut further microcredit interest rate', *The New Age*, Dhaka, 7 January 2013. Online. Available at: www.newagebd.com/detail.php?date=2013–01–07&nid=35905#.UUkl91eXR6g (accessed 22 February 2013).

Joint Learning Network for Universal Health Coverage, see 'UHC'.

Kakwani, N., Soares, F.V. and Son, H.H. (2005) 'Conditional cash transfers in African countries', International Poverty Centre, Working Paper No. 9, New York: UNDP.

Khalily, M.A.B. (2004) 'Quantitative approach to impact assessment of microfinance programmes in Bangladesh: what have we learned?', *Journal of International Development*, 16 (3): 331–53. Reprinted in S.R. Osmani and M.A.B. Khalily (eds), (2011) *Readings in Microfinance: Reach and Impact*, Dhaka: University Press Ltd, pp. 855–98.

Khan, A.A. (2012) 'Move to amend GB ordinance undemocratic', *Daily Star*, Dhaka, 10 August 2012.

Khandker, S.R. (1998) *Fighting Poverty with Microcredit: Experience in Bangladesh*, Oxford and New York: Oxford University Press.

Khandker, S.R, Khalily, M.A.B. and Samad, H.A. (2012) 'Seasonal hunger and its mitigation in North-West Bangladesh', *Journal of Development Studies*, 48 (12): 1750–64.

Langmore, J.V. (2011) 'Poverty reduction through social protection: a potential form of debt-for-development exchange', in R. Buckley (ed.), *Debt-for-Development Exchanges: History and New Applications*, New York: Cambridge University Press.

London School of Economics (2012) 'India's public distribution system: replace or reform?' Report of a conference. Online. Available at: http://blogs.lse.ac.uk//indiaatlse/2012/10/12/indias-public-distribution-system-replace... (accessed 27 November 2012).

McArthur, J.W. (2013) 'Own the goals: what the Millennium Development Goals have accomplished', *Foreign Affairs*, 92 (2): 152–62.

Mahjabeen, R. (2008) 'Microfinancing in Bangladesh: impact on households' consumption and welfare', *Journal of Policy Modelling*, 30 (6): 1083–92.

Mahmud, A.A. (2012) 'NGOs' socio-economic impact in Bangladesh', *The Financial Express*, Dhaka, 2 February 2012.

MFIs in Bangladesh (2013) *Microfinance in Bangladesh: Country Profile*. Online. Available at: www.mixmarket.org/mfi/country/Bangladesh (accessed 23 February 2013).

Mitchison, R. (2000) *The Old Poor Law in Scotland: The Experience of Poverty 1574–1845*, Edinburgh: Edinburgh University Press.

Morduch, J. (1998) 'Does microfinance really help the poor? New evidence from flagship programs in Bangladesh', Department of Economics and HIID, Harvard University, First Completed Draft: 26/2/98.

Morduch, J. (1999a) 'The Microfinance promise', *Journal of Economic Literature*, 37 (4): 1569–1614.

Morduch, J. (1999b) 'The role of subsidies in microfinance: evidence from the Grameen Bank', *Journal of Development Economics*, 60 (1): 229–48.

Morduch, J. and Haley, B. (2002) *Analysis of the Effects of Microfinance on Poverty Reduction*, NYU Wager Working Paper No. 1014 (Issued 28 June). Online. Available at: www.microfinancegateway.org/gm/document-1.9.29382/analysis%20of%20the%20effects.pdf (accessed 6 December 2012).

MRA (Microcredit Regulatory Authority) (2011) *NGO-MFIs in Bangladesh* (Vol. 8), June 2011. Online. Available at: www.mra.gov.bd/images/mra_files/Publications/ngo-mfis%20vol. 8.pdf (accessed 12 February 2013).

MRA (Microcredit Regulatory Authority) (2012) *Microcredit in Bangladesh*. Online. Available at: www.mra.gov.bd (accessed 12 September 2012).

Nandi, A. (2013) 'The health of India's insurance scheme for the poor', Washington, DC and Delhi: Centre for Disease Dynamics, Economics and Policy. Online. Available at: www.c ddep.org/blog/posts/health_india%E2%80%99s_health_insurance_scheme... (accessed 15 February 2013).

Navajas, S., Schreiner, M., Meyer, R.L., Gonzalez-vega, C. and Rodriguez-meza, J. (2000) 'Microcredit and the poorest of the poor: theory and evidence from Bolivia', *World Development*, 28 (2): 333–46.

Naved, R. (1994) 'Empowerment of women: listening to the voices of women', Special issue on Women, Development and Change: *Bangladesh Development Studies*, 22 (2 and 3): 155–79.

NGOAB (2012) *NGO Affairs Bureau Bangladesh: Official Website*. Online. Available at: http://profilebd.blogspot.co.uk/2012/12/ngo-affairs-bureau-of-bangladesh-ngoab.html (accessed 18 February 2013).

NOAB (2012) *List of NGOs as on 22 October, 2012*. Online. Available at: www.ngoab.gov.bd/Files/NGO_LIST.pdf (accessed 25 October 2012).

Osmani, S.R. and Khalily, M.A.B. (eds) (2011) *Readings in Microfinance: Reach and Impact*, Dhaka: University Press Ltd.

Pitt, M. (1999) 'Reply to Jonathon Morduch's "Does microfinance really help the poor: new evidence from flagship programs in Bangladesh"', Providence, RI: Department of Economics, Brown University. Online. Available at: www.microfinancegateway.org/gm/document-1.9.24728/36058_file_01.pdf (accessed 28 October 2012).

Pitt, M. (2012) 'Gunfight at the NOT OK Corral: reply to high noon for microfinance'. Online. Available at: www.brown.edu/research/projects/pitt/sites/brown.../faults6.pdf (accessed 12 January 2013).

Pitt, M. and Khandker, S.R. (1998) 'The impact of group-based credit programs on poor households in Bangladesh: does the gender of participants matter?', *Journal of Political Economy*, 106 (5): 958–96.

Pitt, M. and Khandker, S.R. (2012) 'Replicating replication: due diligence in Roodman and Morduch's replication of Pitt and Khondker (1998)', Policy Research Working Paper No. 6273, Development Research Group, Agriculture and Rural Development Team, November, 2012. Online. Available at: www-wds.worldbank.org/external/default/WDSContentServer/IW3P/IB/2012/11/21/000158349_20121121125524/Rendered/PDF/wps6273.pdf (accessed 21 January 2012).

POPI (2013) *People's Oriented Program Initiative (POPI)*. Online. Available at: http://ecf.cseas.kyoto-u.ac.jp/data/NGO/POPI.html (accessed 18 February 2013).

Prakongsal, P, Limwattananon, S., Patcharanarumol, W., Tisavatikom, K. and Tangcharosathien, V. (2007) 'Assessing the impact of the universal coverage policy on financial risk protection, health care, finance, and benefit incidence of Thai households', *Journal of Health Science*, Abstract available online at: http://ssm.com/abstract=9932089.

PROSHIKA (2013) *PROSHIKA: Over 35 Years in Empowering Poor Men and Women*. Online. Available at: www.proshika.org/report.html (accessed 18 February 2013).

Rahman, A. (2012) *Chairman's Speech at the Opening Ceremony of MRA's New Office*. Address by the Governor of the Bangladesh Bank (in Bengali), 22 December 2012. Online. Available at: www.mra.gov.bd/images/mra_files/speech/governor%20speach_office%20inauguration.pdf (accessed 22 January 2013).

Rahman, H.Z. and Choudhury, L.A. (2012) *Social Safety Nets in Bangladesh: Ground Realities and Policy Challenges (Vol 2: Ground Realities and Policy Challenges)*. Online. Available at: www.undp.org.bd/info/pub/Social%20Safety%20Net%20Volume-2%20qxd.pdf (accessed 27 December 2013).

Rawlings, L.B. (2004) 'A new approach to social assistance: Latin America's experience with conditional cash transfer programs', World Bank Social Protection Discussion Paper Series No. 0416, August, Washington DC.

Republic of Namibia (1998) *Towards Achieving Health for All Namibians*, Windhoek: Ministry of Health and Social Services. Online. Available at: http://books.google.ch/books/about/Towards_Achieving_Health_for_All_Namibia.html?id=r83EHwAACAAJ&redir_esc=y.

Republic of Namibia (2007) *Community-Based Health Care Policy*, Windhoek: Ministry of Health and Social Services.

Roodman, D. (2012) *Due Diligence: An Impertinent Inquiry into Microfinance*, Washington DC: Centre for Global Development.

Roodman, D. and Morduch, J. (2011) *The Impact of Microcredit on the Poor in Bangladesh: Revisiting the Evidence* (Revised 2011), Working Paper 174, Washington DC: Centre for Global Development. Online. Available at: www.cgdev.org/files/1422302_file_Roodman_Morduch_Bangladesh_2.pdf (accessed 22 January 2013).

Sachs, J.D. (2005) *The End of Poverty: How We Can Make it Happen in our Lifetime*, London: Penguin Books.

Scheil-Adlung, X., Juetting, J., Xu, K., Carrin, G. *et al.* (2006) 'What is the impact of social health protection on access to health care, health expenditure and impoverishment? A comparative analysis of three African countries', Geneva: ILO, ESS Paper No. 24.

Sen, A.K. (1981) *Poverty and Famines: An Essay on Entitlement and Deprivation*, Oxford: Clarendon Press.

Sen, A.K. (1995) *Economic Development and Social Change: India and China in Comparative Perspectives*, STICERD No. 67, London: London School of Economics.

Sinha, S. (1998) 'Introduction and overview. special issue on micro-credit: impact, targets and sustainability', *IDS Bulletin*, 29 (4): 1–10.

Sjoblom, D. and Farrington, J. (2008) 'The India National Rural Employment Guarantee Act: will it reduce poverty and boost the economy?', ODI and DFID, Project Briefing No. 7, January.

Stern, N. (2009) 'The rich, the poor, and the planet', *LSE Connect*, 21 (2): 8–9.

Sudarshan, R.M. (2011) 'India's National Rural Employment Guarantee Act: women's participation and impacts in Kerala, Himachal Pradesh, and Rajasthan', IDS, Centre for Social Protection, CSP Research Report 06, January.

Sudarto, S. (2005) *Social Safety-Nets: Indonesia*, Inter-Regional Inequality Facility, Policy Brief 5, London: Overseas Development Institute.

TMSS (2013) *TMSS: Profiles & Reports: MFI Report*. Online. Available at: www.mix-market.org/mfi/tmss (accessed 18 February 2013).

Tomeli, E.V. (2009) 'Conditional cash transfer programs: achievements and illusions', *Global Social Policy*, 9 (2): 167. Online. Available at: http://gsp.sagepub.com/content/9/2/167.

UHC (Joint Learning Network for Universal Health Coverage) (2012) 'Indonesia: Jamkesmas'. Online. Available at: www.joint_learning_network.org/content/jamkesmas (accessed 18 September 2012).

UHC Forward (2012) 'Towards universal health coverage: Indonesia'. Online. Available at: http://uhcforward.org/content/indonesia... (accessed 18 September 2012).

UNDP (United Nations Development Program) (2005) 'Conditional cash transfers in African countries', by N. Kakwani, F.V. Soares and H.H. Son, International Poverty Centre, Working Paper No. 9.

UNDP (United Nations Development Program) (various years) *Human Development Report*, New York: United Nations.

WHO (World Health Organization) (2012a) 'Thailand: health care for all, at a price', *Bulletin of W.H.O.*, 20 July 2012. Online. Available at: www.who.int/bulletin/volumes/88/2/10–010210/en/index.html (accessed 27 July 2012).

WHO (World Health Organization) (2012b) *WHO Country Health System Profile: Thailand* (last updated 27 July 2012), Geneva: WHO.

Wikipedia (2012a) *Mahatma Gandhi National Rural Employment Guarantee Act*. Online. Available at: http://en.wikipedia.org/wiki/Mahatma_Gandhi_National_Rural_Employment_Act... (accessed 20 July 2012).

Wikipedia (2012b) *Public Distribution System*. Online. Available at: http://en.wikipedia.org/wiki/Public_Distribution_System... (accessed 27 November 2012).

Wong, C. (2012) 'Paying for urbanization in China: challenges of municipal finance in the 21st century', in R. Bahl, J. Linn, D. Wetzel and G. Ingram (eds), *Metropolitan Government Finances in Developing Countries*, Cambridge, Ma: Lincoln Institute for Land Policy.

Wood, G. (2003) 'Staying secure, staying poor: the faustian bargain', *World Development*, 31 (3): 455–71.

World Bank (2006a) *Social Safety Nets in Bangladesh: An Assessment* (Bangladesh Development Studies – Paper No. 9), Dhaka: World Bank (January 2006). Online. Available at: http://siteresources.worldbank.org/BANGLADESHEXTN/Resources/FINAL-printversion_PAPER_9.pdf (accessed 12 December 2012).

World Bank (2006b) *The Economics and Governance of Nongovernmental Organisations in Bangladesh*, Dhaka: The World Bank. Online. Available at: http://siteresources.worldbank.org/BANGLADESHEXTN/Resources/NGOreport_Dev_Series.pdf (accessed 22 January 2012).

World Bank (2007) *World Development Report 2007*, Washington DC: The World Bank.

World Bank (2008a) *World Development Indicators 2008*, Washington DC: The World Bank; together with *Poverty Data: A Supplement to the World Development Indicators 2008*.

World Bank (2008b) *World Development Report 2008*, Washington DC: The World Bank.

World Bank (2010) *World Development Report 2010*, Washington DC: The World Bank.

World Bank (2011a) *World Development Indicators 2011*, Washington DC: The World Bank.

World Bank (2011b) *Health Financing in Indonesia: A Reform Road Map*. Online. Available at: http://siteresources.worldbank.org/INTINDONESIA/Resources/Publication.... .PDF file.

World Bank (2013) *Povcalnet* (world poverty statistics). Online. Available at: http://econ.worldbank.org/povcalnet (accessed 19 February 2013).

Wright, G.A.N. (2000) *Microfinance Systems: Designing Quality Financial Services for the Poor*, London & New York: Zed Books, and Dhaka: University Press Ltd.

Yunus, M. (2010) *Building Social Business: The New Kind of Capitalism That Serves Humanity's Most Pressing Needs*, New York: Public Affairs.

Yunus, M. (2011) 'Vision 2050: a poverty-free world: social business – a step toward creating a new global economic order', *Journal of Social Business*, 1 (1): 7–23.

Zaman, H. (2004) 'Microfinance in Bangladesh: growth, achievements, and lessons'. A Case Study Paper conducted for the World Bank: Scaling Up Poverty Reduction: A Global Learning Process and Conference, Shanghai, 25–27 May 2004. Online. Available at: http://info.worldbank.org/etools/docs/reducingpoverty/case/108/fullcase/Bangladesh%20Microfinance%20Full%20Case.pdf (accessed 22 November 2012).

Zepeda, E. and Alarcón, D. (2009 or later, n.d. given) 'Employment-guarantee and conditional-cash-transfers programs for poverty reduction', New York: UNDP Bureau for Development Policy.

Zohir, S. (n.d.) 'NGO sector in Bangladesh: an overview'. Online. Available at: www.ergonline.org/30th_april/april_30/epw/reprint_series3.pdf (accessed 1 October 2012).

Zohir, S., Mahmud, S., Sen, B., Asaduzzaman, M., Islam, M.J., Ahmed, N. and Mamun, A.A. (2001) *Monitoring and Evaluation of Microfinance Institutions* (Final Report: BIDS Study on PKSF's Monitoring and Evaluation), Dhaka: BIDS. The preliminary pages including the Executive Summary are available online: www.pksf-bd.org/index.php?option=com_content&view=article&id=148 (accessed 20 February 2013).

Index

Page numbers in *italics* denote tables, those in **bold** denote figures.